WHAT IS ISLAM?

WHAT IS ISLAM?

Chris Horrie and Peter Chippindale

This edition published in Great Britain in 1997 by
Virgin Books
an imprint of Virgin Publishing Ltd
332 Ladbroke Grove
London W10 5AH

First published in Great Britain in 1990 by Star Books

Revised and reissued in 1991 by Virgin Books

Reprinted 1993, 1994, 1996, 1998, 2001

A catalogue record for this book is available from the British Library

ISBN 0 352 32636 0

Typeset by Medcalf Type Ltd, Bicester, Oxon
Printed and bound in Great Britain by
Clays Ltd, St Ives plc

CONTENTS

PART ONE – FAITH

PART FOUR – THE MUSLIM WORLD

The Koran (Qur'an)
Quotations from the Qur'an are given in brackets, for example
(20:50). The first number refers to the chapter (or 'surah' in Arabic)
and the second number refers to the verse.

Modern editions of the Qur'an reproduce the Book exactly as
it was revealed to Muhammad. It therefore contains what appears
to be punctuation, grammatical and other human errors. In most
editions these 'errors' are indicated with brackets. Square brackets
are used, in addition, to enclose clarifications made by non-
Muslim editors.

PART ONE

FAITH

1.0 THE UNIVERSAL RELIGION

'There is no god but Allah.
Muhammad is the messenger of Allah'.

Recitation of these two phrases in the presence of two witnesses is all that is required for conversion to Islam. Each year millions of people – mainly in the Third World – make this simple declaration and, by accepting the strict obligations of Islamic law, join the fastest growing body of religious believers in the world. The exact number of Muslims is difficult to estimate, but all authorities agree that it will be at least 1,000 million by the year 2000 AD.

Islam is thus the second largest religion after Christianity, which already has over 1,000 million followers divided between Eastern Orthodoxy, Catholicism and Protestantism. And in practice, as many Muslims point out, Christian belief in the highly secularised countries of Europe and North America is often nominal. Therefore, they claim, Islam probably has the largest number of 'true believers'.

Unlike Christianity, Islam could never become a private religion of personal conscience and ethics. Rather it is a complete way of life governing dress, economics, business ethics, rates of taxation, justice and punishment, weights and measures, politics, war and peace, marriage and inheritance, family and domestic life, the care of animals and livestock, sexual relations within marriage, education, diet, cookery, social behaviour, forms of greeting and rules of hospitality. Even the way in which a glass of water is to be drunk is governed by Islamic religious law.

3

Islam's approach to the great religious issues of life and death, the origins and fate of the universe, and the nature of mankind and God (Allah) is both simple and uncompromising.

It holds there is only one merciful, eternal and all-powerful Allah. He is the Lord of everything in existence, including the whole of mankind. He brought the universe into being in an act of creation approximately 8,000 years ago and He will bring it to an end when He wills. The end of the universe will be followed by a Day of Judgement when all mankind will be resurrected, individually called to account, and sent either to Paradise or Hell for all eternity.

Allah has made this known to all mankind through a series of Prophets, starting with Adam and ending with Muhammad ('The Last Prophet' or 'The Seal of the Prophecy').

Allah's final message to mankind was given to the Prophet Muhammad and has been set down in the Koran (Qur'an) which, together with certain stories about the life of Muhammad, dictates everything that a man should know and do in order to enter Paradise.

The spread of Islam has always been based on the strength and simplicity of this religious conviction, with its emphasis on ideas of punishment and reward in the afterlife. It is therefore easy to see why the poor of the Third World – where Islam is growing fastest – should seek solace in the idea of Paradise after death.

But there are also political and social reasons for the religion's continuing success. Islam is a powerful conservative force, bolstering traditional family life and protecting individuals and communities against the enormous and often destructive changes imposed on Third World countries by contact with the developed capitalist or Communist world.

The recent growth of Islam has been particularly marked in African and Asian countries where there was contact with Christian colonial powers. At independence the elites in most of these countries embraced Western or Soviet ideas of secularism, economic development and either liberal democracy or socialism. Now, after decades of political instability, growing poverty and social disintegration, the dream of Western or Soviet-style development has almost without exception ended in disillusionment. It is against this background that the Islamic 'Reformation' known as 'fundamentalism' – literally a return to a simplified and basic form of Islamic law – is taking place.

Western reaction to Islamic fundamentalism has been marked

by revulsion against the reintroduction of Qur'anic punishments such as amputating a hand for the crime of theft. Beneath this is a revival of the ancient European fear that Muslims plan to conquer the world.

These fears are understandable, but are exaggerated because of a basic and widespread misunderstanding of the Islamic duty of *jihad* (Holy War), one of the few aspects of the religion widely discussed in the West.

It is true that all Muslims are obliged to fight to the death in defence of Islam and that the Islamic epoch began with the declaration by Muhammad of *jihad* against the pagans of Arabia. But this Qur'anic duty is entirely defensive. Aggressive war, either to gain worldly power or wealth or to forcibly convert unbelievers, is expressly forbidden in the Qur'an: 'There is no compulsion in religion; truly the right way has become clearly distinct from error' (2:256).

At the same time there is a clear obligation of self-defence, and a duty to fight those who oppress fellow Muslims. The Qur'an says: 'And fight in the way of Allah with those who fight you . . . and kill them wherever you find them, and drive them out from whence they drove you out . . . and fight with them until there is no persecution, and religion should only be for Allah, but if they desist, then there should be no hostility except against oppressors' (2:190-193).

In reality the distinction between war in the name of self-defence and aggressive war is blurred and Muslim states tend to be as warlike as any others. Nevertheless they do require at least a pretext of aiding oppressed co-religionists, and this has always been a factor in conflicts between them in the modern world. But even in conditions of peace, it is unlikely that fundamentalist Islam could ever compromise with the secular societies of the West, or accept Western political ideas and institutions. In particular the cherished Western ideals of nationalism and individual freedom have no place in Muslim thought.

The very word *Islam* translates from Arabic as 'submission' or 'obedience' (to the will and laws of Allah as set down in the Qur'an) and the word *Muslim*, with the same Arabic root, means 'that person or thing which obeys Allah's law'.

It is this trenchant denial of individualism, and the requirement to submit to Divine authority in every minute aspect of life, which seems so alien to the Western mind.

In Islam the issues of 'freedom of choice' and 'human rights', which form central pillars of modern Western political philosophy, hardly arise. The only free choice to be made is whether to obey the eternal laws of Allah and gain salvation, or to disobey and risk eternal damnation. And the only important human right is to be able to follow unhindered the laws given by Allah through the agency of Prophethood.

1.1 The Prophethood

Main Muslim Prophets mentioned in the Qur'an

Biblical Name	Arabic Name
ADAM	ADAM
NOAH	NUH
ABRAHAM	IBRAHIM
ISHMAEL	ISMA'IL
ISAAC	ISHAQ
JACOB	YACOUB
MOSES	MUSA
DAVID	DAWUD
JOHN THE BAPTIST	YAHYA
JESUS (SON OF MARY)	ISA IBN MARYAM
(SHILOH)*	MUHAMMAD

* Non-Jewish Prophet foretold in Genesis and generally taken by Muslims to be a reference to Muhammad.

Whilst the central creed of Islam is simple monotheism – accepting Allah as controlling the fate of all the universe – the second inseparable belief is the Prophethood – Allah communicating with mankind through a series of divinely guided messengers.

Muslims believe all races and nations have had their own Prophets. Islam is therefore not a religion of human speculation and discovery, but of divine revelation of Allah's pre-existing laws, centring on the oneness and unity of Allah, His omnipotence and mercy. In line with this He has also taken care to warn against the dangers of worshipping false gods of any kind.

Unfortunately mankind has repeatedly ignored or forgotten this message from the Prophets and lapsed into paganism and polytheism. Sometimes Allah has punished us for this – for example in the time of Noah (Nuh), when all but the true believers were drowned by the flood. But in most cases, in His mercy, He has sent further Prophets to clarify His message, reveal further elements of His law, or warn of the dangers of disobedience.

There have been an extraordinary number of Prophets. Muhammad said that Allah had sent 124,000 Prophets before him, and twenty-five Jewish-Christian Prophets from Adam to Jesus (Isa) are mentioned in the Qur'an.

Other religions based on the Prophethood – such as Judaism, Christianity and the effectively extinct monotheistic religions of Arab Sabianism and Persian Zoroastrianism – are said to be 'muslim' in the sense that followers accept monotheism and parts of Allah's law.

However, followers of polytheistic religions, paganism and godless ethical cults such as Buddhism, Confucianism, Taoism, Humanism and Marxism are rejected as *kafirs* (non-muslims). But even *kafirs* are believed to be 'muslim' by nature, though in a condition of *kufr* (hiding from Allah) through their own choice. And it is this act of deliberately hiding from the Truth which condemns *kafirs* to eternal damnation, as those who hide from Allah also hide from His mercy.

The Jewish Heritage

Judaism is particularly important to Islam and is the religion it most closely resembles. The Qur'an states that the Prophets Jacob (Yacoub) and Abraham (Ibrahim), who founded Judaism, were the first human beings to fully submit to Allah's law.

Islam's claim to be the true religion of Ibrahim is based on the events surrounding his willingness to show obedience to Allah by sacrificing his son. Both religions agree that Allah, in His mercy, allowed him to sacrifice a ram instead.

The split comes over which of his two sons he was prepared to kill, and was therefore saved. Jews believe it was his younger son Isaac (Ishaq), and both religions then agree that Ishaq's twelve sons founded the twelve tribes of the original Jewish nation. Jews therefore claim Allah intervened directly to bring the Jewish nation into being, and that the original Jewish nation was Allah's chosen people, and He was God of the Jewish nation alone.

The Qur'an directly contradicts this. It says that Ibrahim only had one son, Ishmael, at the time of the proposed sacrifice and

7

that Ishaq was born afterwards as a reward to Ibrahim for his obedience. Ishmael (Isma'il) went on to found the Arab nation, proving Allah chose the Arabs to be particularly blessed and, in particular, to receive the final revelation via Isma'il's direct descendant, Muhammad.

But the Qur'an is quite clear that Allah is the god of all mankind and not either the Israelites or Arabs alone. It chides the Jews for refusing to accept the Prophets Jesus (Isa) and Muhammad and continuing to believe they are His chosen people.

The second chapter (surah) of the Qur'an, much of which is directly addressed to the children of Israel (Banu Isra'il), says: 'Surely those who believe, and those who are Jews, and the Christians, and the Sabians, whoever believes in Allah and the last day and does good, they shall have their reward from their Lord, and there is no fear for them, nor shall they grieve' (2:62). In other words, the Sabian Arabs, Jews, Christians and 'whoever believes', regardless of nation, have the same God – Allah.

The same surah warns Banu Isra'il about their failure to accept the Prophethood of Jesus (Isa) and Muhammad: 'What! whenever then an apostle came to you with that which your souls did not desire, you were insolent so you called some liars and some you slew . . . Evil is that for which [Banu Isra'il] have sold their souls – that they should deny what Allah has revealed, out of envy that Allah should send down his grace on whomsoever of His servants He pleases; so they have made themselves deserving of wrath upon wrath, and there is a disgraceful punishment for the unbelievers' (2:87-90).

After this dire warning Allah tells the Jews to sincerely repent in which case he will be merciful: 'O Banu Isra'il, call to mind My favour which I bestowed upon you and made you excel amongst the nations . . . And [unbelievers] say: Be Jews or Christians, you will be on the right course. Say: Nay! we follow the religion of Ibrahim . . . we believe in Allah and in that which had been revealed to us, and that which was revealed to Ibrahim and Isma'il and Ishaq and Jacob (Yaqoub) and the tribes, and that which was given to Musa and Isa, and that which was given to the Prophets from their Lord, we do not make any distinction between any of them, and to Him do we submit' (2:135-136).

But even those who fail to heed this message and remain practising Jews are awarded a greater status by Islam than followers of pagan or polytheistic religions. Throughout history Muslim rulers have given their Jewish subjects 'protected persons'

(*Dhimmi*) status, free to follow their own religion unmolested, as the Qur'an commands toleration of Biblical religions.

Historically Dhimmi Jews in the Arab world not only enjoyed this considerable freedom, but greatly influenced Islamic culture and commerce and sometimes reached high office in the state. Although the Jews of the Muslim world were discriminated against from time to time they escaped the terrible persecutions periodically inflicted upon them throughout most of Christian Europe.

Most Muslim Middle Eastern countries retained large Dhimmi Jewish populations until the establishment of the state of Israel in 1948, since when many Arab Jews have emigrated there. Life for those remaining, still a sizeable number in Syria, Iraq, Egypt and Morocco, has become more difficult.

Jesus – Prophet of Islam

Christianity, like Judaism, is described throughout the Qur'an as essentially a misguided form of the 'religion of Ibrahim', the true version of which is Islam. The main error of Christians is their misunderstanding (sometimes described by Muslims as wilful slander) of the significance of the Islamic Prophet Jesus, Son of Mary (Isa ibn Maryam).

Isa is regarded by Muslims as the Jewish Messiah, sent by Allah to lead them back to the true path of Ibrahim and take their place amongst the rightly guided Islamic nations. He is described as a Prophet of the Highest Order (*rasul*), a status otherwise reserved for only for the most important Prophets including Ibrahim and Muhammad himself.

The Qur'an confirms Isa's miraculous virgin birth, his performance of symbolic miracles, and the validity of the Gospels as genuine revelations from Allah, but the Book dwells on his rejection by the Jews. His significance as the founder of Christianity is of secondary importance to the central story of relations between the Jews and the Prophets.

Nevertheless the Qur'an reveals Allah to be astonished and angered by the Christian idea that Isa was His son: 'And they say: The Beneficent God has taken a son. The heavens may almost be rent thereat, and the earth cleave asunder, and the mountains fall down in pieces, that they ascribe a son to the Beneficent God. And it is not worthy of the Beneficent God that He should take a son' (19: 88–92).

9

The fifth surah of the Qur'an deals with the story of Isa at length and parts are directly addressed to Christians as fellow 'People of the Book'. The surah warns that the Christian concept of the Holy Trinity is a form of polytheism and bluntly denies the divinity of Isa: 'Certainly they disbelieve who say: Surely Allah is the third of the three; and there is no God but one God, and if they desist not from what they say, a painful chastisement shall befall those among them who disbelieve. Will they not then turn to Allah and ask His forgiveness? And Allah is Forgiving, Merciful. The Messiah, son of Maryam, is but an apostle . . .' (5:73–75).

The same surah shows that Isa, like any mortal, will be tried by Allah on the Day of Judgement. It even reports the conversation which will take place between Allah and Isa: 'And when Allah will say: O Isa, son of Maryam, did you say to men, Take me and my mother for two Gods beside Allah, [Isa] will say:... I did not say to them aught save what Thou didst enjoin me with: That serve Allah, my Lord and your Lord' (5:116-117).

Because Isa was crucified he is not only a Prophet but an Islamic martyr. There is some debate amongst Muslims about the fate of Isa after his death. The Qur'an says he did not die – probably a reference to the privilege of martyrs who are said to remain in a state of bliss until the Day of Judgement. But some Muslims have interpreted this as a literal denial of Isa's crucifixion and there is even a popular belief that Isa returned to the desert, performed additional miracles and lived to be 120 years old.

Although Christians are discussed far less frequently than Jews in the Qur'an, there are signs that, despite their errors, they are believed to be closer to Islam. A passage in the fifth surah addressed to the Muslims says: 'And you will certainly find the nearest in friendship to those who believe to be those who say: We are Christians . . . And when they hear what has been revealed to the apostle [Muhammad], you will see their eyes overflowing with tears on account of the truth that they recognise; they say: Our Lord! we believe, so write us down with the witnesses' (5:83).

The original Arabian and Assyrian Christian Church was certainly much closer to Islam than modern Christianity. Many early Christians subscribed to Arianism, a Christian heresy which, like Islam, believed Isa to have been merely human.

All that divided Arians from Muslims was acceptance of the finality of Muhammad's Prophethood and Qur'anic law. But

Arianism was crushed after the adoption of a coherent Trinitarian doctrine by the Roman Church at the Council of Nicea in the 3rd century AD.

Despite these similar beginnings Christianity and Islam began to diverge in the Middle Ages. Countless wars between Christian and Muslim states left a legacy of bitterness and mutual ignorance expressed as a growing theological gulf.

The idea that the Holy Trinity is just a sophisticated version of One God monotheism was so alien to Muslims that most believed it was the simple polytheistic worship of Allah, his wife Maryam and his son Isa. Medieval Christian reverence for sacred relics like fragments of the Cross led, with some justification, to the accusation that Christians had become pagan symbol worshippers.

Veneration of icons was denounced as pagan idol worship (Classical Islam forbids attempts to represent Allah in pictures). The adoption of the pre-Christian Roman solar calendar and the celebration of Christmas at the winter solstice similarly led to the belief that Christians practised pagan sun-worship.

But Christians, like Jews, have still enjoyed protected Dhimmi status within Muslim states for many centuries. Cut off from the mainstream of Christianity, Dhimmi Arab Christian Churches – such as the Egyptian Copts and Syrian Maronites – have preserved an older, more original version of their religion, whilst absorbing and enriching Islamic culture.

Ironically, in the light of the recent Muslim-Christian civil war, this process was most developed in Syria and Lebanon, where Islamic sub-sects such as the dominant Alawite group adopted parts of Christian doctrine. Until World War Two Dhimmi Christian communities within Muslim territories such as Syria – including the Lebanese Maronites – were unmolested by Muslim rulers.

Pagans and Polytheists

Ancient history shows that Islam's central idea of one all-powerful god – monotheism – is relatively new as a force in world religion. The earliest men and women almost always believed in a hierarchy, or family, of gods controlling different aspects of worldly life. And until the conversion of the Roman Empire to Christianity, followers of monotheistic religions were a small minority.

Today the position has been almost exactly reversed. Polytheism – in the shape of formal religions at least – remains as a major force only in the Hindu and Sikh religions of the Indian sub-continent.

Muslims are implacably opposed to polytheism, the practice of which is a form of *shirk* – either the 'association' of Allah with another god, His division into parts, or the denial of His absolute command of the universe. *Shirk* is Islam's one unforgivable sin – 'far error' as it is put in the Qur'an – and the penalty is eternal damnation.

Surah four is quite clear about the penalty: 'Surely Allah does not forgive that anything should be associated with Him . . . and whoever associates anything with Allah, he indeed strays off into far error . . . These are they whose abode is hell, and they shall not find any refuge from it' (4:116-121).

The sin of *shirk* also applies to Buddhists, Shintoists, Confucianists and followers of tribal religions of Africa because of their worship of idols and the graves of ancestors. The atheistic philosophies of Marxism and Humanism, which propose that God is the creation of the human imagination, are also guilty of *shirk* in the highest degree because they elevate man to a position above Allah.

In recent decades many 'fundamentalist' Muslim scholars have, in addition, denounced the nominally Christian societies of the West as pagan. Passive agnosticism and religious scepticism are widely regarded as *shirk* because of the implicit denial of Allah's omnipotence. The 'worship' of material goods and money, faith in scientific progress, problems of drink and drugs, sexual permissiveness, widespread gambling and the spread of superstitious cults (such as astrology) are all seen as signs of the growing paganism of the Western world.

Thus, although Islam recognises 'Biblical' Judaism and Christianity as being worthy of toleration and respect, the other major world religions, ethical systems, political ideologies and secularised versions of Christianity and Judaism are all fiercely rejected as being, in effect, pagan.

And the struggle against paganism is central to Islam's mission, just as the struggle against the corrupt pagan aristocracy of Mecca and Arabia dominated the life of Allah's last and greatest Prophet – Muhammad.

1.2 The life of Muhammad

The exact date of Muhammad's birth in Mecca is unknown, but it is thought to have been no later than 570 AD, the year the city's territory was invaded by the Christian Emperor of Ethiopia.

His father was called Abdullah, which means 'servant of God' and his mother Aminah ('peaceful'). Both were members of the Hashim clan, a sub-division of the Quraysh tribe which had lately abandoned its nomadic life as desert Bedouins and risen to dominate the trading city of Mecca.

Although the Hashemites could trace their ancestors back to Isma'il and Ibrahim, it seems they had largely lapsed into paganism, although some clan members were Christian or Jewish.

Muhammad had a sorrowful early childhood. His father was dead by the time of his birth and his mother died before he was six, meaning he was raised as an orphan. According to Quraysh law he was to be given to a Bedouin foster mother and sent off into the desert, and would be unable to inherit from his father's estate. So almost from the beginning of his life he was both poor and something of an outcast from Meccan society. Although there are hundreds of traditional 'reports' or 'sayings' (*hadith*) about Muhammad's early life, many are regarded by Muslim scholars as pious inventions or allegories invented centuries after his death.

It is, however, known for certain that when he was eight Muhammad was sent to live with his uncle, a merchant called Abu Talib. From the age of 12 Abu Talib took him with him on his long trading trips, which sometimes lasted for many months. Muhammad first worked as a camel driver, but as both his horizons and business acumen expanded, he became known as The Trusted One (*al-Amin*) for being fair in his dealings and honouring his obligations.

The most important *hadith* about his early life, and the ones with some of the largest degree of unanimity, are about a trip to Syria, where he was recognised by a Christian monk as Shiloh — the non-Jewish Prophet whose coming was foretold in the book of Genesis.

The relevant verses, which form a central part of Islam's mission to the Jews, tell of events immediately before the end of the world. 'And Jacob (Yaqoub)', Genesis reports, 'called unto his sons [The Israelites] and said, Gather yourselves together, that I may tell you that which shall befall you in the last days . . . The

[Prophethood] shall not depart from Judah . . . until Shiloh come; and unto him shall the gathering of the people be' (Genesis, chapter 19, verse 1–10).

It seems that Muhammad, from an early age, believed himself to be Shiloh, the first and last non-Jewish Prophet who would bring the final message and warning to mankind in the 'last days' before the end of the world.

It may have been for this reason that he became something of a mystic, spending long periods of isolated meditation in the desert. From his early twenties onwards he began to have religious experiences and visions of various sorts, but was on the whole confused by their significance. He is also reported to have become an expert on the Jewish and Christian religions and to have engaged in long religious debates with both monotheists and pagans.

At the age of 25 Muhammad's social status changed markedly. He had been employed by a wealthy widow, Khadijah, to run her trading interests and, after they had prospered, she asked him to marry her. He accepted, even though she was 40, and became a person of prominence and wealth. She was not only his first convert but just as importantly she was to prove a faithful, understanding and supportive wife and the marriage was happy. The couple had only one surviving child, a daughter called Fatima who in later life became a fanatical Muslim.

At that time Mecca was a tumultuous melting pot of Christianity, Judaism, and the various pagan religions practised by the desert tribes and Meccan clans. Khadijah's family had been exposed to monotheism, which was growing in popularity in its various forms and it is known that her uncle was a practising Christian.

In contrast, the pagan clan cults of the Quraysh in the city had become decadent, especially in their shameless worship of material goods and worldly wealth and the consequent huge disparities between rich and poor, which Muhammad, with his varied background, was able to appreciate.

These problems, springing from the difficult transition of the Quraysh from nomadic poverty to sedentary merchant wealth, concerned him greatly, and social injustice – especially the treatment of orphans like himself – is the theme of many of the early surahs of the Qur'an.

The cults of the pagan desert Bedouin clans, who visited Mecca only occasionally, were equally divisive, degenerate and cruel.

Human sacrifice and female infanticide were widely practised. Each Arab tribe or clan had its own gods and worshipped idols or natural features in its desert sanctuaries (*harams*).

The most important of these was the House of God (*Ka'bah*), located in Mecca itself. When Muhammad was a young man it contained 360 pagan idols, worshipped by dozens of separate tribes and clans. His clan, the Hashemites, had the honour of guarding it, through tradition which held that the monument had been re-built by their ancestors Ibrahim and Isma'il after the original – believed to have been built by Adam at the beginning of time – had fallen into disrepair.

In its narrowest sense the whole of Muhammad's mission can be summed up by Allah's Qur'anic command to 'Purify my House [The Ka'bah]' (2:125), by smashing the pagan idols within and revealing its true purpose – the worship of Allah alone. And when he began to preach the need to 'purify' the Ka'bah his activities led to bitter civil war.

But before this Muhammad had begun to receive Allah's final message to mankind in the form of the Qur'an through miraculous revelations which did not come until he was – by the standards of the time – already an old man.

1.3 The Koran (Qur'an)

Muhammad received his first revelation during the month of Ramadan in the year 610 AD when he was about 40 years old. He was engaged in one of his regular periods of solitary meditation in a cave known as Hira near the top of Mount Jabal Nur, near Mecca, when he received a visitation from the Archangel Gabriel (*Jibreel*).

Muhammad had experienced religious visions before, but this was quite different. Jibreel commanded him to 'Recite in the name of your Lord', and the Prophet lost control of himself and, Muslims believe, began to speak the actual words of Allah.

In the 23 remaining years of his life Muhammad received a total of 114 separate revelations which were compiled as the Qur'an (the Arabic for 'recitation') after his death. Muhammad was illiterate so he would repeat each revelation afterwards. Some were written down on whatever was available, from parchment to palm leaves and animals bones, but the majority, in the tradition of the times, were memorised.

A year after Muhammad's death they were collected together by his secretary, Zayd, under the supervision of a committee, shown to many of the Prophet's companions, and agreed to be accurate.

But by about thirty years after his death a number of different versions were circulating and being recited, so a definitive 'canonical' version was issued and sent to the four main Islamic cities of Basra, Damascus, Kufh and Medina. Two of these original copies still exist today. One is in Tashkent in Soviet Uzbekistan and the other is in the Topkapi palace in Istanbul, Turkey.

The text is divided into 114 surahs, each containing the words of one revelation. The number of verses, or *ayahs*, in each surah varies from three to 286 and totals 6,239. Each has a title, and 86 have sub-headings indicating they were received in Mecca, whilst another 28 were received in Medina. The Meccan surahs are shorter, more mystical and warn about the dangers of paganism. The Medinan surahs are in general longer and deal in great detail with aspects of Allah's law such as the rules for declaring war, accepting converts, divorce proceedings and the mandatory punishments for various crimes.

The structure of the Qur'an is unusual and, apparently, illogical. In general the longer Medinan surahs, given last, are at the front of the Book and the shorter Meccan surahs, the earliest, at the back.

There is no logical explanation for their order but at the same time Western scholars, attempting to reorganise them on this basis, have found that no other order works without splitting the surahs up into scattered verses. Sunni Muslims hold that the order was dictated by Jibreel to give the Qur'an an esoteric inner meaning reflecting the Divine rather than human order of things.

Acceptance of every word of the Qur'an as the literal word of Allah is a binding obligation on all Muslims. The idea that Muhammad (or any other human or spirit) was the author of the Qur'an, or any part of it, is rejected absolutely.

At the heart of the Qur'an is the simple, repetitive warning that mankind must renounce paganism, accept Allah as the One God of all mankind and live according to His laws. This message is directly addressed to the pagans, Jews and Christians of Mecca, amongst whom Muhammad lived, complete with threats of dire consequences if they failed to mend their polytheistic ways. The first revelation received by Muhammad (by tradition, surah 96) deals with this very theme.

16

In surah 96 Allah describes an unnamed pagan Lord who has prevented his servants from praying to Him and calls on them to take up arms. 'Does he not know that Allah does see?', the surah asks, 'Nay! if he desist not, We would certainly smite his forehead, A lying, sinful forehead. Then let him summon his council, We too would summon the braves of the army. Nay! Obey him not, and make obeisance and draw nigh to Allah' (96:14–19).

In another early revelation Allah openly threatens Muhammad's brother-in-law Abu Lahab, who, as head of his Hashemite clan, had disowned Muhammad and annulled the marriage between his son and Muhammad's daughter Fatima. Allah also shows himself to be equally angry with Abu Lahab's wife, who had ridiculed the idea of Muhammad's Prophethood: 'Perdition overtake both hands of Abu Lahab, and he will perish. His wealth and what he earns will not avail him. He shall soon burn in the fire that flames, And his wife, the bearer of fuel, Upon her neck a halter of strongly twisted rope' (111:1–5).

A sceptic might think the Allah revealed in surah like this is too suspiciously spiteful and parochial to indeed be the God of all mankind. But Muslims still remain absolutely adamant that Muhammad had no role in writing a surah such as this.

The main argument used to defend the Divine authorship of the Qur'an is the incomparable quality of the writing. Much of it is composed in rhyming Arabic and the language is particularly beautiful and graceful. The lengthy surah 81 is held up as an example of absolute mastery of the classical Arabic poetical style and does not resemble anything which could have been composed by anyone with Muhammad's rudimentary education.

The surahs were given in Arabic and, since it would be a sin to alter the word of Allah, Arabic remains the sacred language of Islam. Non-Arabic-speaking Muslims can use translations but the Qur'an is so important to them that many learn Arabic just so they can read it in its original form.

Muslims and non-believers alike agree the full power and beauty of its writing can only be appreciated in the original. But for Muslims it goes further than that. Translations can only be 'interpretations' which cannot truly say what is said in Arabic. The combination of the words and rhythms in the original language – the way the Qur'an sounds when recited – is also an important part of its power.

Muslims think of the Qur'an as a complete philosophy, a

17

comprehensive description of the universe and the entirety of the law by which mankind must live. The longer and later Medinan surahs stress Allah's merciful nature more fully, with extensive friendly practical advice on personal and family matters.

The Qur'an is also the focus of Islamic art. Many individual copies of the Book are major works of art in their own right – with sublime Arabic calligraphy on superb hand-made paper, and high quality decorative leather and metal work. Figurative art is forbidden by classical Islam, especially the creation of images of Allah and the Prophets, and the astonishingly fine decorative art found in many mosques is largely based on Arabic calligraphy, woven into patterns repeating passages from the Book.

Even the most sceptical non-believer, Muslims insist, is forced to admit that the Qur'an is a book of immense beauty and importance – not least because it has now almost certainly become the most widely read and memorised book in the world. The preface to one of the most widely available Qur'an in English, the Tahrike Tarsile translation, puts it like this: 'The Qur'an's miracle lies in its ability to offer at least something to non-believers and everything to believers'.

Learning large parts of the Qur'an by heart is an important part of Muslim religious devotion and children start memorising it at an early age. In many Muslim countries learning the Qur'an by heart forms the basic curriculum of primary school education. Muslims who memorise its contents in their entirety are given the honourable title of *al-hafiz*.

1.4 The Dawn of Islam

After receiving the first surah of the Qur'an Muhammad acted with enormous caution. He realised the pagan Quyrash rulers of Mecca, to whom the blood-curdling threats of the early revelations were directly addressed, would eventually oppose him by force, so for three years he preached privately to the immediate members of his own family. According to tradition his wife Khadijah was the first to accept his Prophethood, followed by his cousin 'Ali and servant Zayd.

Islam first came to the attention of the Quyrash in either 611 or 612 when Muhammad began preaching to the Hashemite keepers of the Ka'bah. The Quyrash and some Hashemite elders denounced him as mad, but no action was taken.

The Quyrash's wealth was based on the dozens of pagan cults who used the Ka'bah as their central shrine. They sold idols, and Mecca's position as a trading city was largely based on contacts made with the visiting tribes. New religions were welcomed as good for business. At first Islam was seen as just another money-making cult and Muhammad was encouraged to use the Ka'bah alongside the others in a spirit of fair play and toleration.

But in 613 Muhammad began preaching to the public at large, rejecting all other religions, demanding the removal of idols from the Ka'bah and therefore threatening trade. As Quyrash hostility grew Muhammad showed himself to be a skilful politician as well as a learned theologian.

Steadily he gathered around him the elders of minor clans and middle ranking merchants through preaching a return to the religion of Ibrahim. Whilst the Quyrash continued to ridicule him, calling him a madman and an impostor, Muhammad remained protected by the complex laws of pagan religious toleration, tribal kinship and blood feud and they were reluctant to act against him.

The confrontation with the Quyrash began in 616. Having fully converted some of the smaller Meccan clans and many individual Christians and Jews, Muhammad began to use his position as one of the Hashemite keepers of the Ka'bah to preach to pagan Arabian tribesmen as they arrived to worship in its precincts.

The other Quyrash tribes now moved to silence him. Their first offer was to make him King of Mecca if he stopped preaching. When he refused they punished him by boycotting merchants belonging to his Hashemite clan.

This caused some of the Hashemite elders to turn against Muhammad and his followers. Some were forced into brief exile in Christian Abyssinia (modern Ethiopia), where the Emperor, Negus, attempted to convert the Muslims to Christianity, but failed.

Negus was nevertheless impressed by their honesty and sincerity. According to tradition, when the Muslims described how the Quyrash had defiled the Ka'bah he wept until his beard was soaked and promised to not help the Quyrash if the Muslims attempted to overthrow pagan rule.

The Night Journey

In 619 Muhammad and the Hashemites arrived at a tactical compromise which lifted the trade boycott and allowed him to return to Mecca. It was also at about this time that Muhammad received one of his most remarkable revelations – the Night Journey – described in the 17th surah and in numerous *hadith* attributed to him.

In the *hadith* Muhammad describes how he was sleeping next to the Ka'bah when he was woken by Jibreel and told to mount a winged animal 'smaller than a mule but larger than an ass'. The animal took him to the ruined site of the Temple of Solomon in Jerusalem, where all the Prophets – including Adam, Musa, Ibrahim, Ishaq, Isma'il and Isa – were assembled. Muhammad said he prayed with all Prophets and was then asked by Jibreel to drink either wine or milk. He chose milk and was told this was the right path for himself and his followers.

The Angel Jibreel then carried him up in the sky and showed him the gates of heaven, where reality begins and ends. Here he received the command from Allah that he and his followers pray 50 times a day, every day. After some discussion with Musa, Muhammad thought this too often and begged Allah to reduce the number to five – a request which Allah, in His mercy, granted. Muhammad then returned to Mecca on the back of his winged beast.

The site of this miraculous happening, which graphically demonstrates the kinship of all Prophetic religions as well as confirming Muhammad as the last Prophet, is now marked by the Dome of the Rock Mosque in Jerusalem, Islam's holiest shrine outside Mecca. The Night Journey is also commemorated in the annual festival of the Night of Ascent (*Laylat al-mi'raj*), one of Islam's most important Holy Days.

Following the Night Journey Muhammad became certain that war with the Quyrash was inevitable and prepared to leave Mecca. He and his followers switched their missionary efforts to the neighbouring, rival city of Medina, 250 miles to the north.

Between 619 and 621 Muhammad converted virtually all the tribal leaders of Medina, many of whom were previously Jews. With his position greatly strengthened Muhammad returned to Mecca and began preaching the need to overthrow pagan Quyrash rule.

Outraged by Muhammad's boldness, the Quraysh now demanded his expulsion from the Hashemite clan, which would have removed the protection he enjoyed as one of the keepers of the Ka'bah and enabled the Quyrash to execute him without fear of a blood feud amongst the clans.

Fearing for their lives, Muhammad and his followers fled from Mecca into desert exile, arriving in Medina on September 16th 622.

The Hijrah

Muhammad's flight into exile (known as the *Hijrah*, the Arabic word for 'emigration') is the most significant episode in the Prophet's life apart from the revelations he received which made up the Qur'an.

It marks the point in the Prophecy when Allah demanded not just a reform of the religious life of Mecca, but a total break with it. It also marks the start of *jihad* (Holy War – both spiritual and physical) against the pagan Quyrash and, ultimately, all those oppressing Muslims and opposing by force the spread of Allah's word.

The date of this declaration of war was later chosen as the first day of the Muslim calendar, with 622 the first year of the Age of Hijrah (*Anno Hijarae* – AH).

By this time most of Medina's population regarded themselves as his followers. Many, in addition, had signed military treaties with his followers in Mecca promising military aid. They now eagerly awaited Muhammad's declaration of war. But instead, after receiving fresh revelations, he decided to first convert the nomadic Bedouins in the surrounding desert.

Muhammad was now following the classical pattern of Arab politics and warfare, based on short-lived confederations of nomadic tribes united around a specific military objective and rewarded afterwards by the fair division of booty.

These confederations, often brought into being by a charismatic figure such as Muhammad, developed quickly. The difficulty was uniting the first two or three tribes. After that, united tribes had such a military advantage the others were forced to join or face destruction.

Between 622 and 628 Muhammad set in motion the biggest tribal avalanche Arabia had ever seen. The tribal chieftains (*shayks*) rapidly converted to Islam and joined Muhammad's army. The process was helped by Islam's being an entirely new religion free from the feuding associations of both the localised pagan cults and the 'foreign' monotheist doctrines of Judaism and Christianity.

Muhammad showed himself to be a brilliant military leader in early skirmishes with the Quyrash and this, along with further revelations promising Allah's support and certain victory, is likely to have persuaded yet more *shayks* to join.

In just six years Muhammad assembled an army of 10,000 Arabs – a huge force for those times – and marched with the people of Medina against Mecca. The force was so overwhelming the city was taken without resistance.

Muhammad issued a general amnesty to the Quraysh and urged them, without pressure, to convert to Islam, which they slowly did. The conquest of Mecca also gave him control of the Ka'bah and he resumed his preaching to pagan pilgrims as they visited the shrine. Conversion was rapid and only nine months after the occupation of Mecca his army had grown to 30,000.

Muhammad's next move was a great expedition to Tabuk, on the trade route to the wealthy north western Arabian territory of Syria, where Damascus had been Mecca's main rival as the predominant Arabic trading and cultural centre. More clans and tribes were converted on the way, whilst settlements of Jews and Christians were offered 'protected minorities' Dhimmi status so long as they did not oppose Islam.

Muhammad died at Mecca on June 8th 11 AH/632 AD. Although Syria, Palestine and north Arabia had not been subjugated, at his death he was the greatest military leader the Arabs had ever known. The basis for Arab-Islamic domination of the whole of the middle East in the centuries that followed had been firmly laid.

However, even before Muhammad's death, there was unease amongst his original followers in Mecca that the religion might easily be corrupted by rapid growth and worldly success. Satan had been defeated on the battlefield, but might he not now work within the religion, as he had done many times before, to turn it into an idol-worshipping mockery?

The Satanic Verses

Throughout his career as a military leader Muhammad had continued to receive further revelations and, as the political power of Islam began to grow, these became lengthier and more detailed.

They often gave precise advice on how further conversions were to be made, finalised the law relating to the conduct of war and peace, and stressed the need for vigilance against non-believers and hypocritical converts.

Many of the more legalistic revelations were given to

Muhammad when he was in Medina and uncertain about the tactics he should adopt. According to legend it was during this time that Muhammad received a 'Satanic' revelation granting Divine status to three pagan goddesses worshipped by a politically important pagan tribe whose support he was keen to enlist.

When he proclaimed this revelation, the legend continues, the pagans agreed to join Islam, greatly strengthening its army. But then Muhammad received another message, revealing these verses had been 'put upon his tongue' by Satan.

Neither the original Satanic revelation nor its denial has been preserved as surah, and no reference can be found in any commonly available edition of the Qur'an. But if the story is true no Muslim can be certain the rest of the Qur'an was not similarly inspired by Satan. The logic underpinning the whole of Islam therefore collapses and becomes a mockery.

The relatively small number of Muslims who are familiar with it fiercely reject the legend as the work of ancient and long-forgotten enemies of the religion. Any person (Muslim or not) who subscribes to the story commits the unforgivable sin of *shirk* (association of Allah with another – in this case Satan) and will certainly be sent to hell for all eternity. In addition, Muslims who repeat the legend also commit the crime of apostophy – reversion from Islam – which is against Qur'anic law and may be punishable by execution in extreme cases.

Despite the extreme reluctance of Muslims to accept even the existence of the legend of the Satanic Verses, let alone the verses themselves, it still persists, suggesting that it may have had some basis in truth. It seems likely that the legend originated as an allegorical warning of the lengths to which Satan would go in his ceaseless attempts to lead men away from the true path.

In the years immediately after Muhammad's death, many of his original followers, especially the groups of fanatical Bedouins known as the *Khariji*, attempted to purge Islam of the 'hypocrites' who had insincerely converted to share in early military successes.

The Khariji's great fear was that Satan would infiltrate his followers into the body of Islam, destroying it from within, and in the bitter civil wars over the succession to the Islamic Empire after Muhammad's death it was common for Muslim factions to denounce each other as Satanic.

2.0 THE FIVE PILLARS OF ISLAM

Any person may become a Muslim by sincerely accepting Islam's basic 'creed': 'there is no god but Allah; Muhammad is the messenger of Allah'. This creed is a contracted form of all the core beliefs of Islam, known collectively by the Arabic title *shahada* ('witness').

But to remain a Muslim they must then accept four obligatory duties, known collectively as the *ibadah*, the Arabic word for 'state of submission', sometimes translated as 'holy slavery'.

The obligations of the *ibadah* were revealed to Muhammad during his period of exile and warfare and clarified by further revelations when he was ruler of Mecca and Medina.

The basic function of the *ibadah*, then as now, is to discipline followers for the purpose of spreading the religion of Islam and weeding out hypocrites and 'lukewarm' converts. The obligations are arduous, and the practical effect is to force the believer to build his entire social and business life around devotion to the religion.

The *ibadah* consists of: ritual prayer five times a day, every day (*salat*); payment of a tax for relief of Muslim poor (*zakat*); fasting for the entire month of Ramadan (*sawm*); and pilgrimage to the Ka'bah and other holy places of Mecca (*hajj*).

Together the *shahada* and *ibadah* are known as the Five Pillars of Islam. Muslims may disagree over some of the finer points of Islamic law, or the significance of events in Muslim history. But the entire body of believers accept the Five Pillars in their entirety. They must be rigorously observed by Muslims to avoid being sent to hell on the day of judgement.

2.1 The Creed (*shahada*)

The simplest form of Islam's creed, the *shahada*, is recited in Arabic as: 'la ilaha illa allah; Muhammadon rasul Allah' (There is no god but Allah; Muhammad is the messenger of Allah). This phrase, known as *kalima*, must be recited in the presence of two witnesses to be accepted into the body of the religion. Thereafter it is recited during prayers, various religious ceremonies and whenever Islam is challenged by non-believers.

The first half of *kalima* — 'There is no god but Allah' — is known as *tawheed* (the unity). This is by far the most important Muslim article of faith and denial. The second half — 'Muhammad is the messenger of Allah' — is known as *risallah* (acceptance of Prophethood). It implies acceptance of Muhammad and all the Prophets as infallible messengers of Allah.

But the *shahada* does not stop at *kalima*. Acceptance of *shahada* involves unquestioning acceptance of seven articles of faith — *tawheed*, *risallah*, and five others: belief in angels (*mala'ikah*); belief in the infallibility of the Qur'an and other Prophetic books such as parts of the Bible (*kutubullah*); belief in the Day of Judgement (*yawmuddin*); acceptance of pre-destination of worldly affairs by Allah (*al-qadr*); and faith in life after death (*akhriah*).

Acceptance of all seven beliefs of the *shahada* without question is the first and central obligation of the Five Pillars of Islam. Denial of any part of the *shahada* amounts to the crime of apostophy (reversion from Islam), punishable under Qur'anic law, in extreme circumstances, by death.

Denial of the *shahada* by a sincere Christian or Jew may be forgivable on the day of judgement, but the open denial by a Muslim will certainly lead, as well as punishment in this life, to eternal damnation in the hereafter.

The Unity (tawheed)

Tawheed is the belief in the oneness and unity of Allah. Although it is summarised as 'there is no god but Allah', the phrase has far greater significance than the literal translation implies. 'Allah is greater than anything else, or anything which can possibly be imagined' would be closer to the real meaning of *tawheed*.

The concept is expressed by Allah himself in the Qur'an as: 'Say: He, Allah, is One. Allah is He on Whom all depend. He begets not, nor is He begotten. And none is like Him' (112:1–4).

Comparing Allah to other gods or humans claiming to represent Him is again rejected by Muslims as the unforgivable sin of *shirk* (association). The importance given to the sin of *shirk* originates in the mission of Muhammad (and Muslims would say all the Prophets) to the pagans, known as 'The Associators' (*mushrikun*).

Acceptance of Prophethood (risallah)

All Muslims must accept that Muhammad and all the other Prophets were chosen by Allah to deliver His literal word to all mankind. Their central mission was to lead humans back from their degeneration into paganism to the 'true path' given to the first Prophet, Adam, at the beginning of time.

Muhammad in turn, according to *hadith*, said he was the last of the 124,000 Prophets, all of whom gave the same basic message of *tawheed* to all the nations in their own languages.

The idea that Muhammad was the final Prophet, or 'The Seal of the Prophecy', is central to Islam, underlining its claim to be the true version of Judaism and Christianity. Allah himself confirmed Muhammad as the last Prophet in surah five (by tradition the last revelation) which states: 'This day I have perfected your religion for you, completed my favour upon you and have chosen for you Islam as your way of life' (5:3).

But Muslims are not permitted to worship Muhammad, or any other Prophet, as Divine or god-like as this would be the sin of *shirk*. The common Western description of Islam as Muhammadanism (probably a confusion with Christianity or Buddhism which are both named after their founders) is an absurdity.

Angels (mala'ikah)

In common with classical Christianity and Judaism, Islam teaches that all mortals (animals as well as humans) are a combination of 'clay' (*hayula*) – tangible but lifeless physical material – and 'spirit' (*jinn*) – the intangible, immortal soul which brings the 'clay' to life.

Spirits ('genies' or *jinn* in Arabic) existed as divine light (*Nur*) before the material world and mankind came into being and the first man, Adam, was fashioned from clay by Allah. But he only came to life when he was invested with a spirit. After the creation of the human race those *jinn* which were not given human form became angels.

Both men and angels were created by Allah to serve Him but, apart from angels not taking human form, there is another important difference between them. Whilst Adam and his offspring were given the freedom to obey or disobey Allah, reaping the appropriate reward or punishment on the Day of Judgement, angels have no free will and are incapable of sin. They can only do Allah's bidding.

Allah has an army of billions of angels — at least one for every human — and His omnipotence is expressed through them.

The angels are arranged in an aristocratic hierarchy with the Archangel Gabriel (*Jibreel*) at the top. All have specific functions, some move the sun and moon around the sky, others deliver thunderbolts that destroy wicked tribes. The angel Israfil has the job of sounding the trumpet which will herald the day of judgement whilst the angel Isra'il, the angel of death, sees to it that we die at the time allotted in Allah's plans.

A whole host of angels known as the Honest Recorders (*Kiraman Katibin*) have been given the job of accurately recording the thoughts, words and actions of every man, woman and child on Earth. In this way Allah is able to know what every mortal is thinking or doing at any time. The constant presence of Allah's angels is an important part of any Muslim's thinking and controls his behaviour.

Allah cannot allow any man to talk to Him directly or to see His form. Inevitably they would compare Him with something or somebody else — the sin of *shirk*. So instead He has spoken to Prophets through angels who are incapable of sin or error and can be relied upon to deliver His words completely and truthfully. The status of a Prophet can usually be judged by the rank of angel who summons a Prophet to receive revelations. Ibrahim, Isa and Muhammad, for example, were spoken to through Archangel Jibreel himself.

Satan (Iblis) — *the fallen angel*

The only angel ever to disobey Allah is Satan. According to tradition, Satan was the King of the Angels at the time Allah created Adam. But he became jealous of Adam, and refused to serve mankind as Allah had commanded. Surah 18 reports: 'And when We said to the angels: Make obeisance to Adam; they made

27

obeisance but Satan [did not].' Then Satan said: 'What! would you then take [Adam] and his offspring for friends rather than me, and they are your enemies?' (18:50).

After this argument Satan was banished from heaven and Jibreel replaced him as Archangel. Satan was bitter about this turn of events and decided to destroy mankind by leading it away from Allah towards paganism and eternal damnation.

Satan misleads men by whispering lies designed to make them believe that they are equal to Allah or can hide their thoughts and sins from Him. He attempts to lead Muslims into pagan ways and encourages them to break the Qur'anic law and corrupt Islam from within.

Satan may also give false revelations, apparently from Allah, and thereby create false Prophets and Messiahs. Some non-Muslims say that Satan misled Muhammad himself in the episode of the Satanic Verses (see 1.4 – The Dawn of Islam).

According to both the Qur'an and *hadith* the only protection against the work of Satan is constant remembrance of Allah and the word of the Qur'an. The need to protect the mind against Satan is one reason why Muslims attempt to learn the Qur'an by heart and pray so frequently. A person is only really safe from Satanic misguidance when his mind is fully pre-occupied with the worship of Allah.

Allah's Books (kutubullah)

In addition to the Qur'an, which Muslim scholars have 'proved' to be the infallible and literal word of Allah (see part 1, section 1.3 – The Qur'an), the *shahada* requires Muslims to accept the basic truth of the Jewish Torah (*Tawrat*) given to Musa (Moses); the book of Psalms (*Zabur*) given to Dawud (David); and the Gospel (*Injil*) given to Isa (Jesus).

The Qur'an mentions these three books as being the authentic word of Allah, but warns that errors (either innocent mistakes or Satanic inventions) have been introduced into them. Muslims maintain that the Qur'an is the only authentic, unchanged and comprehensive version of Allah's word and that it supersedes all the others. They point out that the Bible was altered in translation from Hebrew or Aramaic to Greek, and that words authored by mortals were mixed with those of Allah, committing the sin of *shirk* and rendering most of the book worthless. Nevertheless they accept the Biblical books of the Torah as authentic, though these too – especially the Book of Genesis – are said to contain errors.

According to Muslims, Genesis levels several minor gratuitous insults at various Prophets (Nuh, for example, is said to have been a drunkard) and contains one very serious error. This is Genesis' assertion that Ibrahim proposed to slaughter his son Ishaq (father of the Jewish nation) and not Isma'il (father of the Arab nation) until he was prevented from so doing by merciful Allah. This criticism, made in the Qur'an, underpins Islam's insistence that Allah is the God of all mankind and not just of the Jews.

Islam accepts most of the Christian Gospel as true, but, as it was composed by Isa's followers long after his death, where the Gospel and the Qur'an disagree the Qur'an, as the literal word of Allah, must be taken before the Gospel. The main disagreement between the two books concerns Isa's resurrection, with the fourth surah of the Qur'an denying that the event took place.

The Day of Judgement (yawmuddin)

Just as Allah created the universe and everything within it with the simple command 'Be!', He will bring it to end when He so desires. The end of the world is described in apocalyptic terms in surahs 81 and 82 of the Qur'an which tell how the sun and the stars are extinguished, the mountains crumble and great fires sweep the earth.

On the Day of Judgement the graves will be opened. Those who were sinful on Earth will already have been suffering in the fires of hell, but they may now be saved if they are prepared to sincerely repent. But those who have committed the sin of shirk (association) will remain beyond salvation because they have refused to recognise the existence of Allah and His mercy.

Surah 82 says: 'And when the graves are laid open . . . Most surely the righteous are in bliss, And most surely the wicked are in burning fire, They shall enter it on the Day of Judgement. And they shall by no means be absent from it. And what will make you realise what the Day of Judgement is? . . . The day on which no soul shall control anything for (another) soul; and the command on that day shall be entirely Allah's' (82:4–19).

The timing of the Day of Judgement, or the signs indicating its imminent arrival, are not mentioned in the Qur'an. But there is a wealth of hadith on the subject, much of it attributed to Muhammad himself. And it seems very likely he believed the Day of Judgement would follow relatively shortly after his death. This follows from his belief that he was Shiloh, the first and last non-Jewish Prophet in the line of Ibrahim, whose coming is foretold in the book of Genesis as one of the signs that the world is about to end.

Muhammad probably also shared the view, prevalent amongst Christian and Jewish scholars during his time, that the world was about 5,500 years old and would end before the 6,000th year — about 1100 AD. Even if he himself did not believe this, many of the earliest Muslim scholars — such as ibn Ishaq, a learned former Christian monk and his first 'official' biographer — certainly did.

The *hadith* describe the events immediately prior to the end of the world in stirring and enormous detail. The first sign will be the splintering of Islam in a great many rival sects. Qur'anic law (the *shari'ah*) will be ignored or overthrown. Brutal civil wars will rage throughout the world and the degree of savagery and torture will be so great the living will envy the dead.

Allah will send not a Prophet but the *Mahdi* (the 'chosen one', a Messiah or political ruler) to restore order. *Hadith* attributed to Muhammad describes the Mahdi as 'one of my stock and he will be of broad forehead and aquiline of nose'. The Mahdi will proclaim himself at Mecca and then lead an army of the faithful to Jerusalem, where he will establish himself as ruler of the world and restore order, peace, justice and Qur'anic law.

The Mahdi's rule, however, will last for less than a decade before the people desert him for the anti-Christ (impostor-Messiah) a figure clearly identifiable as he will have only one eye.

The anti-Christ will be enormously popular because he will legalise sin, provide food and material comfort, heal the sick and perform other pseudo-miracles to convince the people they have no need of Allah. Islam will be reduced to a rump of core believers — 'a body of my people will not cease to fight for the Truth', says Muhammad, 'Islam began in exile and it shall end in exile'.

But, just as the anti-Christ is about to destroy this last group of True Believers, the resurrected Isa will descend to earth in armour and kill the anti-Christ in battle at the town of Armageddon in Palestine. Isa will then rule Earth gloriously. There will be peace and plenty for all. Amongst his edicts Isa will order the removal of crosses from the Christian churches.

But this golden age will eventually give way to the physical destruction of the Earth, as described in surah 81, the opening of the graves and the Day of Judgement.

Early Muslim scholars confidently expected this sequence of events to begin around the year 1100 AD (the 6,000th year of creation according to tradition). As a result the preceding century was marked by fanaticism, re-doubled *jihad* and proclamation of Mahdi status by rival Muslim rulers.

When the world did not end Islam was thrown into a theological crisis which speeded up the division of the formerly united Islamic Empire into rival sects and states, many of them led by rulers claiming to be the Mahdi.

Throughout the subsequent history of Islam various rulers and scholars have continued to do this and Muslims still believe that the sequence of events will take place. They believe in it literally, but at the same time know it will be modified for the modern context. Jesus in armour, for example, could be a tank division.

Muhammad Ahmad ibn 'Abd Allah (died 1885), the Sudanese leader who defeated the British General Gordon at Khartoum, is probably the best known self-proclaimed Mahdi in recent history. It is also clear that post-war Muslim leaders such as Abdul Nasser of Egypt, Ayatollah Khomeini of Iran and Colonel al-Qaddafi of Libya have often been regarded as Mahdi by more fanatical followers and, in general, have done little to dispel this myth.

Because of the importance of Jerusalem in the story of the end of the world, the current Arab-Israeli conflict over control of the city has, in the eyes of many Muslims, apocalyptic significance. It explains, to a very large degree, the bitter intransigence of Muslim states towards Israel.

Life after Death (akhirah)

The Muslim Paradise and Muslim Hell are tangible domains, described at length throughout the Qur'an. Paradise is a state of bliss, peace and tranquillity where men are free from earthly concerns and where longed-for comforts − possibly intended to mean sacrifices made whilst on earth such as not drinking alcohol − may be enjoyed at last. Hell is full of fire and the torture of facing eternity without the knowledge of Allah and His mercy.

Those pious Muslims who die as martyrs in the defence of Islam are especially blessed. According to surah two of the Qur'an Islamic martyrs do not die. Instead their souls remain alive in a state of bliss until the Day of Judgement when they will be admitted to Paradise without difficulty.

Predestination (al-qadr)

Muslims must accept that Allah has already decided their fate in advance. There is nothing they can do to alter it. Islam teaches that Allah created the universe with a single command – 'Be!'. His creation is not chaotic, but it has an inner order and purpose beyond human understanding or questioning. All nature is under the command of Allah, as is every aspect of human life. A Muslim attempts to live his life as ordered by Allah, accepting His control of everything he does at every moment of his life.

At the same time Allah has given men free will and the ability to disobey Him if they choose to. The Qur'an is quite clear that Allah expects many people to disobey him or to be led astray by Satan into false religions.

The Qur'an is equally clear that no Muslim can convert an unbeliever to Islam by force. So if a person chooses to ignore the word of Allah and face eternal damnation, that is their right.

Predestination is the last of seven articles of the *shahada* together forming the first of the 'Five Pillars'. Everything else in the Qur'an relates to the laws (the *shari'ah*) which Muslims must follow in order to enjoy a successful, happy and holy life leading to salvation after the Day of Judgement.

The most important of these laws – the four obligations of the *ibadah* – form the remaining four of the Five Pillars.

2.2 Obligatory prayer (*salat*)

According to the rules of *ibadah*, *salat* prayers must be offered five times each day, every day – before sunrise (*as-subh*), noon (*az-zuhr*), mid-afternoon (*al-asr*), immediately after sunset (*al-maghreb*), and before midnight (*al-isha*). The most important is the evening *salat*, *al-maghreb*.

Whenever possible a Muslim must offer prayers in congregation at the mosque, where women and men pray separately, but these congregational prayers are only obligatory on Friday at noon. Otherwise Muslims may pray on their own, always facing in the direction of Mecca, on any clean surface (usually a mat kept especially for this purpose).

In Sunni Islam congregational prayers are led by any member of the congregation well versed in the Qur'an and beyond moral reproach. What is preached will be decided by the mosque's own

Imam (resident Qur'anic scholar) except in Islamic monarchies such as Saudi Arabia and Morocco where the lesson may be decided centrally by state officials.

In Shi'i Islam prayers are led by either the Imam (who has a broader political and leadership function than a Sunni Imam) or a mullah – a Shi'i priest-teacher.

The masjid and mosque

The word mosque is derived from the Arabic term *masjid* ('place of prostration') where *salat* is offered to Allah in congregation.

The simplest *masjids* are desert prayer grounds (*musalla*) consisting of a small square marked off by pegs with stones indicating the direction of the Ka'bah in Mecca. This is perfectly adequate for offering *salat* so long as it is maintained in a state of ritual purity with all traces of dirt – especially blood, urine, excrement, wine or animal fat – painstakingly removed.

Any structure or space may be used as long as the rules of ritual purity are observed. In Britain the first *masjids* used by immigrant Muslims from the Indian sub-continent were often in disused cinemas, warehouses or large Victorian houses.

The magnificent mosque architecture surrounding *masjids* in many Muslim countries is entirely optional in strictly theological terms. No building regulations appear in the Qur'an. Mosque architecture is nevertheless sacred in origin because it follows the pattern of the first mosque built by Muhammad and his companions around their *masjid* in Medina.

Mosques built according to the Muhammadan pattern enclose the *masjid* within either a large hall or open courtyard depending on weather conditions. The central piece of architecture is the *mihrab*, an arch which indicates the direction of the Ka'bah. Usually the *mihrab* is protected by a dome originally copied from the Orthodox Christian church architecture of Byzantium.

The stunningly beautiful early Arabian mosques, dating from the Golden Age of Baghdad, follow this simple design of courtyard and dome. The best example of early mosque architecture is the astonishing 7th century AD Dome of the Rock mosque in Jerusalem which marks the site of the desecrated Temple of Soloman and Muhammad's miraculous Night Journey to the gates of Paradise.

The distinctive minarets – tall, thin towers used to call the faithful to prayer – are a later, Ottoman Turkish invention. The

Ottomans also began the tradition of placing crescents on the tops of domes and minarets to indicate the direction of Mecca.

The crescent is a symbolic reminder that mortal life, like the phases of the moon, comes and goes within an allotted time. It usually appears above three or five spheres representing descending levels of reality. At the top is Allah, the absolute reality, whilst the bottom sphere represents the lowest level of reality – the physical world as experienced by humans.

The great mosques of Arabia and Persia are decorated with quotations from the Qur'an in Arabic or Persian with the flowing calligraphy woven into delicate and repetitive patterns often lavishly adorned with gold and bright blue lapis tiles. In other parts of the world mosques incorporate local architectural tradition. The great Djenna mosque of Mali, central Africa, is square and made from dried mud and tree trunks. The mosques and Islamic architecture of Mogul India, including the Taj Mahal, reflect Hindu influences.

However the mosque is decorated, its design is dominated by the need for cleansing and purification before prayer. All mosques, however humble, have a plentiful supply of clean, drinkable water and this can make them important social institutions in many parts of the Third World.

The more splendid mosques often have fountains and streams running through beautiful gardens adjacent to the *masjid*. Muhammad himself said that the mosque should be a beautiful place: 'between my house and my pulpit is a garden of the gardens of Paradise'.

Call to prayers (adhan)

Before each prayer session a mosque official known as the *Muezzin* (caller) chants the call to prayer (*adhan*) from the tallest point of the mosque, usually the minaret. The *adhan* is made with a series of rhythmic Arabic phrases devised by Muhammad himself. These days the *adhan* is often a tape recording broadcast through loudspeakers.

The *adhan* begins with the phrase 'Allah is the greatest' ('*Allah akbar*') which is repeated four times. This is followed by four more phrases – 'I bear witness that there is no god but Allah; I bear witness that Muhammad is Allah's messenger; rush to prayer; rush to success; Allah is the greatest' – each of which is repeated twice.

34

The *adhan* ends with the phrase: 'There is no god but Allah' — the *tawheed* or central dogma of the faith. *Adhan* for the dawn prayer session includes the phrase 'Prayer is better than sleep' between 'rush to success' and 'Allah is the greatest'.

Ritual washing (wudu)

Elaborate ritual washing (*wudu*) must take place before prayers, and most mosques are equipped with baths and clean, drinkable water which must, according to custom, be given free to allcomers. The Qur'an specifies the way in which a Muslim must wash to remove all sacrilegious uncleanliness. Any traces of urine, excrement, blood or unclean substances such as wine or the blood or fat of animals must be removed from the body and clothes.

Before using the water the Muslim must first sniff it three times to ensure it contains none of the unclean substances. He must then wash his arms up to his elbows and his feet up to his ankles, rinse out his mouth, wash his ears and pass wet fingers three times through his hair and across the back of his neck. If the Muslim has had sex he or she must wash the entire body before the next prayer session.

Wudu becomes invalid if the Muslim visits the toilet, passes wind, burps, falls asleep or bleeds from a wound between the act of washing and praying. If any of these things happen the process must be repeated.

Then, facing the Ka'bah in Mecca, he assumes the *qiyan* (standing) position, with head bowed and hands folded in front of him. At the direction of the prayer leader he bows forward in an L-shape, the *ruku*, keeping the legs and back straight.

He then resumes *qiyan* before prostrating himself (*sajda*) with his legs tucked under his body and his forehead on the ground. (Shi'i Muslims rest their foreheads on small cakes of dried mud gathered during pilgrimage to Karbala, the site of the martyrdom of Husayn — the second Shi'i Imam — in Iraq.)

Each cycle of standing, bowing and prostration is known as a *ra'kah* and the number of *ra'kahs* varies between two and four according to the time of day.

The Qur'an is quite clear about the social, as opposed to religious, function of *salat*. The aim is to discipline believers into unconditional acceptance of Islam and submission to Allah, and expose non-believers by their lack of zeal.

In practice the requirements of *salat* are so arduous only a limited form is practised by many Muslims and in highly secularised Muslim countries like Turkey or Soviet central Asia most believers only attend the mosque on the obligatory Friday noon *salat*. But in Muslim countries such as Saudi Arabia where Qur'anic law is strictly applied, observance is total and everything comes to a halt five times a day following the call to prayers.

2.3 Poor Tax (*zakat*)

The Qur'an specifies that all Muslims who live above subsistence level must pay *zakat*, the poor tax for the relief of poorer Muslims. *Zakat* is not charity, but the rightful and legal claim of the poor against the rich. Charity, which is also an obligation placed on the rich by Islam, must be paid in addition, according to conscience.

As *zakat* is an annual wealth tax, rather than income tax, it is not payable unless a Muslim has amassed some capital. The scale of payments, fixed by *hadith*, varies according to the type of property held, starting with a basic rate of one fortieth (2.5%) of the individual's total capital, including savings, jewels and land.

In oil-rich Muslim countries like Saudi Arabia individual liability for *zakat* can in theory be enormous. But the actual amount paid may be purely nominal as the Qur'an specifically forbids the establishment of a bureaucracy to collect the tax. Instead the money must be paid out of a sense of duty, on pain of punishment in the afterlife. Even in oil-rich Brunei – where *zakat* is the only tax – there is no system of accounting.

Although rampant inequality exists in many Islamic nations, in theory the religion is wedded to egalitarianism – a commitment which began with Muhammad's warnings to the rich and worldly merchants of Mecca.

The basic teaching of the Qur'an is that all worldly wealth is unclean unless it is used in the service of Allah and Islam and the Book is full of warnings of the terrible fate awaiting those becoming rich through 'usury' or failing to share their wealth with other Muslims. One passage tells of a rich man in hell being burned by white-hot coinage.

The rich man may only 'purify' his wealth, which he is then free to enjoy with the blessing of Allah, by paying *zakat*.

2.4 Fasting (*sawm*)

To show obedience to Allah and willingness to forgo the pleasures of this life, every Muslim must fast each year for the whole 30 days of Ramadan, the ninth month of the Islamic calendar. This is the month, according to tradition, when Muhammad received the first surah of the Qur'an from Allah after being called by the Archangel Gabriel at Hira.

From dawn to dusk Muslims may not eat, drink, smoke or have sex. Ramadan builds up to the 'Night of Power' (*Laylat al-Qadr*), generally on the 27th day but dependent on the arrival of the new moon. This commemorates the actual day the revelation began. The most devout Muslims spend the last ten days of Ramadan in continuous prayer, ending with the Feast of Breaking the Fast (*'Id al-Fitr*), one of the few occasions when Muslims may celebrate and take part in festivities.

Every Muslim who has reached puberty must take part in *sawm* (fasting). There are exemptions at the time for the sick and women nursing newly-born babies, but they must make up for any days missed by fasting at other periods throughout the year.

The Qur'an permits all Muslims to rise one hour before dawn and eat a special large breakfast called *suhur* to help them through the day. Some Muslims, especially in Muslim minority countries like Britain, practise only a limited form of fasting by giving up something like smoking or eating rich foods.

The spread of Islam to lands far north and south of Arabia has caused many practical difficulties for observance of *sawm*. In far northern or southern latitudes it often falls, according to the Muslim lunar calendar, in the summer when the time between dawn (first glow of sunlight) and sunset (last glow of the sun) can be as much as 20 hours. This applies to Britain, and there is much inconclusive debate amongst British Muslims on how to deal with the problem. In the past the requirements of *salat* and *sawm* have been one reason why Islam has been restricted to tropical latitudes, where the times of prayer and fasting do not vary considerably. A Muslim community could not exist within the Arctic Circle without breaking the laws of *salat* and *sawm*.

2.5 Pilgrimage to the Holy Ka'bah, Mecca (*hajj*)

Hajj translates from Arabic as 'visitation of Holy Places' (of

Mecca). All Muslims must attempt it at least once during their lifetime. The focus of *hajj* is not Mecca as such, but the Great Mosque which encloses Islam's holiest shrine, the Holy *Ka'bah* (Arabic for 'House of Allah').

The Ka'bah is a cube-shaped stone building, believed to have been built at the beginning of time by Adam for the exclusive worship of Allah. The fate of the shrine is symbolically linked to Islam's battle against mankind's repeated reversion from the true religion of Allah-worship into paganism.

In the centuries after Adam's death his offspring became pagan, allowed the Ka'bah to fall into disrepair and filled the remains with pagan idols. About 3,500 years ago the Prophet Ibrahim smashed the pagan idols and re-built the temple. But by the time of Muhammad's Prophethood the Ka'bah had once again degenerated into a pagan shrine. This time Muhammad cleared out the idols and defeated the pagans. And it was here that he first preached Islam, gaining converts from the pagan tribes worshipping there.

To take part in *hajj* Muslim men must be sane, free from serious physical infirmity and – most importantly – able to provide for their dependants whilst they are away. This is one of the main reasons why Muslims fear getting into debt.

Muslim women may take part in *hajj*, subject to various restrictions. During it each must be accompanied by a male chaperon (*mahram*), who must be a man she is legally unable to marry – for example her father or brother. Preparations for *hajj* start in the last days of Ramadan, especially after the night of *Laylat al-Qadr* (Night of Power), with the process of entering the state of cleanliness and physical and spiritual consecration known as *ihram*.

Before leaving for Mecca pilgrims (*hajji*) pray almost continuously and perform extended versions of elaborate washing rituals (*wudu*) required before prayer. *Hajji* also shave, and cut their hair and nails.

They then don the special *ihram* costume consisting of two unsewn pieces of clean, white cloth, one tucked around the waist covering the legs down to the knees and the other wrapped around the shoulders. Both men and women wear sandals rather than shoes and women in addition wear extra garments entirely covering their legs and face.

Once *hajji* have entered the state of *ihram* they are not allowed to remove their ritual dress, even when sleeping. No Muslim in a state of *ihram* may wear tailored clothes, jewellery or perfume. A male pilgrim may not shave or cut his hair, and no pilgrim is allowed to harvest crops, hunt animals, arrange to be married, or have sex even if they are married already.

The pilgrims then make their way to Mecca by any transport or method they choose. Some make epic journeys on foot from faraway Muslim countries like Indonesia and central Africa, but today most fly. Once at Mecca they can not enter the precincts of the Great Mosque surrounding the Ka'bah until the first day of the month of Dhu al-Hijjah, two months after Ramadan.

On entering the Great Mosque the *hajji* performs a ceremony known as *tawf* – the core ritual of *hajj* – which involves circling the Ka'bah seven times anti-clockwise. Most attempt to touch or kiss the 'black stone', about a metre square, which Muhammad himself placed in the wall of the shrine. Numbers are often too great to allow contact with the stone and *hajji* may instead raise their right arm in its direction, keeping it raised.

Men make the first three laps at a jogging pace and walk the last four. After each lap there are ritual declarations of faith and prayers. Women must walk slowly for all seven laps.

Once the *tawf* is completed most *hajji* drink from the *Zamzam* stream which flows through the basement of the Great Mosque, though this is not obligatory. The stream has religious significance, according to *hadith*, as Hagar, the concubine of Ibrahim, and her son Isma'il were wandering in Mecca unable to find water. Just as they were about to die of thirst Hagar dug her heel into the ground and Allah caused a spring to come to life. The water gushed so quickly she had to shout '*zam! zam!*' – the Arabic for 'stop! stop!' – hence the stream's name of *Zamzam*.

The significance of this story for Muslims is that it shows Allah's mercy towards Isma'il, the founder of the Arab nation and direct ancestor of Muhammad. If Allah had allowed Isma'il to die, Muhammad would not have lived and mankind would never have received the final prophecy.

The salvation of Hagar and Isma'il is commemorated by drinking from the *Zamzam* and by *sa'ayee*, the second obligatory ritual of the day, during which *hajji* believe they are following the exact path taken by the pair as they searched for water. The *hajji* passes seven times between the nearby peaks of as-Safa and Marwa at an increasing pace, quoting whatever passages they have memorised from the Qur'an.

The Saudi Arabian royal family, which has taken upon itself responsibility for the upkeep of the Holy Places, has considerably modernised the setting for today's age, with a wide, air-conditioned, marble-lined corridor between the two peaks to accommodate the huge numbers of people performing *sa'ayee* at any given time.

After *sa'ayee* the *hajji* returns to the campsites (*mawaqueets*) outside the precincts of the Great Mosque – which these days includes several five star hotels as well the more traditional tents – where they must remain in a state of *ihram* until sunset on the 8th day of the month. How long this is depends which day they choose to begin *tawf* and *sa'yee*.

They then move to Mina, about eight kilometres east of Mecca, and spend the night at prayer. At sunrise the next day they travel en masse to Mount Arafat, in the hot desert fifteen kilometres east of Mina, for the climax of *hajj*. Most people now travel in buses or private cars along the new ten lane motorways.

After arriving at Arafat pilgrims spend the afternoon standing in prayer. Up to two million pilgrims of all races and classes can be seen on the slopes of the mountain on this day, rendered anonymous by their *ihram* costume and chanting – truly one of the most remarkable sights in the world.

At sundown the pilgrims return along the motorways and flyovers to Mina to prepare for the feast of sacrifice ('*Id al-Adha*) on the following day, the most important in the Muslim calendar.

'*Id al-Adha* celebrates Ibrahim's willingness to sacrifice his own son Isma'il to show obedience to Allah, and Allah's mercy in allowing Ibrahim to substitute a ram thus allowing Isma'il and his offspring (including Muhammad) to live. During '*Id al-Adha* Muslims are required to slaughter a live animal in commemoration and at Mina the *hajji* slaughter hundreds of thousands of sheep, camels and cattle in the culmination of their pilgrimage.

At the same time every Muslim in the world, whether taking part in *hajj* or not, is called upon to slaughter an animal in his home for the feast. Sometimes, especially in countries where Muslims are a minority, liberal-minded mosque officials will accept money as a substitute for the ritual slaughter, but this is rare even amongst Muslims in Britain. It is common, however, for British Muslims to preside over the sacrifice at an *halal* (lawful) butcher's shop rather than in the kitchen of their own home.

In India and Indonesia the slaughter of cows is sometimes a cause of strife between Muslims and Hindus, who worship the cow as sacred. And in Mina and Mecca the disposal of the hundreds of thousands of sacrificed carcasses has created a growing public health problem as the number of pilgrims has increased and the number of poor Arabians who used to live off the sacrifices has declined.

Following the feast in Mina *hajj* ends with the ritual of *ramyee*. Pilgrims throw stones (a ritual form of Muslim execution) at three pillars symbolising Satan which they pass on their way back to Mecca. *Hajji* throw seven stones at each, chanting: 'Allah is the greatest!' (*Allah akbar!*).

In practice these days sheer numbers prevent many *hajji* from getting near enough to take accurate aim, and serious injuries have been caused by over-enthusiastic *hajji*, too far away to hit the pillars, throwing stones which land on those closer to the front.

In an attempt to solve overcrowding problems the Saudi Arabian royal family has employed Western architects to build tiered walkways, ten lane highways and stadiums to ease movement between the various holy sites.

This has brought widespread complaints that the holy places have now been turned into a nightmare landscape of motorways, flyovers and towering western-style hotels on the sacred campsites overlooking the Ka'bah. This has been coupled with complaints about high prices charged by *hajj* tour operators, sponsored by the Saudi government.

The government is also accused of having too tolerant an attitude to rich Muslims, who perform *hajj* from the comfort of air-conditioned limousines and five star hotel rooms, paying poorer Muslims to stand in the queues for them.

But, despite these complaints, most *hajji* are profoundly moved by the experience and often return to their communities as truly changed people.

During *hajj* they may also have joined one of the bewildering array of Islamic sects and sub-sects which use it, in the tradition of Muhammad, to preach their version of the true faith. The Shi'i Muslims (as found in Iran) have been particularly active in this missionary work in recent years and have also attempted to politicise the event by turning *hajji* against the Saudi royal family, whom they regard as usurpers.

The *hajj* has been disrupted twice in recent times. In 1979 pro-Libyan revolutionaries stormed the Great Mosque as part of a failed coup attempt. The culprits were beheaded by the Saudi royal family. In 1983 plans for a similar attempt to storm the mosque by Iranian extremists was foiled by intelligence work.

2.6 Defence of Islam (*jihad*)

Shahada, salat, zakat, sawm and *hajj* make up the Five Pillars of Islam. But these obligations are only the absolute minimum a Muslim can do in order to serve Allah. The truly pious Muslim takes on many more obligations and most important, the responsibility of responsibilities, is *jihad*, sometimes described as the 'sixth pillar' of Islam.

The literal translation of *jihad* is 'striving' (to serve Allah), but it is usually translated in the West as 'Holy War', which Muslims agree is a reasonable translation. All Muslims must constantly wage *jihad* to the best of their practical ability. In particular a fellow Muslim attacked for practising Islam must be defended by the rest of the Muslim community.

The duty to participate in *jihad* for the defence of Islam is, according to the leading fundamentalist Muslim scholar Sayid Abdul Ala Mawdudi, 'just as much a primary duty of Muslims as daily prayers or fasting. One who shirks it is a sinner. His very claim to being a Muslim is doubtful. He is plainly a hypocrite who fails in the test of sincerity and all his *ibadah* (religious observance) and prayers are a sham, a worthless hollow show of devotion'.[1]

[1] 'Towards Understanding Islam'. UK Islamic Mission, 1980. Mawdudi was founder of the Ja'mat-i-Islami Party in Pakistan, one of the first modern 'fundamentalist' movements. Mawdudi played an important role in the campaign to make secular Pakistan the world's first 'Islamic Republic'.

3.0 THE MUSLIM YEAR

The Islamic calendar consists of 12 lunar months, totalling 364 days, and does not correspond with the Western calendar which is adjusted to ensure winter and summer solstices are always on the same date. Use of the lunar calendar ensures religious festivals and Holy Days do not coincide with pre-Islamic pagan seasonal festivals or fertility cults.

As a result important events such as the Muslim new year, the start of *hajj* and the Ramadan fast move steadily around the seasons and take place on different days of the Western calendar every year.

Over the next ten years or so the Muslim new year will take place in summer, slowly moving back into the spring. The 1410th year of the Muslim age (dated from Muhammad's declaration of war against Mecca – *Anno Hijarae* or AH) began on August 4th 1989 AD. But the first day of the year 1421 AH, for example, will begin on the 6th April 2000 AD.

Islam has only two major 'official' Holy Days. The most important is the Feast of Sacrifice (*'Id al-Adha*) on the 10th day of Dhu al-Hijjah, the twelfth month of the Islamic year. The second, the Feast of Breaking the Fast (*'Id al-Fitr*) marks the end of the annual fast for the whole of the ninth month of Ramadan.

Classical Islam officially recognises only these two Holy Days, but in practice Muslims celebrate many more. Some of these additional festivals like *Mawlid an-Nabi* (Prophet's Birthday) resemble ceremonies from other religions Muslims have come into contact with – in this case the Christian Christmas.

During periods of extreme orthodoxy Islamic authorities have attempted to ban 'pagan' festivals like this, but they persist.

i. *Muharram* ('The sacred month')

The year begins with the month of Muharram and the first festival, *Ashura*, takes place on its tenth day. Ashura began as the Jewish feast of Passover and still celebrates the Israelite flight from Egypt. According to Islamic tradition it is also the day on which Noah left the ark. To distinguish Ashura from Passover Muslims fast for two days instead of one. Since the early Middle Ages Ashura has had a special importance for Shi'i Muslims as the anniversary of the martyrdom of Muhammad's grandson (via his daughter Fatima) Husayn ibn 'Ali (see Part Three – Islamic Sects, Shi'i (Shi'ite Islam)).

ii. *Safar* ('The month which is void')

By tradition Safar is the month in which Muhammad once suffered a serious illness and was unable receive any further revelations from Allah – hence the title. Exceptionally devout Muslims spend most of it in mourning to commemorate the Prophet's illness. But the last Wednesday of the month is sometimes celebrated by a carnival day commemorating Muhammad's return to health.

iii. *Rabi al-Awai* ('The Spring')

The title of the third Muslim month is incongruous since, being lunar, it is not linked to the spring or any other season. For the next ten years in the northern hemisphere Rabi al-Awai will fall in the autumn or early winter.

The origin of the title is unknown. It may have been left over from the earlier pagan solstice-based Arabian calendar, or a mystical reference to its main event – Muhammad's birth-death day.

Most of the month is devoted to commemorating the birth and death of Muhammad which, according to tradition, took place on the same day, the 12th of the month. The festival of 'Id-Mawlid al-Nabi which marks the day was first celebrated in 1207 in what is now Iraq and associated with the growth of heretical Sufi teaching about the personal survival of the soul after death (for Sufi Islam see Part Three – Islamic Sects, Sufi'ism).

During 'Id-Mawlid Muslims give each other presents, dress in bright clothes and burn incense and candles. 'Id-Mawlid's similarity to Christmas, with the doctrinal danger of worshipping

Muhammad instead of Allah, has led to its being banned during periods of extreme Sunni orthodoxy.

iv. *Rabi al-Thani* ('The month following Spring')

The fourth month has no special significance for orthodox Sunni or Shi'i Muslims but is celebrated by Sufis, especially in India and Pakistan. One of the largest Sufi monastic orders, the Qadiriyah, was founded during this month in the 11th century AD.

Sufis dress in bright clothes and hold carnivals to celebrate the death of their 'saint' 'Abd al-Qadir, founder of the order. This activity is regarded as deeply heretical by Shi'i and, especially, Sunni Muslims.

v./vi. *Jumada al-Qula* ('The first month of dryness') and *Jumada-th-Thaniyyah* ('The second month of dryness')

The fifth and sixth months are set aside for preparation of the intense series of festivals which begin half-way through the following month of Rajab. Any form of public religious devotion, except *salat* (prayer), is banned by Sunni Muslims during these months, though local Shi'i martyr worship and Sufi saint worship does take place.

vii. *Rajab* ('The revered month')

Some Muslims mark the first day of Rajab with the minor festival of Ragha'ib, when it is believed that Muhammad was conceived by his mother Aminah. But the main preoccupation is increasing religious observance leading up to the 27th day, the most widely observed festival of the year even though it is not recognised by classical Islam − The Night Festival of the Ascent (*Laylat al-Mi'raj*).

During Laylat al-Mi'raj Muslims commemorate Muhammad's miraculous 'Night Journey' from Mecca to Jerusalem on the back of a winged beast. The site of the miracle where he was shown the gates of heaven and hell is now marked by the Dome of the Rock mosque in Jerusalem, to which many Muslims make a minor pilgrimage to celebrate the festival.

On the 13th day Shi'i Muslims celebrate the martyrdom of 'Ali (son-in-law of Muhammad), the first Shi'i Imam. As at the festival commemorating Husayn, the Shi'i mark 13th Rajab with huge displays of public grief and declarations of willingness to die the death of the Muslim martyr.

viii. *Sha'ban* ('The month of division')

The festival of Laylat al-Bara'ah ('Night of the Battle of Badr' or, popularly, 'Night of the Fates') takes place on the night of the full moon and formally commemorates Muhammad's conquest of Mecca.

Its real significance, however, is the superstition that this is the night on which Allah reviews all mankind and determines the fate of each believer (just as He determined that Muhammad should conquer Mecca).

Just as al-Mawlid is the unofficial 'Muslim Christmas', Laylat al-Bara'ah is the unofficial Muslim version of Diwali, the Hindu 'festival of lights' when Hindus make pacts with their gods to ensure good luck for the coming year.

As such the festival is clearly pagan in origin and although ferociously discouraged by Sunni Muslim authorities (especially in Pakistan) remains popular in countries with Hindu populations like India, Bangladesh and Indonesia.

Believers often pray all night, presenting Allah with a type of confession of their sins over the past year before they beg forgiveness. This directly contradicts a central point of orthodox Muslim theology – that Allah cannot be addressed directly and anyhow has already predestined believers' fates.

The day is also the key Shi'i festival of *al-Mahdi* – the mystical birthday of the 'concealed' twelfth Imam descended from Muhammad, who will one day be resurrected or re-born and lead *jihad* to rid Islam of the Sunni 'usurpers'.

ix. *Ramadan* ('The month of great heat')

The ninth month, Ramadan, is the most demanding of the Islamic year. All Muslims must fast for its entire 30 days in accordance with the *ibadah* rules of *sawm*. Throughout the month all secular festivities are banned and in those countries where Qur'anic law is enforced, those breaking any part of the *ibadah* are severely punished.

Ramadan climaxes with the festival of *Laylat al-Qadr* ('Night of Power') on the 27th.

According to tradition this is the night on which Muhammad

received the first surah of the Qur'an and he is thought to be at his most active in the world on this night. According to *hadith* if a Muslim spends it at prayer this is believed to be more effective than 'a thousand months' of prayer during other times of the year.

Many Muslims – especially those preparing to take part in *hajj* in the following months – do pray all night, repeating a highly demanding routine (the *tarawih*) based on cycles of 20 and 23 repetitions of the *qiyam-ruku-sajada* (prostration) ritual of *salat* prayers.

x./xi. *Shawwal* ('The month of hunting') and *Dhu al-Qa'dah* ('The month of rest')

The first day of the tenth month begins with the festival of *'Id al-Fitr* (feast of breaking the fast) which ends the fast of Ramadan and is therefore a source of a huge officially-sanctioned celebration. In Turkey it is known as the 'sugar festival' (*Seker Bayrami*) when large amounts of sweets are eaten. In stark contrast to Ramadan, Muslims tend to be in high spirits throughout the tenth and eleventh months.

xii. *Dhu al-Hijjah* ('The month of *hajj*')

The tenth day of Dhu al-Hijjah is the holiest in the Islamic calendar and commemorates the willingness of the Prophet Ibrahim to sacrifice his son Ishmael (Isma'il) to show submission to Allah.

It is on this day that every Muslim must ritually slaughter an *halal* (lawful) animal such as a sheep, goat, cow or camel. The focus of *'Id al-Adha* is the valley of Mina, near Mecca, where pilgrims end their *hajj*.

The Shi'i have one additional festival, *'Id al-Ghadir*, the day on which they believe Muhammad announced he should be succeeded by their first Imam, 'Ali. But apart from this *'Id al-Adha* brings the religious year to a climax, and there are no further festivals until the cycle begins again with Ashura on the tenth day of the first month of Muharram.

47

MONTH	FESTIVALS
1 *Muharram*	Ashura (10th) two days of fasting to commemorate the passover and the deliverance of Nuh (Noah). Shi'i Muslims also celebrate the martyrdom of Imam Husayn.
2 *Safar*	Entire month of mourning for the sufferings of Muhammad.
3 *Rabi al-Awai*	'Id-Mawlid al-Nabi (12th) birth-death day of Muhammad.
4 *Rabi al-Thani*	Sufi celebrations of the death of 'saint' 'Abd al-Qadir.
5 *Jumada al-Qula*	No religious festivals.
6 *Jumada th-Thaniyyah*	No religious festivals.
7 *Rajab*	Ragha'ib (1st) celebration of the conception of Muhammad. Laylat al-Mi'raj (27th) festival of Muhammad's 'Night Journey'.
8 *Sha'ban*	Laylat al-Bara'ah (approx 10th) the 'Night of the Fates'. Also Shi'i festival of the al-Mahdi – the 'expected one'.
9 *Ramadan*	Entire month of fasting (*sawm*). Laylat al-Qadr (approx 27th) the 'Night of Power'). Celebration of the first revelation given to Muhammad.
10 *Shawwal*	'Id al-Fitr (1st) the feast of breaking the Ramadan fast.
11 *Dhu al-Qa'dah*	The month of rest.
12 *Dhu al-Hijjah*	Climax of *hajj* (first nine days). 'Id al-Adha (10th) 'Feast of Sacrifice' Islam's holiest day. 'Id al-Gahadir (18th) Shi'i festival adoption of Imam 'Ali by Muhammad as his true successor.

4.0 ISLAMIC LAW – The *shari'ah*

The Islamic concept of law and justice is entirely different from that of the secularised countries of the West. Muslims believe Allah, through the Qur'an, revealed the universal laws which govern not just the affairs of man but the very laws of nature.

Any man who disobeys these universal laws will find himself at odds not just with secular authority but with his own nature and that of the rest of creation. And, since all Muslims must accept that their every action and thought is recorded by Allah's angels, there can be no escaping punishment for disobedience following the Day of Judgement.

The body of detailed Islamic law – the *shari'ah* (Arabic for 'what is prescribed') – is based on the later surahs of the Qur'an. The fifth, one of the last to be revealed, is also one of the most important sources of the *shari'ah*. It begins with the injunction: 'O you who believe! fulfil the obligations' (5:1) and ends with the words: 'Allah's is the kingdom of the heavens and the earth and what is in them; and he has power over all things' (5:120).

This surah also deals with dietary law and prohibits drinking and gambling, which are linked to pagan rites: 'Liquor and gambling, idols and divining arrows are only a filthy work of Satan; give them up so that you may prosper' (5:90). The same surah prescribes the punishment for theft: 'As for the thief, both man and woman, chop off their hands. It is the reward for their own deeds and exemplary punishment from Allah' (5:38).

The first part of the earlier surah 24 deals with sexual behaviour and prescribes punishments for adultery and false accusations of adultery: 'As for the fornicatress and the fornicator, flog each of them [giving] a hundred stripes . . . And those who accuse free women then do not bring four witnesses, flog them [giving] eighty stripes, and do not admit any evidence from them ever; and these it is that are the transgressors . . . Allah's curse will be on him if he is a liar' (24:1–7).

Muslims believe that legalistic later surahs such as these represent Allah's revelation of the law in its entirety. But it is also accepted that, in some cases, the laws thus revealed are lacking in detail. For example the Qur'an says that Muslims must pray frequently and wash themselves before so doing. But it does not say how often prayers should be offered or the way in which Muslims should wash.

To find these things out a Muslim must turn to *hadith*.

Tradition (hadith)

The second source of *shari'ah* law is the collected deeds and sayings of Muhammad and his earliest followers known as *hadith* (Arabic for 'traditional reports or sayings').

The 33rd surah says: 'Certainly you have in the Messenger of Allah [Muhammad] an excellent exemplar . . .' (33:21). This is understood by Muslims as endorsement of the infallibility of Muhammad's *hadith*.

The rituals and obligations of the Five Pillars of Islam – including the *shahada* (basic creed) – as well as much of the criminal law originate from *hadith*.

Legal consensus (ijma)

The process of *ijma* is a method of framing laws based on agreement between jurists. *Hadith* has Muhammad saying: 'My community shall never be in agreement in error'. It is a consensus decision which along with *hadith* and the Qur'an legitimises law.

A perfect *ijma* decision is possible, with everybody in agreement, but this position is often difficult to reach because of the lack of previous authorities. *Ijma* therefore usually means that consensus exists amongst the large majority.

Analogy (qiyas)

Where legislation is required for social problems not dealt with in sufficient detail in either the Qur'an or *hadith*, Muslim rulers and law-makers must use analogy (*qiyas*) to frame legislation or new religious doctrines. This arises when situations which Muhammad or the Qur'an cannot have foreseen arrive and therefore cannot be dealt with by either the Book or *hadith*.

For example the Qur'an specifically prohibits the consumption of 'wine', but does not mention any other alcoholic drinks. By using *qiyas* Muslim jurists have extended the prohibition to other alcoholic drinks which cropped up later, such as whisky. When Islam was faced with the problem of drug-taking *qiyas* dealt with it by making it analogous with drinking alcohol.

4.1 Islamic Jurisprudence (*fiqh*)

Fiqh is Islamic jurisprudence − the science of Islamic law. It is through *fiqh* that Islam demonstrates how it covers all aspects of life, by including those things which in the West would be considered private and beyond the scope of the legal system − such as style of dress.

Fiqh divides all human behaviour into five categories: forbidden (*haram*); discouraged (*makruh*); neutral (*mubah*); recommended (*mustahabb*); and obligatory (*fard*).

The obligatory (*fard*) category covers the Five Pillars of Islam including mandatory prayer, alms-giving, fasting and so on. These *fard* requirements are legally binding on all Muslims. Failure to carry out a *fard* obligation is both a sin and a crime punishable in *shari'ah* courts.

Forbidden (*haram*) behaviour is also both sinful and criminal. Anything mentioned as unlawful in the Qur'an and Old Testament falls within the *haram* category including all the prohibitions of the Ten Commandments. In addition the Qur'an explicitly prohibits the eating of certain food.

No Muslim may eat animals which have died from natural causes or which have not been ritually slaughtered. This ritual slaughter must be carried out by a clean knife cut to the throat and accompanied by a prayer said over the carcass. Only meat produced in this way is lawful (*halal*); everything else is *haram*.

Pig meat is *haram* however it is produced, as is the meat of any carnivorous animal. A Muslim may not drink blood, eat dried blood, drink alcohol or eat any substance with even a drop of alcohol in it (2:168−173).

The discouraged (*makruh*), recommended (*mustahabb*) and neutral (*mubah*) categories deal mainly with such things as

51

manners, charity, personal habits and social life. The law here is based mainly on the vast literature of *hadith*.

For example Muhammad once said: 'When a man drinks, he should not breathe into the beaker' and this now forms part of the *shari'ah* in the discouraged (*makruh*) category. He also said: 'Allah is polite and likes politeness' and so polite behaviour forms part of the *shari'ah* in the recommended (*mustahabb*) category. There are thousands of such sayings.

Discouraged (*makruh*) behaviour is not sinful but it is criminal and Muslims can be punished in a *shari'ah* court – especially if they deliberately persist with discouraged behaviour.

Much of what would be called civil law in the West is covered by the recommended (*mustahabb*) category of the *shari'ah*. Muslim courts will endeavour to reconcile the parties where there are disagreements but, if they fail, the party failing to follow *mustahabb* behaviour may be punished. Some of the most important *mustahabb*-based laws include those governing funeral rites, marriage and family life.

Funeral Rites

Islamic graves are simple and sometimes anonymous because the erection of a headstone is seen as a form of idol worship. No coffins are permitted.

The corpse is washed according to the rules of *wudu* (ritual ablutions, as before prayer) and simply wrapped in white sheets (three for a man, five for a woman) before being placed in the ground laying on its side with feet facing towards the Ka'bah in Mecca. There is no elaborate ceremony and only a few short prayers are said over the grave. Islam does not encourage extended periods of mourning.

It is the duty of every Muslim to attempt to say the contracted form of the *shahada*, 'la ilaha illal lah; muhammadon rasul Allah' (there is no god but Allah; Muhammad is the prophet of Allah) as his last words on earth.

Age of Majority (balogh)

Legal majority is established by evidence of puberty. Unless proved otherwise boys of 12 or less and girls of nine or less are assumed to be minors. But both are assumed to have reached puberty by fifteen. As soon as puberty is established Muslims become full legal citizens, bound by the *ibadah* and with full criminal liability for their actions. They may also become married, sign binding contracts and take a full part in the life of their mosque.

Duty of Keep the Peace (Alaykuim)

Muslims have a general responsibility of civility and respect for other Muslims based on dozens of *hadith* and Qur'anic verses. The *hadith* recommends a Muslim to greet another Muslim with the ritual salutation 'As-salamu Alaykuim' (peace be on you). The other person replies: 'Wa-alaykuim as-salam' (peace be on you also). If any of the Prophets are mentioned in conversation they should also say 'peace be upon them'.

The Qur'an says that slander, blasphemy, ridicule and the use of offensive names are crimes as serious as physical assault or murder and should be punished accordingly.

In the Middle Ages the punishment for false accusation – especially false accusation of rape on the part of women – was removal of the tongue by its root. This form of punishment may still take place in remote areas, though reports are rare.

The Qur'an and *hadith* also emphasise that Muslims should be fair and honest in commercial dealings and refuse to charge or accept the payment of interest on loans. Beyond this there are dozens of verses in the Qur'an and hundreds of *hadith* encouraging good manners, respect for elders, kindness to children and the like. Most of these further instructions have the *mustahabb* legal status which means they are recommended – and may be taken into consideration when weighing more serious legal matters – but are not obligatory.

Dress

The Muslim rules of dress are also designed to prevent offence as well as making observance of *salat* (ritual prayers) easier. Men are required to cover their bodies from their navel to the knees and woman must cover their entire bodies from the head to the ankles.

Other than this there is no prescribed form of dress, although *hadith* emphasises simplicity and avoidance of tight clothes which would make bending during *salat* difficult. No particular colours are recommended except white which must be worn during *hajj*. The Shi'ah have a preference for black clothes symbolising their continual state of mourning for the martyrs. Other groups, such as the Bedouin Ibadites, prefer blue. These choices are cultural rather than Qur'anic.

Muslims tend to keep their heads covered at all times. This is a sign of respect for Allah's angels who symbolically reside in the skulls of men and women and must therefore be protected. Usually this takes the form of a small cap similiar to the Jewish skull-cap.

Women, in addition, usually cover the cap with a shawl over the head. In some Muslim countries men wear additional headgear over the cap or instead of it. But no hat or turban may be worn which prevents the forehead touching the ground during *salat* and this accounts for the brimless hats, such as the fez, popular in some Muslim countries. Brimmed Western hats such as the trilby are often worn by secular Muslims in countries like Turkey (as are moustaches) as a deliberate sign of secularism.

Women's legal status

Muslim women are required to accept that they have different roles from men in most respects, and are expected to be obedient, firstly to their fathers and then to their husbands – unless they ask her to do something which would break other parts of the *shari'ah*.

The fourth surah of the Qur'an describes a woman's father or husband as her 'master', with the right to beat her if she does not obey. The same surah says: 'Men are the maintainers of women . . . the good women are therefore obedient [to their masters] (4:34). And the second surah, whilst revealing the laws of divorce in great detail, says of women: 'And the men are a degree above them' (2:228).

The *shari'ah* requires both men and women to take part in the obligations of the Five Pillars, but communal prayers at the mosque on Fridays are optional for women and tend to be predominantly male affairs. No woman is allowed to lead prayers.

Islam has a strong menstruation taboo and no woman may attend the mosque during her period. In some Muslim countries – especially amongst the Shi'ah – it is the practice to confine women until their period is over (*purdah*). The taboo is understandable given the great emphasis placed on avoidance of blood, especially during the frequent prayer sessions, but is still basically cultural and not Qur'anic.

In some Muslim countries women are required to cover their

entire bodies in the presence of men other than members of their immediate family. This law is based on passages of the Qur'an which instruct women not to wear jewellery (and, by analogy, make-up) and to cover their hair, breasts and 'private parts' in public (33:59 and 24:30-31).

But forcing women to cover their entire bodies − as in much of Arabia and Iran − is again cultural rather than Qur'anic, as are many other examples of discrimination against, or maltreatment of, women throughout the Muslim world. These include the practice of removing parts of the female genitals, so-called 'female circumcision', which is widespread in Muslim Arabia and Africa.

Whilst the Qur'an does place restrictions on Muslim women, it also guarantees them the right to own and inherit property, to participate fully in political affairs and to sue for divorce − in short a complete, separate legal identity.

Muslims often point out that these rights, available in theory to Muslim women since the time of Muhammad, have only been introduced in Europe comparatively recently. And in the Third World − where Islam is mainly to be found − there is no doubt that the application of the *shari'ah* can improve the social position of women considerably.

Marriage (an-nikh)

Muslim marriages are simple contracts specifying the obligations and duties of both the bride and the groom in advance. The *shari'ah* gives the bride the right to negotiate over the contract and specify such matters as the value of the dowry (*mahr*) to be paid by bridegroom and, since Islam permits polygamy, whether he may or may not take further wives. The mahr need not be particularly valuable and, if the bride agrees, it may even be a token sum of money or a simple gift such as a new set of clothes.

In practice most Muslim marriages are arranged and the bride has little choice in the matter. This, however, is a cultural rather than a religious practice, common in peasant-based cultures throughout the world regardless of religion.

Nevertheless, the pressure on Muslim girls to accept the husband selected by their parents is intense, even in countries like Britain. But there are signs that increasing numbers exercise their legal right to repeatedly object to marriage contracts and therefore effectively turn down proposals.

Both the Shi'i *shari'ah* and the most widespread version of the Sunni *shari'ah* grant women the right to contract for their own marriage. Only the minority versions of the *shari'ah*, found mostly in Indonesia, Malaysia, North Africa and Saudi Arabia, deny it.

All versions of the *shari'ah*, however, prevent a Muslim women from marrying a non-Muslim male. A Muslim man, on the other hand, can marry any virginal women subscribing to a faith based on scriptures recognised in the Qur'an, such as Christianity or Judaism.

Polygamy

The Qur'an and *hadith* assume that large numbers of Muslim men will be killed waging *jihad* in the defence of Islam. Polygamy was legalised specifically to take care of the large number of widows likely to be left behind.

The relevant surah, number 4, was given to Muhammad shortly after the Quyrash inflicted a terrible defeat on his army at the battle of Uhud. It says: 'And if you fear that you will not deal fairly by the orphans, marry the women who seem good to you, two or three or four; and if you fear that you cannot be fair to so many, then one only . . .' (4:3).

This has been interpreted to mean that a Muslim man may take up to four wives, as long as he can provide for them and all their children. In practice the vast majority of Muslim men only take one wife these days and if they have a second the reason is usually that their first wife could not bear them children. And in many Muslim countries (for example Syria, Iraq and Pakistan) a polygamous marriage requires specific permission from the state. In Tunisia and Algeria they have been abolished, and even in conservative Morocco there is a law allowing divorce if a first wife objects to a polygamous second or subsequent marriage.

Throughout the Muslim world the *shari'ah* gives polygamous wives additional rights. They must, for example, be given a separate home of their own and they are entitled to an equal proportion of their husband's time, attention and estate.

The position is rather different for Muslim rulers and conquerors. The Qur'an says that military victors may take 'the captives that your right hand possess as [wives]' (4:3). Throughout Muslim history kings and generals have remarried the wives of their defeated opponents, usually to gain kinship with the aristocracy of newly conquered peoples.

The most recent example of this was Muhammad ibn Sa'ud, the founder of Saudi Arabia, who married the wives of the dozens of tribal rivals he killed whilst creating his state in the 1920s. The Ottoman Turkish sultans also took hundreds of wives for similar dynastic purposes and the practice of mass polygamy spread downward through the aristocracy of their Empire creating, in the European mind, the legend of the rapacious, harem-keeping Muslim male.

Divorce (talaq, khul and faskh)

The customs preceding a divorce in an attempt to hold a failed marriage together vary enormously in the different Muslim nations.

But once the position is irretrievable the *shari'ah* provides three types of divorce proceedings. The first, *talaq*, is simple unilateral renunciation of marriage by the husband. Under the rules of *talaq* a husband may divorce his wife, or wives, at will, provided he is not insane and has not made the declaration in jest or whilst drunk (drunkenness is a separate offence against *shari'ah* law).

No formalities are required other than his public declaration of the fact. The Shi'i variant of the *shari'ah* requires four witnesses. The wife usually keeps her dowry and the husband has to provide for the children and give her additional maintenance for a short period.

Although *talaq* is still available in most Islamic nations, its practice is rare and it has been abolished outright in the Soviet Muslim republics, Afghanistan, Algeria and Tunisia. Divorce by mutual consent (*khul*) is much more widespread and takes the form of a legal renunciation of the original marriage contract.

The *shari'ah* also provides for divorce at the request of the wife, usually on the grounds that the original contract has been broken. She can ask for this in exchange for repaying the dowry.

The availability of this form of female divorce, known as *faskh*, is granted to all Muslim women in theory but in practice availability varies from country to country. The most liberal conditions are found in Afghanistan, the Soviet Muslim republics, Turkey and Egypt. The most restrictive, from the point of view of the wife, are found in Saudi Arabia, Iran and the Gulf.

The exceptional grounds of renunciation of Islam – apostophy – by either husband or wife leads to immediate judicial dissolution of the marriage.

57

Inheritance

The *shari'ah* laws governing inheritance are extremely complex, creating twelve separate categories of relatives entitled to fractions or multiples of one sixth of the estate remaining after funeral expenses. In general, at each stage, women are discriminated against by having exactly one half of the claim of any male in the same category, since it is assumed that men will have a duty of care to their wives.

4.2 Punishment (*qisas* and *hadd*)

Just as Islamic theology has no place for redemption of the individual mortal soul in the eyes of almighty Allah, the *shari'ah*'s penal code has no place for the rehabilitation of the individual offender in this world.

The code is extremely crude and severe and is based entirely on the doctrine of *qisas* – retaliation on behalf of the community as a whole. *Qisas* has its origins in the Old Testament doctrine of 'an eye for an eye; a tooth for a tooth' – the principle revealed by Allah to Moses (Musa) when He first revealed His law to the Israelites.

The punishment for murder or attempted murder is beheading; for theft, amputation of the right hand; for adultery and false accusation of adultery or blasphemy, stoning to death; and for drunkenness, severe flogging to the point of death.

Together these severe punishments are known as *hadd* – the Arabic word for the process of 'limitation' – and, like most things in Islam, can only be understood in the context of Muhammad's mission, the problems he faced and the revelations Allah gave in order to help him overcome those problems.

The society in which Muhammad lived was almost entirely lawless and disputes dragged on for generations, with rival tribes exacting endless revenge on each other in the form of blood feuds.

In the process of creating the Islamic state Muhammad brought the feuds to an end and replaced the endless quest for revenge with simple and inescapable 'retaliation' (*qisas*) against the guilty parties. This is why the severe *shari'ah* punishments are known as *hadd* – the Arabic for 'limitation' (of feuds).

The logic behind the punishments at the time was simple –

it is better to mete out swift and severe punishment than allow an incident like the theft of a camel, adultery or murder to become a tribal feud killing hundreds.

The Qur'an and *hadith* contain several warnings that these severe *hadd* punishments should be given sparingly and only when the offender has either been accused by four eyewitnesses of spotless moral character or, preferably, has confessed to the crime.

When the European powers established their rule in large parts of the Muslim world they found it was difficult to obtain a conviction in a *shari'ah* court, even when the circumstantial or forensic evidence was overwhelming. And, because of the Qur'anic injunction to use the *hadd* sparingly, *shari'ah* courts had a reputation for arbitrary action.

It was entirely possible that two offenders convicted of identical crimes of theft on the same day would be treated entirely differently. One, who may even have committed the greater offence, would walk free with only the punishment of hell awaiting him, the other may have his hand chopped off.

It was mainly for these reasons that the *shari'ah* courts were superseded by more workable and efficient European-based systems of criminal law in the 19th and early 20th centuries. Only in the Arabian peninsula, where tribal conditions have scarcely changed since Muhammad's time, did the complete *shari'ah* and *hadd* system remain unchallenged throughout the European colonial era.

The re-introduction of *hadd* punishments in countries such as Pakistan, Iran, Mauritania and Sudan after independence is part of a general desire to return to Islamic fundamentals. As far as can be seen, reintroduction of *hadd* punishments has done little to curb crime and there are strong signs that in Sudan, Iran and Afghanistan the Qur'anic warning to use *hadd* punishments sparingly has been ignored.

Amnesty International has estimated the number of executions in Iran as over 1000 a year since the Islamic Revolution and there are similar reports of widespread vengeance in the parts of Aghanistan under control of the 'fundamentalist' Mujahideen rebels. Use of *hadd* punishments on this scale obviously has more to do with contemporary politics than a strict interpretation of the Qur'an.

PART TWO

ISLAMIC HISTORY

Important Historical Centres

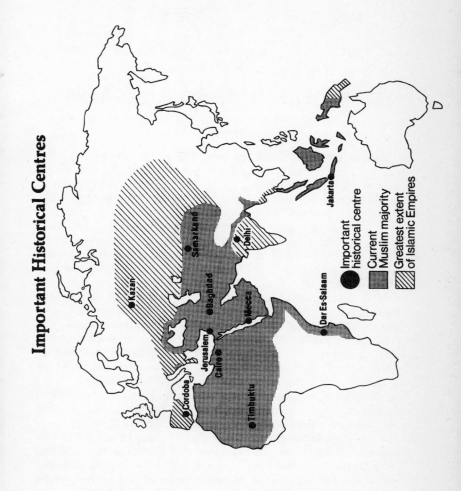

Cordoba

Timbuktu

Cairo

Jerusalem

Kazan

Baghdad

Mecca

Samarkand

Delhi

Dar Es-Salaam

Jakarta

● Important
historical centre

Current
Muslim majority

Greatest extent
of Islamic Empires

1.0 THE ISLAMIC EMPIRE (622–1258)

The Muslim calendar takes the year 622 AD as the start of the Islamic epoch. The date marks the *hijrah*, when Muhammad and his followers were driven out of Mecca and settled in Medina, 480 kilometres to the north east, founding the first Islamic state and declaring war on the pagans.

Islam's choice of 'year zero' is highly significant. It shows how the religion, from the very beginning, was a political creed to establish the rule of Allah on earth. This mission has always been equal to and inseparable from Muhammad's purely religious and spiritual mission as a Prophet.

In the last ten years of his life Muhammad inflicted total defeat on his original enemies – the pagan Quyrash aristocracy of Mecca – and by doing so united all the Arabic tribes in submission to both his rule and that of Allah. The later Medinan surahs of the Qur'an, delivered to Muhammad after he became the ruler of Medina, Mecca, and most of Arabia, are preoccupied with the laws under which the new state should be governed.

The Medinan surahs also address the immediate political problem he faced – holding together the fragile alliance of tribal leaders he had painstakingly constructed. Tribal alliances were not new in Arabia but they usually disintegrated after the short-term military objectives had been met and the spoils divided up.

Muhammad received help from revelations which stressed above all else the need for all believers to be united so they could carry out further expansion and avoid military defeat.

The third surah, for example, is addressed directly to the fractious tribal leaders: 'Be not disunited, and remember the favour of Allah on you when you were enemies, then He united your hearts so by His favour you became brethren; and you were on the brink of a pit of fire, then He saved you from it' (3:102).

The same surah also lays down detailed instructions for the care of the widows and orphans created by the battles in defence of Islam, and says how the booty should be shared between warriors and the new Islamic state.

But the Qur'an gave no guidance on the key question – how a successor was to be chosen after the Prophet's death. It was left to Muhammad himself to solve this tricky problem.

The traditional method of dynastic succession, probably acceptable to the tribes, was out of the question. Although Muhammad had a daughter, he had no son. And as he had been proclaimed the last Prophet none of his subsequent followers could also claim leadership as a new Prophet.

1.1 The Succession to Muhammad

In the event Muhammad nominated Abu Bakr, who had been his closest friend, was a fellow member of the Hashim clan and had risen to be the leading general of the Islamic army. Abu Bakr himself stipulated he would have to face election and ratification by all the tribal leaders.

After Muhammad died in 632 Abu Bakr was duly elected *Caliph* (ruler), but despite this some of the tribes immediately rebelled. Abu Bakr put down the tribal rebellion which broke out following Muhammad's death and went on to conquer northern Arabia and parts of Syria and western Persia before dying in battle just two years after his election.

He was succeeded by his nominee, 'Umar ibn al-Khattab, as the second Caliph amid a renewed successional crisis and threats of revolts. 'Umar, however, soon established his rule beyond question by sheer military skill and a stunning series of conquests which brought huge wealth back to Mecca.

'Umar inflicted defeat after defeat on the Christian superpower of Byzantium, conquering all of Syria, Palestine, Egypt and parts of North Africa. The capture of Jerusalem, the Holy City of all the Ibrahimic religions, was most significant to Muslims because of Muhammad's 'Night Journey' and the miraculous revelation of the gates of heaven and hell.

After 'Umar's death, the Dome of Rock mosque, a magnificent architectural achievement, was constructed on the site on Temple

Mount and became a Muslim shrine second only in importance to the Holy Places of Mecca.

'Umar's successes to the east were even greater. The powerful Persian Empire was utterly destroyed and all of its territory as far as central Iran was incorporated into the Empire.

'Umar was undoubtedly a messianic figure who believed he could conquer the whole world. He conscripted the entire Arab nation and forbade any occupation other than warrior. As a result Arabs formed a military caste, doing no other work and effectively looting new territories. The Arab warrior class depended on conquered peoples, especially the highly literate Persians, to administer the Empire.

'Umar was stabbed to death by a resentful Persian administrator in Basra in 644. Unlike Muhammad and Abu Bakr he had not nominated a successor but instead appointed a six man council (the *Shura*) to select a new Caliph. The two main candidates were 'Ali ibn Abi Talib, the husband of Muhammad's daughter Fatima and a member of Muhammad's Hashim clan, and 'Uthman ibn 'Affan, a member of the more distantly related 'Umayyad clan.

The Shura offered the Caliphship to 'Ali on condition he did not proclaim a Hashemite dynasty. But 'Ali refused these conditions and so the position went instead to his rival 'Uthman.

'Uthman's succession was controversial and contained the seeds of a civil war which was to threaten the very existence of the original Arab Islamic Empire and still divides Muslims today.

For the first five years of his reign 'Uthman enjoyed the support of the most of the clans opposed to 'Ali's Hashemite dynastic ambitions, as they were certain they would downgrade their own status. Continuing military success also made 'Uthman popular. But after 650 the pace of conquest slowed and taxes had to be introduced to replace the previous supply of fresh booty. 'Uthman was accused of misusing state funds, nepotism and plotting to establish a dynasty of 'Umayyad Caliphs to follow him.

1.2 The Khariji revolt

Opposition to 'Uthman was strongest amongst Muhammad's original followers, known as the *Khariji* ('successionists'). They included many of his closest friends and relatives, and many Bedouin tribal leaders who had been the first converts outside Mecca and Medina. They were fanatical Muslims determined to uphold the traditions of Mecca at all costs.

The Khariji suspected that many of the tribes and peoples who had since joined the body of Islam and with whom they were now required to share the spoils were opportunists and fortune seekers. They even feared some might – as both the Qur'an and Muhammad had warned – actually be 'Satanic', working to destroy Islam from within.

Under the first two Caliphs, Abu Bakr and 'Umar, conquered peoples had been allowed to convert to Islam by simply accepting the obligations of the Five Pillars. But in some cases they had only had to accept the *shahada* (the duty to recite the creed: 'There is no god but Allah; Muhammad is the messenger of Allah').

As a first step the Khariji insisted that acceptance and performance of all the duties of the Five Pillars were the bare minimum condition for conversion to Islam. They then categorised the people who had accepted the Five Pillars as 'Common Believers' (*Mu'minum*). But they said these converts could only be regarded as proper Muslims if they also led sin-free lives. It followed that any Muslim committing an act forbidden by Qur'an, or failing to carry out additional 'good deeds' had renounced Islam and became a non-believer (*kafir*).

Khariji doctrine was rejected by 'Uthman as it would have been a serious brake on the Imperial expansion which was the source of his power. His answer was to sponsor a rival sect, the *Murji'ah* ('those who postpone judgement') which taught that judgement of a Muslim's piety should be left to Allah – not the Khariji. Those who broke the *shari'ah* (Qur'anic law) were to be punished, but still regarded as Muslims. Non-believers could join Islam if they outwardly observed religious law and accepted the rule of the Caliph.

The establishment of the Murji'ah infuriated the Khariji. When 'Uthman was convincingly accused of breaking the *shari'ah* by stealing from state funds, the Khariji proclaimed him a Satanic anti-Muslim (*kafir*), demanded his overthrow, and declared war on his 'Umayyad clan.

In 656 'Uthman was killed in Mecca by a rioting Khariji mob and the Shura immediately appointed 'Ali ibn Abi Talib as the fourth Caliph.

The Caliphship of 'Ali was welcomed by all but the most extreme Khariji groups. As a member of the Hashim clan he was a much closer relative to Muhammad than 'Uthman and, most importantly, he was married to Muhammad's daughter Fatima.

67

Following her father's death Fatima had become prominent in Khariji circles, and 'Ali himself shared many Khariji ideas.

'Ali promised to root out 'Umayyad corruption and growing Syrian and Persian influence in the Imperial administration, but within a year was challenged by Mu'awiya, the 'Umayyad governor of Damascus and cousin of 'Uthman.

Mu'awiya pledged himself to avenge the death of 'Uthman, to destroy the Khariji and overthrow 'Ali's Khariji-backed Caliphship. Based amongst the newer converts of Damascus, he started an inconclusive and costly civil war against 'Ali and the traditionalists of Mecca.

'Ali's army was composed mainly of Bedouins, Kharijis and Meccan clansmen, while the Syrian and Persian forces supported Mu'awiya and the 'Umayyads. The result of the civil war was to halt external expansion of the Empire, and Byzantium was able to recapture important possessions such as Alexandria in Egypt.

After the costly Battle of Siffin in 658, 'Ali proposed arbitration. Mu'awiya accepted, but the Khariji were outraged, accusing 'Ali of breaking the *shari'ah* by failing to wage *jihad* against the 'Satanic' 'Umayyads.

The 4,000 Kharijis in 'Ali's army, about one tenth of the total manpower, declared war on him, but 'Ali put down the revolt at the Battle of Nahrawan, killing all but a few hundred.

Mu'awiya and the 'Umayyads, meanwhile, broke off negotiations, resumed the civil war and over the next three years captured most of the Empire's territory. 'Ali's death, however, came not at their hands but through a vengeful Khariji survivor of the Battle of Nahrawan.

After his defeat of the Khariji 'Ali had declared his own dynasty, and was therefore succeeded by his eldest son Hassan, but Hassan lasted a mere six months before admitting defeat and accepting Mu'awiya Umayyad as Caliph. A year later he was murdered by the 'Umayyads and the Hashemite claim to the Caliphship passed to 'Ali's second son, Husayn.

1.3 The Shi'ah (*Shi'ites*)

Mu'awiya attempted to end the continuous crisis over the Caliphship by proclaiming an 'Umayyad dynasty based on simple patriarchal succession. Then, to reduce the influence of the Hashim clan and Khariji-type traditionalists he moved the capital of the Empire from Mecca to the 'Umayyad stronghold of Damascus.

The measure worked. The surviving Khariji repeatedly rebelled but were easily defeated and by the end of the 8th century, after vicious persecution, were effectively extinct, only surviving in isolated Bedouin communities in remote desert areas. Their modern descendants are known today as the Ibadites and live in small nomadic desert communities, observing a version of the *shari'ah* completely unchanged since the original Khariji revolt (see Part Three – Islamic Sects, The Ibadiyah (Ibadites)).

The remaining non-Khariji members of 'Ali's defeated army, now led by his son Husayn, became known as the *Shi'ah* (sometimes called the Shi'ites) from the Arabic word for 'partisans'.

The Shi'ah saw the 'Umayyads as Satanic usurpers who had stolen the Caliphate from the Hashemites in order to destroy it. Unlike the Khariji, whose puritanical tradition they largely inherited, the Shi'ah continued to present a serious threat to 'Umayyads.

Their first major rebellion came in 680 when Husayn took on the 'Umayyad army at the Battle of Karbala in Iraq. But he was hopelessly outnumbered, his army was destroyed and he was killed.

Thereafter Shi'i Islam became predominantly a creed of rebellion and martyrdom and Husayn's death is commemorated by the Shi'ah in their most important religious festival of the year – Ashura.

The 'Umayyad Caliphs then gave free reign to the Murji'ah movement, established by 'Uthman to counter Khariji 'fundamentalism'. The Murji'ah ('those who suspend judgement') developed the relatively permissive theological and legal doctrines later to form the basis of *Sunni* Islam (from the Arabic word for followers of the 'smooth path').

Murji'ah doctrines were tailored to the political needs of the Caliph and designed to help Imperial expansion and government. They taught that subjugated peoples could convert to Islam, regardless of their actual commitment to the faith. All they had to do was accept 'Umayyad rule and carry out the duties of the Five Pillars, even if they did so uncomprehendingly. It did not matter if new subjects were insincere, as conversion would come later – perhaps even in generations – through constant practice of the Five Pillars.

The 'Umayyad Caliphs were efficient but tyrannical rulers. They introduced currency, regularised taxation and set up a crude system of justice. The new legal system was based on the Murji'ah principle that breaches of the *shari'ah* should be dealt with in 'Umayyad courts, but offenders still be allowed to profess Islam. The question of who was a sincere Muslim and who was a Satanic Muslim, which had caused the original civil war, was to be left to Allah on the Day of Judgement.

Although Shi'ah revolts continued the 'Umayyads were extremely successful in their Imperial expansion, capturing vast new territories in the west, including all of North Africa, Spain and southern France.

In 732 they began the conquest of northern Europe but were turned back when they were narrowly defeated at the Battle of Poitiers, less than a hundred miles from Paris, by a Christian army led by the Frankish general Charles Martel. In the east they gained the territory of modern Pakistan as far as the river Indus and mounted expeditions against Chinese armies in central Asia.

As more tribes and peoples were converted – from the Atlantic coast of Spain across to northern India and the borders of China – the number of religious practices and faiths held in the name of Islam multiplied enormously, which was just what the Khariji had feared. The 'Umayyads regarded their Empire first and foremost as Arab and had effectively turned Islam into a religiously decadent political tool for expanding Arab rule.

In the new territories 'Umayyad rule was based on granting generals the right to loot in return for a tribute of one fifth of their gain to the 'Umayyad treasury in Damascus. These local Arab rulers often became fabulously rich in their own right, like Musa the Great, conqueror of North Africa and Spain, who personally owned 300,000 black slaves captured from the Vandal kingdom of Carthage.

But non-Arab Muslims were not allowed to share in the spoils and Christian or Jewish Arabs were often given legal privileges over them. Arab Christians even became governors of non-Arab Muslims in parts of the Empire, which caused huge resentment amongst local Muslim populations.

The Persian Muslims, seeing themselves as more cultured than the Arabs, were particularly bitter about this doctrine of Arab superiority. In 749 a group of Shi'ah-influenced Persians led by Abu al-Abbas al-Saffah exploited a new successional wrangle within the 'Umayyad clan itself to attack in their heartlands of Syria and Egypt.

Al-Abbas struck when most of the Arab army was in Europe on another attempt to conquer France and the rest were demoralised by repeated defeats at the hands of Martel's Christians. In 750 Al-Abbas decisively defeated the 'Umayyads at the Battle of Zab in Egypt, captured Damascus and slaughtered almost the entire 'Umayyad aristocracy.

Those who managed to flee made their way to Spain where, in 755, the Abbasids allowed them to become *Emirs* (subject rulers) of their own Iberian 'Umayyad Caliphate.

1.4 The Golden Age of the Abbasids

With the fall of the 'Umayyads the Shi'ah believed their time had finally come. They had played a major part in al-Abbas' victory and now demanded their current Imam (supreme religious and political leader) Ja'far as-Sidiq, great-grandson of the original Shi'ah martyr Husayn, be installed as Caliph.

Al-Abbas was sympathetic, but died in 754 whilst still negotiating. His son al-Mansur turned on the Shi'ah, murdered the Shi'i Imam and within five years had crushed the Shi'ah as a coherent military force.

Al-Mansur declared himself Caliph and pronounced an Abbasid dynasty, and although groups of Shi'ah revolted throughout the five hundred years of Abbasid rule which followed, they were never successful. Al-Mansur's first act was to consolidate his clan's domination of the Empire by the construction of Baghdad as an Imperial capital city, on the River Euphrates in the heart of the second major area of ancient Arab settlement, Iraq.

This massive project used up the greater part of the captured 'Umayyad treasury. Building work took forty years, employed 100,000 Persian architects and craftsmen, and claimed the lives of hundreds of thousands of exhausted slaves.

When it was completed Baghdad was by far the most advanced and civilised city in the world. It had amenities like a sewerage system, fountains and street lighting and was graced by hundreds of fine public buildings including mosques, law schools, universities and *madrasas* (college-hospices and institutes of medical science).

The Abbasids soon emerged as enlightened rulers and great

patrons of the arts and sciences. Learning flourished, especially after the conquest of parts of central Asia held by the Chinese introduced the science of paper making. Greek philosophical tracts, gathered from other conquered territories, were translated, published and made widely available. By 850 there were over 700 lending libraries in Baghdad.

In this atmosphere dozens of heterodox religious sects emerged, debating theology and law and trying to impose some order on the doctrinal chaos and legal arbitrariness inherited from the 'Umayyads. The most important of the new learned sects was the *Mu'tazilah*, a rationalist group strongly influenced by the Greek philosophical texts.

The Mu'tazilah introduced into Islamic theology and legal thinking the new concept of human free will over which Allah had only a limited influence. According to its teaching a person was responsible for his own actions, regardless of his knowledge of the Qu'ran. This meant he could be judged for his moral actions on earth, without reference to his status as a Muslim. These doctrines led to the establishment of courts of law with rules of evidence.

Judges were allowed to weigh the evidence without reference to the Qur'an in all cases and the science of *fiqh* (Islamic jurisprudence), based on the work of jurists in addition to the literal word of the Qur'an and *hadith* (sayings and customs of Muhammad and his companions), was born.

These practices enraged traditionalists, especially Arabs and the Shi'ah, who denounced the new rationalist doctrines as Satanic. They demanded a return to the principle of predestination, where all matters were decided by Allah in advance, with total reliance on the Qur'an and Muhammadan *hadith* to settle legal disputes.

In the years that followed Muhammad's death vast numbers of *hadith* attributed to him circulated throughout Arabia. Some were clearly authentic, and others were clearly fabricated to serve the political purposes of the various factions which emerged amongst the Muslims immediately following his death.

The first major compilation of Muhammadan *hadith* was made by the Abbasid lawyer Muhammad ibn Isma'il Bukhari (died 870) and is known as the *Sahih al-Bukhari* ('authentic according to Bukhari'). Bukhari examined a mass of *hadith* and found the overwhelming majority to be the invention of rival factions. Bukhari included only 7,000 *hadith* as authentic after, according to tradition, examining 60,000.

Islam as it is practised today is largely based on the Sahih al-Bukhari. The rituals and obligations of the Five Pillars of Islam – including the *shahada* (basic creed) – as well as much of the criminal law originate from Muhammadan *hadith* collected by Bukhari.

In addition to Bukhari's collection other Abbasid lawyers produced five more books of *hadith* which are today regarded as entirely authentic. These six books of *hadith* are known as the 'smooth path customs' (*Sunnah*) from which Sunni Muslims take their name.

Once the *hadith* had been authenticated in this way the rationalists were prepared to compromise and re-introduce *hadith* as a vital part of the legal system. The basic shape of Sunni Muslim law was defined by the great Abbasid lawyer 'Ali ibn Isma'il al-Ash'ari (died 935) in his book 'The Elucidation of the Foundations of Religion'.

Al-Ash'ari shaped Sunni'ism as a combination of rationalist judicial reasoning (*fiqh*, *qiyas* and *ijma*) and traditionalist reliance on the legal verses of the Qur'an and *hadith*. And the four main legal schools founded by the Abbasids during al-Ash'ari's lifetime – the *Maliki, Hanafi, Shafi,* and *Hanbali* – remain the four sources of modern Sunni law.

Al-Ash'ari's legalism brought great stability and led to the rapid development of political and legal institutions. The first 200 years of Abbasid rule became a Golden Age for the Islamic Empire with subjects guaranteed a large measure of peace, protection, and access to rationalist courts with rules of evidence and well defined procedures.

The economy boomed and Baghdad became the centre of a thriving network of trade routes. The sciences of mathematics, astronomy, architecture, chemistry, medicine and navigation all flourished. A vast collection of art treasures was created and amassed. The Qur'an was translated into Persian and other languages, and the foundations of national literatures laid in many parts of the Empire – not least Persia itself, where many works of superb poetry and fiction were written.

The army was reformed and Turkic horsemen recruited from the territories in central Asia steadily replaced Arabian tribesmen as its cutting edge. The ferocious Turks, backed up by the Persian scientific discoveries, gave back the momentum of the early 'Umayyad days and there were spectacular new military successes in central Asia and India.

The Emirate System

The Abbasids continued the 'Umayyad policy of allowing local rulers to run outlying areas of the Empire with little interference from central government. But the old 'Umayyad anarchy, when local conquerors were free to do as they pleased, was progressively phased out with the introduction of the Emirate system.

The first Abbasid Emirate was established in Spain by surviving members of the 'Umayyad aristocracy who had fled there following the fall of Damascus. Rather than pursuing the civil war the Abbasids allowed the 'Umayyads to rule Spain in return for payment of tribute and acceptance of their overlordship. The 'Umayyad rulers were given the title of *Emir* (subject Caliph) and their state known as an Emirate.

The system was developed by succeeding Abbasid Caliphs and widely applied throughout the Empire to prevent it disintegrating into rival national states. The duties of the Emirs varied according to the strength and financial circumstances of the Abbasids.

In periods of Abbasid strength Emirs were little more than local governors and tax collectors but when central government was weak – especially in the latter part of the dynasty – Emirs effectively became independent sovereign rulers. From the 11th century onwards an increasing number of Emirates declared themselves fully independent Caliphates.

In general the rival Caliphs restricted their ambitions to their own states, except for the pro-Shi'ah Fatimid Emirs (and, after 1022, 'Anti-Caliphs') of Egypt, who repeatedly staked a claim to rule the entire Empire.

The Fatimids sponsored a fanatical Shi'ah sect called the Assassins who terrorised the Abbasid lands for two centuries from their base in Syria. But they never managed to muster an army strong enough to seriously challenge Baghdad.

The Abbasid Caliphs, secure in their palaces, steadily began sinking into decadence, and the Caliphs became distant, semi-divine figures, inhabiting a Chinese-style 'forbidden city' in the centre of Baghdad. But as early as the 9th century the Caliphship had already become a largely ceremonial institution, only one part of an increasingly complex legal and constitutional system.

The actual administration of the state, justice and religion passed to the plurality of law schools and government departments, whilst control of the army passed to shifting

74

alliances of Seljuk Turkish generals and Persian lawyers. Plots and conspiracies were rife and groups resembling political parties emerged to lobby for the interests of various factions, with the Turks beginning to emerge as the most powerful force.

Meanwhile the fabulous wealth and growing decadence of the Abbasid court became legendary throughout the world. Caliph al-Mutawakkil, who ruled from 847 until 861, had 4,000 concubines whilst his successor, Caliph al-Mustain, owned a carpet 400 metres square, sewn from gold, silver and silk thread and studded with diamonds and rubies representing the eyes in figures of birds. From the 10th century onwards it was normal for Caliphs to appear in solid gold armour during court ceremonial.

The Caliphs were to live in powerless splendour for another 400 years, attempting to keep alive the myth that they were rulers of a united Islamic Empire destined one day to rule all the world. But, in reality, by the end of the 12th century the Abbasid Empire had degenerated into a loose federation of autonomous Emirates. Baghdad, still enormously wealthy as a trading centre, was under day-to-day control by a group of Seljuk Turks with a large force of military slaves, many black, and known as the Mameluks.

The most serious secessions of the late 12th and early 13th centuries were by the Turkic Ghaznevid Emirates in northern India. The Ghaznevids declared themselves to be fully independent Sultans (the Turkish word for Caliph) and in so doing opened up a split in the Empire.

The growing pagan Mongol Empire founded by Genghis Khan was quick to exploit it and the Abbasids were able to put up little resistance when the Mongol armies of Halagu Ill-Khan (Khan of the West), the grandson of Genghis Khan, swept into Persia in the 1250s.

In 1258 Halagu captured Baghdad itself and put the entire population of one million to the sword. Palaces were looted and libraries destroyed.

The events of 1258 were a calamity for Islam, the Persian nation and the whole of mankind. Human culture was set back at least a century by the destruction of centres of learning and the murder of hundreds of scholars and scientists.

The Mongol destruction of the Abbasid Empire also brought an end to the dream of maintaining a unified Islamic Empire. Islam would henceforth remain both divided and predominantly Asiatic in outlook.

2.0 OTTOMAN SUPREMACY (1259–1650)

After the Mongol invasion and the sacking of Baghdad, the Islamic Empire split into three main parts which began to develop separately, diverging more and more as the centuries passed.

After converting en masse to Islam in about 1300, the Mongols turned their attention back to their central Asian homelands. The central area of the old 'Umayyad and Abbasid Empires, including Persia, Iraq and Arabia, became a backwater.

The centre of what remained of Arab culture moved west to Egypt and north Africa, where Arab rulers served the new Turkic and Mongol Emperors as Emirs. Arab influence was almost completely extinguished at the centre of the new Islamic Empire.

And although Arabic remained the sacred language of Islam, Turkish and Persian were to become the dominant languages for teaching, art, literature, politics and diplomacy.

The Mongol Khan Tamberlaine moved his capital to Samarkand, in what is now Soviet central Asia. From there he built a mighty Islamic Empire stretching from Kiev and Moscow in the West, to China in the East, which was also to form the basis of the great Islamic Mogul Empire in northern India, and the brief but brilliant flowering of Islamic culture in central Asia.

In the west, power passed to first to the Seljuk Turks and Mameluks whose greatest military achievement was the decisive defeat of the Christian Crusader states on the Palestinian and Syrian coasts. The Mameluks and Turks continued the anti-Crusader campaign north into the ancient Christian Byzantine heartland of Asia Minor (the territory of modern Turkey), a conquest almost completed by 1300.

Meanwhile, further afield, the distant Muslim lands south of the Sahara, where the first Negro Muslim communities had been established in the late Abbasid period, went their own way, ignored by both the Mongols and, later, the Ottomans.

2.1 The Ottoman Sultanate

The most important of the three independent centres of Islamic civilisation as far as the modern Western world is concerned was the Ottoman Empire. After an unpromising start, the Ottomans succeeded in bringing about what the 'Umayyads and Abbasids had fruitlessly attempted for almost 600 years – the conquest of Christian Byzantium and the subjection of the Byzantine lands of Asia Minor and the Balkans.

The ground for this had been laid in the last century of the Abbasid Empire, when the Seljuks – the ferocious Turkic horseback warriors from central Asia – were being used as 'shock troops' in the centuries-long war against Byzantium.

After Baghdad fell to the Mongols, the Seljuks declared an independent Sultanate in eastern and central Asia Minor. There they were joined by wave upon wave of fellow Turkic warrior tribes fleeing from the Mongol expansion in central Asia. Just as the Abbasids had employed the Seljuks as 'shock troops', the Seljuk Sultans now used the newly arrived Uzbek Turkic tribes to strengthen their army and expand westwards. But again, like the Abbasids, the Seljuks became decadent and allowed actual power to pass to the Uzbek generals (*pashas*).

In 1301 Ozman, an Uzbek of the Ottoman clan, overthrew the Seljuk aristocracy and proclaimed himself Sultan of Asia Minor. The Seljuks were relegated to becoming Emirs of the older, eastern part of the realm.

The new Ottoman state was religiously heterodox. The Sultans were Sunni, in the tradition of their former Seljuk-Abbasid masters, but many of their soldiers were Shi'ah and, steeped in the cult of Shi'i martyrdom, vicious fighters.

The Ottomans inflicted a series of defeats on the declining Christian Byzantium and the Ottomans quickly expanded westwards to threaten the capital of Constantinople, which was then by far the most important Christian city in the world.

Constantinople was conquered in 1453 by the Ottoman Sultan Mehmed II, who slaughtered much of the population and forced the rest into exile. Churches, including the great Cathedral of St

Sophia, were converted into mosques and the city was renamed Istanbul ('city of Islam').

The effect of the fall of the Byzantine Empire on Christian Europe was enormous and the large numbers of scholars who fled to Italy were influential in the city states in sparking off the Renaissance and increasing trade with the east.

The centre of Christian Orthodoxy was forced north to Moscow, becoming the spur for consolidating the Russian nation. And, after the defeats and factional sectarianism which characterised the early Christian Crusades, Western or Roman Christianity was galvanised by the need to stop further westward Ottoman expansion.

At first the rule of the Ottoman Sultans was unstable and constantly threatened by the rebellious inclinations of Shi'i soldiers. To counterbalance their influence the Sultans formed groups of fanatical fighters – the Orders of Janissaries (from the Turkish phrase *Yeni Ceri* – new soldiers), manned by the children of captured Christian Byzantine slaves who were raised as fanatical Sunni Muslims.

When Mehmed died in 1481 he nominated his eldest son Bayezid as the new Sultan and the Shi'ah promptly revolted in favour of Bayezid's brother, Jem. The Janissaries suppressed the revolt and from then on became the decisive force in Ottoman politics. After 1500 Bayezid attempted to reduce their power but they switched their support to his son Selim, who in 1512 defeated his father in battle and proclaimed himself Sultan.

With Janissary support Selim laid the foundations for a world Ottoman Empire based entirely on the despotism of the Sultan. The Shi'ah were ruthlessly suppressed and retreated to Persia, joining with local groups of Shi'ah eventually forming their own state under the Safavid Shahs. Shi'i Islam thereafter remained a largely Persian-Iranian faith and the new state was in continual conflict with the Ottomans throughout the centuries that followed.

To end further successional disputes Selim confined his son Suleyman to the harem in the Imperial Palace and introduced the policy of fratricide (murder of brothers). Under this system whenever a new Sultan ascended to the throne his brothers would be locked in cells. As soon as the new Sultan had produced his first son the brothers would be slaughtered. The Sultan's sons would then be confined in the harem until their father's death and the cycle would begin again. By the 17th century the system had grown to the point where Sultans had between 1,500 and 2,000 concubines and produced dozens of sons, only one of whom would become Sultan while all the others would be killed.

Although the Ottoman court retained many of the traditions of the Abbasids inherited through the Seljuks, their method of rule in their expanding domains was more similar to that of the earlier 'Umayyads, whom many Sultans conspicuously tried to emulate.

Ottoman rule also had the hallmark of the Sultan's nomadic Turkic ancestors. The idea of developing territory and investing in it for future gain was alien. Land and peoples were exploited to the point of exhaustion and then more or less abandoned in favour of new ground.

This short-term policy meant the Empire relied on continuous expansion for stability. Newly-conquered lands became the property of the general (*pasha*) who had won them, who was left free to deal with the local population and resources as he saw fit. Usually this meant slavery, ruthless exploitation and brutal rule.

The Ottoman Empire reached the peak of its power during the rule of Selim's son, Suleyman the Magnificent (1520–66), and his grandson Selim II (1566–74). Its power was already in decline by 1683 when the second, and last, attempt was made to conquer Vienna. Victory would have opened up central and western Europe but, without the conquest of these lands, and no new significant wealth to distribute to the pashas, the Empire lost momentum and went into slow decline.

2.2 Safavid Persia

The first people to benefit from Ottoman decline were the Shi'ah Safavid Shahs of eastern Persia.

The Safavid dynasty had been founded much earlier by a Sufi, Safi al-Din (died 1334), who converted to Shi'ism and turned it into a revolutionary Persian nationalist movement. The guerilla army of the Safavid Shahs – known as the Red Heads because they wore bright orange turbans – had first fought the Mongols in 1250 and then the Ottomans, but in 1501 they declared independence when the Ottomans outlawed Shi'i Islam in their territory, strengthened by important Shi'ah elements from the Ottoman army who had fled from persecution.

Under Safavid rule eastern Persia once again became a great cultural centre, with a flowering of the arts and sciences. The influence of the monastic-type Sufi orders, founded in Persia during the Golden Age of the early Abbasids, was all-important in enabling Abbasid culture and learning to survive the Mongol holocaust. And with the rise of the Ottomans the Safavid benefited from their geographical position at the centre of the trade routes of the ancient world and became rich on the growing trade between Europe and the new Islamic civilisations of central Asia and India.

Safavid art was particulary fine and survives in collections of Persian carpets dating from the period. The Safavid Shahs also encouraged portrait painting, especially of miniatures. Islamic portrait painting is almost unknown outside Safavid Persia because of the danger of presenting images of Allah. But as Shi'ah the Safavids were religiously heterodox, and the existence of portraiture says much about the prevailing liberal religious climate.

As the Ottoman military threat receded in the 17th century the Safavid Shahs became increasingly decadent. Power passed to the Shi'ah *ulama* (religious council of wise men), which eventually deposed the Shahs and proclaimed the world's first 'Islamic republic' in the late 18th century. But the republic lasted only for a few years before eastern Persia was once again conquered, this time by the Turkic Sunni rulers of neighbouring Afghanistan.

After the conquest a division of powers was agreed between the new Afghan Shahs and the Shi'ah *ulama*. The Shahs controlled the state and foreign policy, and could levy taxes and make secular laws. The *ulama* retained control of religious practice, and enforced the *shari'ah* (Qur'anic law) in personal and family matters. The *ulama* thus became an important and permanent theocratic institution in Persia, which it has remained.

The *ulama* continued to tolerate non-religious Shahs right up until the 1970s but finally overthrew the monarchy in 1979, claiming total power exercised through its highest officials, the Ayatollahs. From the time of the Safavids the *ulama* has believed that it rules as a 'caretaker' government on behalf of a mystical 12th Imam descended from 'Ali, the first Shi'ah martyr, who, as 'The Twelfth' will appear on earth shortly before the end of the world.

2.3 The Mogul Empire

As the Ottoman Empire entered its long period of decline, the Mongol Islamic civilisation of the Mogul Emperors in India moved into the ascendant. Al Babr, the first Mogul Emperor, was a direct descendant of Genghis Khan. He captured the Turkic Ghur'iat Sultanate of Delhi in 1526, imposing his rule on most of northern India. The Empire he founded produced an astonishingly sophisticated civilisation based on religious toleration, a mixture of Persian, Mongol and Indian culture, and cross-fertilisation between Islam and Hinduism.

Ghur'iat rule in India had been based on Turkish racial and Islamic religious superiority. Hindu temples had been destroyed or crudely converted into mosques and Hindu subjects forced to pay a punitive tax known as the *jiyaz*. The economy of the Sultanate was backward and, like that of the Ottoman Empire, based on slavery and looting newly conquered territories. The Ghur'iats were popularly known as the Slave Sultans.

Al Babr changed all this. Hinduism was tolerated and new temples were built with his permission. Trade with the rest of the Islamic world, especially Persia and through there to Europe, was encouraged. The importance of slavery diminished and peace was made with the Hindu kingdoms of southern India which had previously been subjected to looting expeditions.

The third Emperor, Abu Akbar, who was a Sufi, took the policy of religious toleration even further by breaking from Islam entirely. The Emperor proclaimed an entirely new state religion of 'God-ism' (*din-i-ilahi*) − a jumble of Islamic, Hindu, Christian and Buddhist teaching with himself as deity. It never spread beyond his court and perished with him.

His son, Emperor Jahangir, readopted Islam as the state religion and continued the policy of religious toleration. His court included large numbers of Indian Hindus, Persian Shi'ah and Sufis and members of local heterodox Islamic sects. He also began building the magnificent monuments and gardens by which the Moguls are chiefly remembered today, importing hundreds of Persian architects to build palaces and create magnificent gardens in cities such as Lahore, Agra and Delhi.

Jahangir's approach was typified by the development of Urdu as the official language of Empire. Urdu is a sort of 'Esperanto' of the Muslim east, using Arabic script, but with a predominantly Persian vocabulary and Hindi grammatical structure. Although it lacks precision it has greater flexibility than any of the languages from which it is derived and allows great subtlety of expression. Under Mogul rule many great works of Urdu literature and poetry were written, inspired by a mixture of Muslim and Hindu cultures. Urdu is still widely spoken in India and is the official langauge of modern Pakistan.

The architectural achievements of the Moguls peaked during the reign of Jahangir's religiously heterodox successor, Jahan, between 1592 and 1666. Jahan commissioned the Taj Mahal, with its distinctively Persian dome, as his mausoleum and the Red Fort in Delhi as his palace.

The Gardens of the Red Fort are especially fine and the Islamic art of gardening – important because the Qur'an describes Paradise as a garden – reached new heights under the Moguls. The Persian inscription on the entrance to the Red Fort and its gardens reads: 'If there is Paradise on Earth, it is here! it is here! it is here!'.

Jahan's son Aurangzeb, who was to be the last great Mogul Emperor, abruptly changed his father's policies and embarked on a determined campaign of Islamisation. Thousands of Hindu temples and shrines were torn down and the punitive Ghur'iat *jiyaz* tax was reimposed. In the last decades of the 17th century, Aurangzeb invaded the Hindu kingdoms of central and southern India, conquering much territory and taking many slaves.

Under him the Mogul Empire reached the peak of its military power, but his rule was unstable. The Muslim governor of the newly conquered Mogul territory of Hyderabad in central India rebelled, establishing an independent Shi'ah state and re-introducing religious toleration of his overwhelmingly Hindu subjects. The Hindu kingdoms also fought back, often supported by the French and British, who used them to tighten their grip on the sub-continent.

The establishment of the Hindu Marathi Empire in central India as a direct response to Aurangzeb's expansionism cut off Mogul territories in the south and east, such as Madras and Bengal, from Delhi. The great eastern Mogul city of Calcutta came under the control of the British East India Company in 1696 and in the decades that followed Europeans or European-backed Hindu princes conquered most of the Mogul territory, reducing the Empire to an impoverished rump around Delhi.

Aurangzeb's sectarianism caused Mogul creativity and enterprise to dry up and the Empire went into decline. He left a legacy of bitterness between Muslims and Hindus which continues to this day, whilst the Mogul Emperors who followed him effectively became British or French puppets. The last Emperor was deposed by the British in 1858.

3.0 THE RISE OF ISLAMIC 'FUNDAMENTALISM' (1650–   )

In the 17th and 18th centuries the Ottoman Empire became steadily more corrupt and was thrown into constant internal crisis by the failure to maintain momentum through military conquest.

In the east the martyrdom-seeking warrior bands of Shi'ah Safavid Persia wore away Ottoman numerical supremacy by attrition and finally won independence. Newly independent Persia blocked the only route for Ottoman expansion into India and the Far East and forced them to turn once again to Europe. But for the first time the Muslim world found western expansion blocked by European powers reinvigorated by the Renaissance and able to match its scientific and military skill.

The germ of the European Renaissance had come, ironically, from the 'Umayyad Emirate of Cordoba. The Spanish Catholic civilisation which replaced the Emirate absorbed much of its tradition of learning, especially the science of navigation, making Spain the first great modern European power and laying the foundations for its conquest of the New World.

To the north, Ottoman expansion was prevented by the emerging power of Russia, whose rulers could be just as despotic and ruthless in battle as the Sultans. From the early 1600s settlements of Cossacks – Mongol warrior bands loyal to either the orthodox Christian Tzars of Russia or the Catholic kings of Poland and Lithuania – began to encroach on the Ottoman territories in the Ukraine and western central Asia. The Ottomans were therefore hemmed in to the territory they had gained at the height of their power, yet still had a system of government entirely dependent on military expansion. The Sultans, confined within the warren-like harem of the Imperial Palace, proved to be incapable of reform, and the Empire stagnated and then started fragmenting.

Territory was lost both to straightforward annexation by the European powers, especially Russia, and local Pashas and Viziers (an Ottoman version of the Abbasid Emirs) who established autonomous rule supported by their European allies.

After the Ottomans' defeat in the first full-scale Russo-Turkish war in 1774, their decline accelerated and they lost naval control of the Black Sea and most of the Muslim lands bordering its north coast. As a condition of the peace settlement the Sultans were forced to accept the Russian Tzar as official protector of the Christians in the Balkans, with the right to intervene in Ottoman territory in their defence.

After this the Ottoman Empire became known as 'the sick man of Europe' – despotic, religiously degenerate and slowly and inevitably falling under European control. The last two centuries of decline are only significant for the Islamic reform movements which periodically erupted and a common theme of which was the demand for a return to a 'pristine' form of Islam, based on the fundamentals of Qur'anic law. The first and in many ways most important of these 'fundamentalist' revolts took place in Arabia under the Wahhabi movement in the last years of the 18th century.

3.1 The Wahhabi revolt

The first modern 'fundamentalist' was, without doubt, Muhammad ibn Wahhab (died 1787), a camel trader from Uyaynad near Mecca in what was then the backward Ottoman province of Hejaz. After studying in Iraq and Persia Wahhab settled in Mecca where he preached that the Ottomans and their local collaborators had 'usurped' the position of keepers of the Ka'bah. Like the Quyrash in Muhammad's time, the Ottomans had allowed the Holy Places to fall into disrepair (both actual and spiritual), flouted Qur'anic law and effectively become pagan.

Wahhab cast himself in a similar role to Muhammad, advocating purification of the religion and a return to the traditions of the Hanbali Sunni legal school – the most Arab-orientated and traditional of the four Abbasid schools – and rejection of the decadent Hanafi'ism of the Ottomans.

He then began preaching his austere version of the Qur'an to Arabian tribesmen as they arrived for *hajj* in Mecca, just as Muhammad had done, and soon gathered a small, dedicated band of followers known as the Wahhabi. In 1778 the Wahhabi declared *jihad* on the Ottomans and captured the governor's headquarters in Mecca, murdering him and smashing the jars of wine he kept in his cellars.

Wahhab then attempted to assemble an Arabian tribal confederation along Muhammadan lines, starting with an important alliance with Muhammad ibn Sa'ud, the Ottoman Emir of the Najd desert region of central Arabia. The alliance was consolidated in traditional Arab manner by Wahhab's marriage to ibn Sa'ud's daughter shortly before his death in 1787. Thereafter leadership of the Wahhabi movement passed to ibn Sa'ud and his clan.

In 1802 ibn Sa'ud launched a full scale war on the Ottomans and rival tribes continuing to support them in the name of the Wahhabi cause. Ibn Sa'ud captured Mecca, Medina and Karbala – the holy city of the Shi'ah in Iraq – but was defeated by the Ottoman rulers of Egypt, who recaptured the Hejaz in 1813. But the Wahhabis were not crushed and managed to retreat to the Sa'udi tribal lands where they remained in a state of open rebellion against the Ottomans (and later the British and their tribal allies) until they finally conquered almost the whole Arabian peninsula and proclaimed the Kingdom of Saudi Arabia within its present borders in 1934. The Saudi state enforced the strict Hanbali version of the *shari'ah* and became the first modern 'fundamentalist' Muslim state.

3.2 Ijitihadi'yah (Sunni Modernisers)

The Wahhabi revolt inspired Muslims throughout the world to question the Ottoman Sultans' tangle of arcane practices, mysticism and authority-worshipping cults which had grown up in the name of Islam and swamped its basic simple principles.

This intellectual movement became known as the *Ijitihadi'yah* (those who question tradition) and gained strength throughout the Muslim world in the 19th century. Although the Ijitihadi'yah began as a movement for return to Qur'anic fundamentals, by the middle of the century it had gone much further by questioning traditional literal interpretations of the Qur'an in a way not seen since the days of the rationalist Mu'tazliah in 9th century Baghdad.

This trend was most developed in Egypt, where in the 1880s Muhammad 'Abduh, the Grand *Mufti* (chief legal officer) produced a greatly simplified 'fundamentalist' version of the *shar'iah* (Islamic law). 'Abduh encouraged total devotion to Islam and scrupulous practice of the Five Pillars but at the same time denied that the Qur'an in its entirety was the inspired word of Allah. He denied the literal accuracy of the Qur'anic and Biblical creation story claiming, like many modern Christians, that it was allegorical. He also demanded full legal equality for women, an end to polygamy, and preached the equality of all religions and peoples.

'Abduh was accused of apostophy (reversion from Islam) by Egyptian traditionalists and forced into exile. In Paris he formed a nationalist political association, *Urwah al-Wuthaq* (Unbreakable Bond), and began agitating for a full-scale revision of Islam to make it a rational and modernising creed capable of leading the Muslim nations to independence and equality with the West.

The Ijitihadi'yah movement quickly gained followers throughout the Muslim world and, apart from Egypt, became an influential force in the growing nationalist movement in British India, where it was led by Ameer 'Ali and, above all, Muhammad Iqbal (died 1938), founder of the Muslim League. Like 'Abduh, Iqbal attempted to introduce Western rationalism and scientific thinking into Islam. He baldly proclaimed, for example, that the appearance of man on Earth had 'absolutely nothing' to do with the creation story contained in the Qur'an. He also said that the Qur'an was capable of human interpretation and joined in Western scholastic attempts to reform its apparently illogical structure.

Iqbal argued that Islam, freed from European influence and internal decay, could flourish into a civilisation far superior to Europe, which he saw as dominated by a Godless worship of technology, mindless industrial growth, devastating warfare, colonial exploitation and racialism. To him Islam was the religion most able to enshrine the common spirituality of all mankind.

Many of these principles were upheld by nationalist movements which secured independence for their countries immediately after World War II, but the reality of independence did not bring with it the rationalist spiritual revival thinkers such as 'Abduh and Iqbal had hoped for and Sunni modernism has found itself increasingly on the defensive.

Today, more than half a century after the Ijitihadi'yah achieved their aim of secularising most of the Muslim world, 'modernised' Islamic rationalism is steadily being pushed aside by a revival of Wahhabi-type fundamentalism.

3.3 The Muslim Brotherhood

The Wahhabi revolt, with its call for a return to Qur'anic fundamentals and the overthrow of 'Imperialist' and 'pagan' rulers, shone like a beacon in a world where Muslim states had fallen under the control of European powers. Throughout the Muslim world small groups of intellectuals began to preach versions of the Wahhabi creed, saying domination by the 'pagan' European colonialists was Allah's punishment for straying from the true path.

A Wahhabi-type movement calling itself Islamic Jihad developed in India in the middle of the 19th century. But like similar movements elsewhere (for example, a Sufi-inspired rebel movement in the Muslim lands of the Russian Empire) it lacked mass support throughout the 19th century and was easily suppressed.

The first effective Islamic fundamentalist movement within the British Empire began in 1929, when a Sufi called Hasan al-Banna founded the Muslim Brotherhood (al-Ikhwan al-Muslimum) in Egypt. Al-Banna's aim was the destruction of the British-inspired secular constitution which had been imposed on Egypt in 1923 and its replacement with a Saudi Arabian-type Islamic constitution. He modelled the Brotherhood on the lines of a militant Sufi monastic order, combining evangelism for fundamentalist Islam with underground revolutionary activity against the British-backed government of King Farouk. Members came from all walks of life and pledged to put Qur'anic law into action within their own families. The Brothers adopted religious dress, strictly practised the ibadah (Islamic personal laws), and violently attacked nominal Muslims who drank alcohol, gambled, fornicated or adopted other types of Western behaviour.

Throughout the 1930s and '40s the Brothers carried out military training in the desert, established arms dumps and mounted occasional terrorist attacks on both political opponents and establishments such as casinos and drinking parlours, becoming a constant thorn in the flesh of the British and Egyptian secular authorities.

In 1948, after the defeat of Egypt and the other Arab nations in the war against Israel, the Brotherhood rose in open insurrection. At first the Brothers allied themselves with Gamal Abdul Nasser, a socialist and nationalist leader with strong support in the army. They played an important role in the 1952 revolution which deposed King Farouk and established Nasser as President of the new Egyptian Republic.

In the same year the Jordanian branch of the Brotherhood assassinated King Abdullah al-Hashim who, Arab nationalists believed, had gained the Jordanian throne from the British as a reward for helping create the state of Israel.

Nasser, however, emerged not as a 'fundamentalist' but as an Arab nationalist committed to modernising Egypt along socialist and not Islamic lines. The Brotherhood turned against him and attempted to assassinate him in 1954. Nasser retaliated by hanging six leading Brothers, jailing dozens more and forcing thousands into exile – mainly in conservative Saudi Arabia and Pakistan.

Sayyid Qutb, one of the Brotherhood's jailed intellectuals, used his time in prison to clarify the movement's aims. He described it as no longer a simple movement for the introduction of *shar'iah* law in Egypt, but an international *jihad* against Western Imperialists, Russian and Chinese Communists and Muslim secularists. The Brotherhood's goal was nothing less than the purification and unification of the whole Muslim world into a single Islamic republic with Qu'ranic law extended to every aspect of life and politics.

Qutb's work was published throughout the Muslim world but was especially popular in Pakistan where the immediate post-independence enthusiasm for Western-style secularism had turned into disillusionment.

Fundamentalist movements had been active on the Indian sub-continent since the Islamic Jihad group in the mid-19th century but this was now boosted by the Brotherhood and growing support from increasingly wealthy and powerful fundamentalist Saudi Arabia.

In 1956 agitation by the Brotherhood's Pakistani allies, the Ja'mat-I-Islami Party (founded in 1932), led to the declaration of an Islamic Republic in Pakistan and the progressive replacement of secular with *shari'ah* law.

The Brotherhood remained illegal and severely repressed in

Egypt and most other parts of the Arab world throughout the 1960s. The international leadership of the movement passed to the group of exiled conservative Brothers in Saudi Arabia who were encouraged by the government and increasingly became seen as its tool.

In 1970, when President Sadat ended Nasser's policy of reliance on Soviet aid in favour of the newly oil-rich Saudis, part of the price was acceptance of a degree of Saudi-style 'Islamisation' and the return of the Brothers to Egypt.

Although the Brotherhood is still technically illegal in Egypt, the organisation now acts as an intermediary between the Saudi and Egyptian governments and therefore wields great power and influence.

The Egyptian Brotherhood's many 'front' organisations include the Egyptian Union of Islamic Students, which constantly agitates for Saudi Arabian- and Pakistani-style 'Islamisation'. The Brotherhood also dominates the shell of the otherwise dead Wafd Party, which forms the tame official opposition in the Egyptian parliament.

Yet not all the Egyptian Brothers accepted the new and cosy relationship with the government imposed on the organisation by the Saudi Arabians. In the late 1970s a militant group split off to form an armed underground movement called *Takfir wa'al Hijrah* (The Excommunicated in Holy Flight). The name comes from the Hijrah, Muhammad's flight from Mecca to Medina. In 1981 the group was involved in the assassination of President Sadat.

The Brothers are also active in a number of other countries and during the 1980s were accused of sponsoring subversive fundamentalist agitation in Sudan, Algeria, Morocco and Tunisia, where the local branch uses the name Islamic Tendency. And in the early 1980s the Brothers were largely responsible for the adoption of Islamic Republic status by Mauritania.

Syria has been a particularly important target for the Brothers. In 1982 they gained control of the city of Hama and attempted a fundamentalist uprising against President Assad – a bitter enemy of their Saudi backers.

Today the Brotherhood is a mainly conservative force which agitates with varying degrees of violence for 'Islamisation'. It is especially popular with Arab businessmen and there is little doubt many of its middle class members are chiefly there to curry favour with the Saudi government in the hope of acting as business as well as political agents.

3.4 The Iranian Revolution

In Islamic countries revolutionaries do not look to the future. Instead they look to the past. This is often a difficult concept for Westerners to grasp, but the fact is that the most radical Muslims are simultaneously the most conservative, believing the ideal society existed in the time of Muhammad.

In this sense the Shi'ah of Iran are the most fundamentalist. The roots of modern Iranian fundamentalism go back to the martyrdom of 'Ali and Husayn by the 'Umayyad 'usurper' Caliphs in the 7th century.

The 1979 Iranian revolution was carried out in the name of Shi'ah martyrs to recreate the perfect Muslim political state they died attempting to defend. Ayatollah Khomeini, in his book *Islam and Revolution* (1981), put it like this:

'Unfortunately, true Islam lasted only for a brief period after its inception. First the 'Umayyads and then the Abbasids inflicted all kinds of damage on Islam. Later the Shahs ruling Iran continued on the same path; they completely distorted Islam and established something quite different in its place . . . the Arabism of the *Jahiliyya* (pagan, pre-Islamic age of ignorance).

'Sunni-populated countries,' Khomeini continued, 'believe in obeying their rulers, whereas the Shi'ah have always believed in rebellion.' Shi'i fundamentalism therefore not only involves introduction of the *shari'ah* (Islamic law) but also demands the overthrow of Sunni rulers and monarchs. For this reason the 'fundamentalism' of Iran and that of a Sunni country such as Saudi Arabia or Pakistan are hostile to each other.

The practical, as opposed to ideological, roots of the Iranian revolution only stretch back to the 17th century – a relatively short time-scale for Muslim political rivalries – and the coming to power within the country by the *ulama* (council of wise men). Over the centuries the *ulama* developed into a body similar to the Roman Catholic conclave of cardinals and their Imam became, in effect, the Shi'ah 'Pope'. The priesthood they developed was a ramified, well-organised, hierarchical structure spreading its influence into every town and village. No other Muslim country has ever had anything as comprehensive.

At the bottom of the hierarchy are the common believers, organised into groups by thousands of *mullahs* (priest-teachers), with above them the *Hojjat-ul-Islam* (provincial judges), *Ayatollahs* (judges of appeal) and Grand *Ayatollahs* who form the *ulama*.

Above them all is the *ulama's* elected Imam.

By the middle of the 18th century, force of circumstance meant that the *ulama* accepted rule by a Shah. But the Iranian Shahs (unlike the kings of Sunni Saudi Arabia or Morocco) never became head of the religion. And the *ulama* system was so well established that no Shah could rule without the Imam's support.

In effect a 'concordat' was reached by the *ulama* and the Shahs. The *ulama* controlled the religious and private lives of the population, and the Shahs controlled foreign policy and raised taxes. This system remained in force until the late 1970s when the last Shah, Reza, began to threaten the power of the Shi'ah clergy with modernising reforms. The Shi'ah at first supported secularising left-wing opposition to the Shah through the 'Red Mullah' movement led by Ayatollah Shariati.

The followers of Shariati fused the revolutionary rhetoric of Marxism with the traditional Shi'i suspicion of monarchical rule. But the movement was based mainly amongst the foreign educated middle classes and the small working class of the oil fields.

The more conservative Shi'i landowners, peasants and, above all, bazaar merchants, remained opposed to both the modernising capitalist reforms of the Shah and the proposed socialist policies of the 'Red Mullahs'. This more conservative opposition was ignored by the Shah, and many of his advisers at first believed the conservative Shi'ah would support the regime against the 'Communist threat'.

The conservatives found a spokesman in Ayatollah Khomeini, a traditionalist critic of Shariati. Khomeini remained aloof and passive as the Shah crushed the 'Red Mullah' movement but, after Shariati's death in 1977, he stepped forward to lead the conservative or 'fundamentalist' opposition. Khomeini outlined his thoughts in a series of lectures entitled 'The Coming Rule of the Jurists' which resulted in his expulsion from Iraq and exile to Paris in 1978.

Typically, Khomeini's thinking about the political situation in 1970s Iran was dominated by the events of the 7th century. In his book *The Coming Rule of the Jurists* Khomeini compared the Shah to Yaziz 'Umayyad, the Satanic 'usurper' who martyred Husayn ibn 'Ali.

Khomeini called for *jihad* against the Shah and the establishment of an Islamic Republic run by the *ulama* as the divinely guided 'viceroy' of Allah. These teachings passed by word of mouth through the ramified network of *mullahs* and *Ayatollahs*.

The revolutionary message, no longer couched in the Marxist-influenced jargon of the educated middle classes, sparked a wave of religious revivalism. The rumour spread that Khomeini was the miraculously-born and long-awaited 'Twelfth' Imam descended directly from Muhammad who, according to Shi'ah doctrine, would overthrow all unjust rulers and reunite Islam. His austere features and prophet-like religious dress deepened the impression that he was indeed some sort of messianic figure, even though he quietly denied it.

It was this wave of religious feeling that overthrew the Shah in 1979 and enabled Khomeini to outmanoeuvre his more radical and liberal rivals within the revolutionary movement.

The new revolutionary regime immediately introduced the Shi'ah version of the *shari'ah* which has since formed the basic constitution of the country.

Whether the Iranian model can serve as a model for Islamic fundamentalists elsewhere is another matter. No other Islamic country has a majority of Shi'ah, though Iraq, Syria, Saudi Arabia and some Soviet central Asian republics have sizeable minorities. But in none of these are the *ulama* and the Shi'ah clergy as well-organised or autonomous from the state as they were in pre-revolutionary Iran.

4.0 CHRONOLOGY

4.1 MUHAMMAD AND THE CALIPHS

c570. **Birth of Muhammad of the Meccan tribe of Quraysh (Muhammad the prophet).**

610. Muhammad receives first revelations from Archangel Gabriel during meditation on Mount Hira.

622. **The Hijrah. Muhammad and followers flee into exile in Medina.**

622 (16th July). Muhammad and followers sign pledge of Aqaba with chieftains of Medina declaring Holy War (*jihad*) against Mecca. Signing of pledge regarded as the new year of the first year of the Islamic age (1 AH).

630. Islamic army of 10,000 Medinan Arabs and desert Bedouins directed by Muhammad and father-in-law Abu Bakr conquer Mecca with no resistance.

630–32. Muhammad leads military expeditions to Syria.

632 (June 8th). Death of Muhammad. Abu Bakr (father-in-law of Muhammad) elected successor (Caliph) by congregation of leaders of converted tribes.

4.2 THE CIVIL WAR and THE 'UMAYYAD EMPIRE

634. Death of Abu Bakr. Election of 'Umar as second Caliph.

634–645. 'Umar's conquests include Damascus, Jerusalem, Alexandria, Persia and Libya.

c640. Khariji sect establish religious courts to examine who amongst the newly converted tribesmen are true believers and who are not.

644. Death of 'Umar. Election of 'Uthman of the 'Umayyad tribe as third Caliph.

656. 'Uthman assassinated by Kharijis. Election of 'Ali ibn Abi-Talib (son-in-law of Muhammad) as fourth Caliph supported by Kharijis. Civil war between 'Umayyads and supporters of 'Ali – the Shi'ites (Shi'ah) or 'partisans of 'Ali'.

661. Mu'awiya 'Umayyad (cousin of 'Uthman and military governor of Damascus) becomes fifth Caliph after assassination of 'Ali. Resumes civil war against Shi'ah and Kharijis. 'Umayyad dynasty of Caliphs established (ruled until 750).

680. Shi'ah revolt peaks with the battle of Karbala. Husayn, son of 'Ali, leads a force of only 100 warriors against a much larger force and is slaughtered by the 6th Caliph, Yazid 'Umayyad. Reconquest of Mecca by the 'Umayyads, dispersal of the Kharijis to increasingly remote areas.

685–705. Caliphship of Abdul Malik 'Umayyad who unifies the Empire after civil war, founding a centralised state in Damascus. Flexible definition of Islamic faith adopted to ease mass conversion and growth of Empire. (Kharijis persecuted and effectively extinct after 750).

698. Conquest of Carthage.

711–21. Peak of 'Umayyad power reached under Caliph Walid. Conquest of Kabul (Afghanistan), settlement of Transoxia and the Indus area. Renewed attacks on Constantinople, conquest of most of Spain and southern France including Toulouse. Islam, now the largest Empire the world had ever known, sets about the conquest of central and northern Europe.

732. Death of Zayd ibn 'Ali, founder of the Bedouin Zaydi Shi'i sect as found in modern Yemen.

732. 'Umayyad armies defeated by Charles Martel, Christian general, at battle of Poitiers, north west France, loss of Toulouse, retreat to Spain.

732–750. Renewed unsuccessful Shi'i and Khariji rebellions, fuelled by dissatisfaction amongst converts with high taxes needed for continuous war.

750. Army of Persian Islamic converts raised by Abu' al-Abbas of Ctesiphon – capital of ancient Babylon – defeats 'Umayyads at battle of Zab. Entire leadership of the 'Umayyad clan killed to end any further doubt over the succession, except for Abdur-Ahman 'Umayyad who escaped to the remotest part of the Empire – Spain.

4.3 THE ABBASIDS and THE GOLDEN AGE

750. Abu' al-Abbas proclaims his own dynasty (The Abbasids) and renews persecution of the Shi'ites and Kharijis. Construction of Baghdad.

751. Defeat of the Chinese army in Transoxia opens the way for Islamic conversion of the Turkic tribes of central Asia.

875. The Samanid clan of Transoxania (Samarkand and Bukhara area) are given Emir status to rule on behalf of the Abbasids.

898. Death of Hakim al-Tirmidi, author of 'The Seal of the Saints' (*Khatm al-awliya*), first Sufi-type mystical tract.

c900. Hundred years war with the Jewish Khazars of the Volga Valley. Conversion of the Bulgar Kings of Kazan. Foundation of Islamic power in Russia.

912. Abd ar-Rahman, an 'Umayyad, becomes Emir of Cordoba, introduces the first rationalist regime in Islamic Spain which becomes a centre of learning henceforth. In same year the Christian kingdom of Asturia is established in north west Spain by Christian Norman invaders.

962. Ghaznevid clan, Turkic people, settle in Afghanistan and establish autonomous Sultanate within the Islamic Empire.

969. The pro-Shi'ite Fatimid clan conquer most of North Africa in the name of 'Ali (the first Shi'i Imam) and his wife Fatima (daughter of Muhammad). City of Cairo founded as Fatimid capital.

c970. Foundation of neo-Khariji Qarmatarian (Qa'rmat'iyah) sub-sect of the Egyptian Ismaelites in Cairo.

992. Crucifixion in Baghdad of early Sufi thinker al-Hallaj for blasphemous teachings. Start of Sufi intellectual counter-reaction to al-Ash'ari's Sunni conservatism.

998. Mahmud the Great of the Ghurs, a Turkic tribe originally from central Asia, converts to Islam and declares himself the semi-independent Abbasid Emir of Punjab and Afghanistan at the eastern fringe of the Empire.

999. Qarmatarians establish utopian communist state on east coast of Arabia. Crushed by Abbasid military power within five years.

1001. The Ghurs begin a 200 year *jihad* against Hindu princes of northern India (the Rajputs) culminating in the establishment of the Sultanate of Delhi (founded 1206).

1008–28. Civil war over the succession to the 'Umayyad Emirate of Cordoba. Dissolution of the Emirate into rival smaller states is exploited by Christian forces who begin the 'Reconquista' in earnest.

1021. Al-Hakim, a prince of the pro-Shi'ite Fatimid dynasty in Egypt, is proclaimed the resurrected Isma'il (the repudiator prophet) who will overthrow Sunni Abbasid rule. His failure to do so causes the Ismaelites to split into many factions.

1037. Fall of Asturia, Spain, to Christian Reconquista forces.

1058. Death of Sunni Imam al-Mawardi, recorder of the Sunni statutes of Government (*Al-akham, al-sultaniyah*).

1082. First Islamic communities founded in Java (Indonesia) under the rule of the Hindu kings of Sumatra and Java. Growing spice trade with the Abbasid Empire.

1095. Pope Urban II declares the first Christian Crusade with the objective of reuniting the Eastern and Western Roman Empires and reconquering Jerusalem.

1099. Christian Crusader Kingdom of Jerusalem established by Godfrey of Bouillon.

1144. Reconquest of Crusader territory in Asia Minor by the Emir of Mosul, a Seljuk Turk.

c1100. Expected date of the end of the world according to Muhammad's early followers. Wave of religious fanaticism sweeps Islam and many sects formed.

1147. Launch of Second Christian Crusade under the leadership of King Louis VII of France.

c1150. Al-Ghazali, a Sunni jurist and scholar at the Abbasid court, reforms Sunni and Sufi theology along rationalist lines.

1150–71. Further splits amongst the Ismaelites leads to foundation of the mystical Tayyibiyah sect and the warlike Assassin sect, which establishes a fortress-kingdom in the Alamut Valley in Iran.

1157. Fall of northern Spanish provinces of Leon, Portugal, Castile, Navarre, Aragon and Catalonia to the Christian Reconquista.

1166. Foundation of the first Sufi monastic-type order (the Qadiriyah) by Sufi 'Abn al-Qadir al-Jilani of Baghdad. Rapid development of Sufi 'zawiyah' college-hospices throughout the Islamic world. Henceforth the Sufi orders dominate the intellectual life of Islam.

1171. Saladin of the Kurdish Ayyubid clan overthrows and replaces the Fatimid dynasty of Cairo in the name of the Sunni faith and loyalty to the nominal Abbasid rulers of the Empire. Ayyubid dynasty makes Egypt the foremost Islamic military power of the Crusader period.

1187. Reconquest of Jerusalem from the Christian Crusaders by Saladin.

1189. 3rd Christian Crusade, led by Holy Roman Emperor Frederick Barbarossa (Redbeard), begins.

1191. Fall of Acre to Christian Crusaders. Peace treaty between the Crusaders and Saladin. Christians granted right of pilgrimage to Jerusalem as well as permanent administration of the coastal strip of Palestine from Tyre to Jaffa.

1192. Muhammad the Ghur, nominal Abbasid Emir of the Punjab, defeats the remains of the Hindu Rajput armies and occupies Delhi after the battle of Taraori.

1202. Pope Innocent III announces 4th Crusade. Objective is reconquest of Jersualem and the destruction of Ayyubid Egypt and the Remains of the Christian Byzantine Empire. In the event Crusaders do not get beyond Constantinople, the capital of Byzantium, which they successfully subjugate.

1206. Muhammad the Ghur proclaims himself Sultan (supreme ruler) of Delhi and independent from the Abbasids. Proclaims his own dynasty – the Ghur'iat 'Slave' Sultans.

1219. Western territories of the Ghur'iat Sultans of Delhi occupied by Mongol Khan. Start of Mongol destruction of the original Islamic Empire.

1221. Advance of Genghis Khan into the Punjab. Makes peace with the Ghur'iat in return for tribute.

1227. Death of Genghis Khan. Partition of pagan Mongol world Empire into four parts. Genghis Khan's son Halagu declares himself Ill-Khan (ruler of the west) and begins making raids into Abbasid territory in eastern Persia and northern India.

1228. 5th Christian Crusade begun by Frederick II, Holy Roman Emperor. Conquers Acre and obtains Jerusalem by means of a treaty with the Ayyubid Emir of Egypt, El'kamil.

1236. Christian Reconquista forces occupy Cordoba, seat of the Arab 'Umayyad Emirs of Spain.

1240. Death of Iban al-'Arabi, grandmaster of the Sufi order in Granada, southern spain and first formulator of the humanist Sufi creed 'Unity of Being'. Sufi influence in Islamic Spain leads to great period of scientific discovery – the Alhambra (age of brilliance).

1243. Muslim Ottoman Turks begin arriving in Asia Minor in a westward movement before waves of invading Ill-Khan pagan Mongols. Ottomans place themselves at the service of the Seljuks (fellow Turks and administrators of the late Abbasid Empire) as a caste of warriors and palace guards in the continuing war with the fading Christian Byzantine Empire.

c1240. Decadent Ayyubid Sultanate of Egypt revived by Turkic administrator-warriors.

1244. Reconquest of Jersualem by the Mameluke Turks. Crusaders never again possess Jerusalem.

1248. King Louis IX of France begins the 6th and penultimate Christian Crusade. Captures Damietta, near Suez, but is defeated at the battle of Mansura and taken prisoner by the Mameluke-Ayyubids.

c1250. Foundation of Alawite (Alawiyan) Ismaelite sub-sect in Syria. They refuse to recognise the Assassin (Niziriyah) Imams.

1251. The pagan Ill-Khans conquer most of Islamic Persia.

1254. Louis IX returns to France after payment of heavy ransom and increasing the fortifications of Acre, the last Christian stronghold in the Holy Land.

1258. Catastrophe for Islam. The Mongol Halagu Khan destroys Baghdad, a city of one million people. Fall of the Abbasids and end of the unified Islamic Empire.

4.4 THE MONGOLS AND OTTOMANS

1257-9. Sufi order founded by the Shi'ah Safi al-ha'din (Aladin) secretly in Baghdad with the aim of preserving Persian Islamic culture and converting or overthrowing the Ill-Khans.

1259. Ill-Khan conquest of Syria (Damascus and Aleppo put to the sword).

1260. The Mameluke Caliphs of Jerusalem defeat the seemingly invincible Ill-Khans at the battle of Ain-Jalut (spring of Goliath) near Cairo.

1270. 7th and final Christian Crusade launched by Louis IX of France, but comes to an end in Tunis where Christian forces are wiped out by plague.

1291. Acre, the last Crusader fortress, falls to the Mamelukes and Christian Crusades are never repeated. Henceforth the Holy Land is in Turkish possession until the end of World War One.

c1300. The Ill-Khans convert to Islam, possibly because of contact with the impressive and persuasive Sufi tradition of Baghdad. After their conversion the Ill-Khans continue to rule the land conquered from the Abbasids.

1301. Ozman of the Ottomans usurps the Rum Seljuk Sultans (independent Islamic rulers) of Asia Minor and proclaims himself Sultan of the Ottoman Empire. Rum Seljuks become minor Emirs of Ottoman territories.

1316. Alah'din Khalji, Ghur'iat Sultan of Delhi, repulses the Mongol Ill-Khans from north west India and frees the Sultanate from Mongol tribute and overlordship.

1325. Muhammad ibn Tughluk becomes Sultan of Delhi and conquers the whole of the Indian sub-continent (except for Ceylon). Serious rebellion, however, begins amongst Hindu subjects within five years.

1326. Death of Ozman the Ottoman. His son Orkhan Ozmani becomes Sultan and rules small area in what is now central Turkey.

1327. Orkhan Ozmani conquers Byzantine city of Brussa, 100 miles south of Constantinople on other side of Bosphorus, and declares it capital of the newly founded Empire of the Ottomans. Turkic clans were therefore in control of both the eastern and western extremities of the Empire – the Ottoman Turks in Asia Minor and the Ghur'ati Turks in India.

1328. Civil war in declining Christian Byzantium. John Cantacuzene challenges Emperor Andronicus II and allies himself with Orkhan's Ottoman state.

1337. Orkhan Ozmani subjugates ancient Byzantine province of Nicomedia (renamed Ismid in Turkish) and establishes ramified state with own currency and institutions.

1347. John Cantacuzene overthrows Byzantine Emperor Andronicus II using Orkhan Ozmani's Ottoman troops. As Emperor, gives the Ottomans a base at Gallipoli, just south of Constantinople, their first territory on the European continent.

1349. Ottoman conquest of Epirus expands their control to the whole of Asia Minor (territory of modern Turkey).

c1350. Hindu subjects of the Sultanate of Delhi begin rebellion culminating in the independent Hindu state of Vijayangar in south-central India. The Hindu success is followed by rebel Muslim groups who establish themselves as semi-autonomous Emirs in the various regions of the sub-continent.

c1350. Ottoman Empire adopts and sponsors the Sunni Hanafi legal school which serves to legitimise their rule and spread their influence against the Persians and Seljuks who sponsor the rival Shafi school.

1354. The Ottomans occupy the Gallipoli base granted to them by Byzantine Emperor John VIII (John Cantacuzene).

1359. Death of Orkhan of the Ottomans, succeeded by Murad Ozmani, who invades the Balkan territories of European Byzantium.

1361. Conquest of Adrianople by Murad Ozmani. Foundation of Ottoman Balkan Empire. Reduction of Byzantium to Constantinople alone and John IV to the status of 'Christian Emir'.

1370. The Mongol Khan Tamberlaine gains control of territory of the Mongol Golden Horde (ruled by his blood relatives since the death of Genghis Khan and the division of his Empire into four parts) for Islam. Territory includes Moscow and Kiev, the Crimea, Caucasus, northern Asia Minor and southern Ukraine which become the Islamic Khanates of Crimea, Kazan and Astrakhan.

1389. Ottomans destroy all effective resistance in the south Balkans at the battle of Kosovo on Serbian-Albanian border.

1398–9. Tamberlaine's advance into India. Destruction of Delhi, looting of the Punjab, destruction of Turkic Ghuri'at Empire and restriction of Sultanate to Delhi and its immediate surrounding. The Punjab is ravaged and looted but not annexed.

1402. Tamberlaine defeats the Ottomans at the battle of Angora (near site of modern Turkish capital of Ankara) and checks Ottoman expansion for 50 years.

1404. Tamberlaine's followers, the Timurids, capture Afghanistan and establish a capital at Herat which becomes one of the largest and most prosperous cities of Islam.

1405. Death of Tamberlaine, the Mongol ruler responsible for most of present day Islam's following in central Asia, the Volga-Tartar region and northern Black Sea areas such as Crimea.

1405–50. Ottomans steadily regain territory from the Ill-Khans following the death of Tamberlaine. Difficulties over the succession.

c1450. Small but thriving Islamic Sultanates established on the north coast of Java (Indonesia) to control spice trade.

1453 (29th May). Fall of Constantinople to Muhammad Ozmani, Ottoman Emperor. Constantinople's name changed to Istanbul ('city of Islam') and thereafter serves as the capital of the Ottoman Empire. Decree of fratricide to prevent successional disputes.

1459–63. Ottoman conquest of southern Balkans – Greece, Bulgaria, Serbia and Bosnia.

1461–75. Ottoman conquest of the Mongol Khanate of Crimea

and last isolated bastions of Byzantium in eastern Asian Minor – Caramon ('little Armenia') and Trapezus (in what is now the extreme north eastern corner of modern Turkey, on the Black Sea coast).

4.5 OTTOMAN SUPREMACY

1481. Death of Muhammad the Conqueror, Ottoman Sultan who had conquered 200 cities and 12 kingdoms during his 30 year reign. Muhammad proclaims himself 'ruler of all the faithful' and 'al-Mahdi' – the 'chosen one' – who would unite the Islamic world in the name of Sunni Islam.

1492. Conquest of Granada by Queen Isabella of Spain. Reconquista complete. End of brilliant Sufi-inspired Spanish Arab Islamic civilisation. Sufi sciences of navigation, medicine and mathematics absorbed by the Spanish monarchy.

1501. Isma'il Safavid, a Shi'ah of the Sufi Safavid dynasty, is declared Shah (Persian word for ruler) of Persia after successful uprising against Sunni Ill-Khans.

Ottoman army sent to aid the Khan defeated by the Shi'ah Qizilbashi army (the Red Heads – so called because they wore red turbans with 12 folds to commemorate the 'expected' Twelfth Shi'ah Imam).

1507. Al-Babr, a Muslim Ill-Khan expelled from Baghdad by the Safavids, captures Afghanistan from the Timurids and establishes an independent principality. Allies with the Ottomans for a two-front war against Shi'i Persia.

1511. The Christian Portuguese capture Malacca, the leading Hindu Malay city state. The Malay and Javanese (Indonesian) Hindu princes ally with Islam in a failed attempt to expel them. Thus Islam becomes a military force in Indonesia and Malaya for the first time.

1516. Assassin-led Shi'ite Syrian army defeated by the Ottomans (Sunnis of the Hanafi school) at the battle of Dabik, near Damascus. Rapid decline of Assassins as autonomous military force.

1500–1550. (Ottoman conquests in the reign of Sultan Suleyman the Magnificent 1520–66):

1512 Moldavia (Eastern Rumania)
1516 Syria and the Holy Land
1517 Egypt (forcing exile of Shi'ah Ismaelites)

1521 Belgrade (capital of Serbian Empire)
1522 Rhodes (defeat of Knights of St John, Crusader state)
1526 Jedisan (southern Ukraine – final defeat of Mongol Khans)
1529 1st siege of Vienna (trade monopolies secured)
1529 Acceptance of vassal status by Ayyubid Emirs of Algiers
1534 Western Persia and Baghdad (remains of Abbasid culture)
1538 Sultan proclaimed guardian of Mecca and Medina
1541 Transylvania (Central Rumania)
1541 South and eastern Hungary (partitioned Austrian Empire)
1550. Acceptance of vassal status by Libyan Ayyubid Emirs (also Tunis 1574)

1526. Al-Babr, the Mongol Khan Sultan of Kabul, invades India founding the Islamic Mogul Empire of north and central India.

1530 Al-Babr dies in Kabul. Afghanistan partitioned between al-Babr's Mogul Empire in the east and the Safavid Shi'ah Shahdom of Persia in the west.

c1550. The largest Indonesian harbour-state, Acheh, converts to Islam and becomes an independent Muslim Sultanate. Islamic influence grows rapidly in Java with military support from the Mogul Empire.

1583. Mogul Emperors enact Edict of Toleration of other religions. Sufi'ism becomes widespread throughout India.

4.6 OTTOMAN DECLINE and SHI'I PERSIA

1606. Ottomans defeated in renewed attempt to conquer Vienna. The way to further expansion in Europe remains blocked by growing Austrian military and Venetian-Spanish naval power. Whilst the Ottomans are preoccupied with Vienna the Shi'i Shah Abbas ('Abbas the Great') of Persia defeats an Ottoman Uzbek (Mongol) army in Azerbaijan and threatens the Anatolian heartlands of Ottoman Asia Minor.

1624. Death in India of Ahmad Sirhindi, formulator of modern orthodox Sufi theology. Growth of Sufi movement both within and beyond the Ottoman Empire independent of Sunni establishment.

1639. Ottomans grant peace treaty to Safavids in return for recognition of their rule in Iraq, including Baghdad, which henceforth declines into a provincial town. The Ottoman-Persian border remains in force until 1918.

1640. Safavids move the capital of Persia to Isfahan which becomes one of the leading cities of contemporary world culture (128 mosques, 48 Sufi colleges, 273 public baths, many public buildings, fountains, monuments, etc.) Arts and sciences flourish, especially portrait painting.

1648. Shi'i *ulama* (religious council) of Persia challenges divinity of the Shi'i Safavid Shahs. Ayatollah Ahmad Ardabili defines modern Shi'ah creed that rule of 'the Twelfth' is vested in the *ulama* which should be composed of the wisest and most learned Qu'ranic scholars to be found in the realm.

1652–1694. Reign of the powerless 'Four Drunken Shahs' in Shi'ah Persia. Institution of Monarchy discredited by degenerate court. Riots against un-Islamic morality – e.g. smashing of jars of wine found in the royal cellars, etc. Growing power of the Shi'i *ulama*.

1659. Day to day control of the Ottoman Empire passes from the Sultans to the Albanian Grand Vizier Muhammad Kuprulu who organises a final, futile Ottoman push against Vienna. The events marking Ottoman decline in the late 17th century are as follows:

1664 Peace of Vasvar. Gain of southern Hungary

1671 Hungarian peasant uprising against the Ottomans

1683 2nd siege of Vienna. Ottomans defeated by Polish army

1684 Liberation of Hungary by Papal army

1688 Liberation of Belgrade (Russia joins Papal Alliance)

1691 Liberation of Transylvania (central Rumania)

1696 Tzar Peter I conquers parts of Crimea

1697 Liberation of Sarajevo and parts of Serbia

1690s Uprisings of Christian peoples of Ottoman Balkans.

1691. Islamic Mogul Empire in India reaches peak of power under Aurangzeb.

1694. Ayatollah Muhammad Majlisi deposes last Safavid Shah, Sultan-Husayn 'the drunkard' and rules Shi'ah Iran on behalf of the *ulama* (exactly the position in Iran today). Majlisi weakens the state by persecuting monarchists, Sufis and the Sunni minority.

1696. The Mogul city of Calcutta comes under the jurisdiction of the British East India Company.

1709. Mir Veys Khan leads a successful rising of the Afghan tribes against Persian Shi'i Safavid rule. By 1720 all Afghanistan is independent under the rule of the Asaduallah Khans.

1722. The Asaduallah Khans capture the Persian capital of

Isfahan and overthrow the Safavid dynasty. Persia again comes under Sunni rule. The Asaduallahs repulse a Russian attack from the north and an Ottoman attack from the west.

1726. Whilst the Asaduallahs are preoccupied with subjugating Persia, reforming its institutions and limiting the power of the Shi'i *ulama*, their Afghan homeland is conquered by Nadar Qajar, a Mongol-Uzbek tribesman from central Asia.

1729. Nadar Qajar subjugates Afghanistan and captures Persia from the Asaduallahs after the battle of Damghan.

1732. The Asaduallahs rise against Nadar Qajar and re-establish their rule in Afghanistan.

1736. Nadar Qajar, a Sunni, elected Shah of Persia by gathering of his tribes and with consent of the Shi'i *ulama* and founds Qajari dynasty of Persian Shahs.

1737. Shah Nadar recaptures Afghanistan and threatens the western borders of the Mogul Empire.

1740s. Shah Nadar raids the western Mogul empire looting Delhi, but not establishing rule. The fabulous booty taken from the Mogul treasury includes the Peacock Throne, used in subsequent coronations of Persian Shahs.

1747. Death of Shah Nadar. His descendants become the Qajari dynasty of Sunni Persian Shahs, but Afghanistan again rebels. Ahmad Khan Abdali elected King of Afghanistan by tribal assembly. Founds Durrani dynasty of Afghan Kings.

1768-74. During the first Russo-Turkish war, 'infidel' Russia becomes the official protector of the Christians of the Balkans, conquers parts of Crimea and the north coast of the Black Sea, and gains naval superiority in the Black Sea.

1793. **Death of ibn al-Wahhab, a fanatical Sunni Hanbali revivalist from Mecca, which is under decadent Turkish Ottoman rule. (Al-Wahhab was the originator of modern Sunni conservative 'cleansing' fundamentalism.)**

c1800. Al-Wahhab's follower Shah Wali-Allah of Delhi founds Islamic Jihad, powerful modernising fundamentalist movement in British Indian Raj.

4.7 THE COLONIAL PERIOD

1803–15. Revolt by fundamentalist followers of al-Wahhab (Wahhabis) in Arabia leads to establishment of a shortlived traditionalist Hanbali Sunni state with its capital at Riyadh. The

Wahhabis seek British help, but this is not to come until a century later during the 1914-18 war, and the Wahhabi state is temporarily crushed by Ottoman army.

1803. British General Lake conquers Delhi. Mogul Empire becomes a British protectorate.

1805. Muhammad 'Ali, the modernising Ottoman Vizier of Egypt, declares effective independence from the Ottoman Sultan.

1809. The British grant protection to the Durrani Kings of Afghanistan who are under pressure from Russian expansion in the north and Indian Sikh expansion in the east.

1818. Barakazi tribe rebels against the British-supported King of Afghanistan and takes Kabul and Peshawar. The Barakazi divide the country into small fiefdoms (*sardars*) allowing Sikhs to capture eastern provinces and independence to southern provinces. Muhammad Barakazi establishes the much weakened kingdom of Afghanistan under the rule of his dynasty the Muhammadazi-Barakazi.

1820. British pact with Arab *shayks* of the Gulf brings support for revolts against the Ottomans and effective British control of the area.

1831–40. Muhammad 'Ali, ruler of independent Islamic state of Egypt, annexes Ottoman provinces of Sinai, Gaza, Palestine and Syria.

1839. The Qajari Shah of Persia attacks the weakened kingdom of Afghanistan with Russian support. British General Burns repulses the attack and Afghanistan becomes an effective protectorate of the British Indian Empire.

1844. Baha'i sect founded during a wave of anti-clerical feeling in Persia.

c1850s. Continuous rebellions and uprisings in Afghanistan against the British-supported Kings until Amanollah Shah installs himself as King and is granted 'complete independence' by the British.

1861. Lebanon established as an independent state under French protection with Egyptian-Syrian toleration.

1875. Ottoman Empire declares public bankruptcy. Urgent reform movement (including the abolition of torture) culminated in the first Ottoman 'constitution' which, in theory, gives rights to subjects and recognises the equality of religions within the Empire. The constitution, however, is regarded as an heretical western imposition and the Sultans pointedly ignore it.

1880s. Modernising Egyptians encourage Sufi orders of Tijani,

Sanusi, in missionary work in Sudan and the western sub-Sahara.

1880. Death of Jamal al-Din al-Afghani, leader of early and effective modern fundamentalist movement in Egypt.

1880. Ghulam Ahmad founds theologically degenerate pantheistic Sunni Ahmadiyah sect in East Punjab.

1882. Direct British rule in Egypt and the introduction of Anglo-Muhammadan law with the consent of Egyptian Sunni elites. Chief Egyptian legal officer (Grand Mufti) Shayk Muhammad Abduh (1849-1905) founds a modernist legal reform movement.

1888. Death of Namik Kemal, leader of the 'Young Turk' secularising reform movement in Ottoman Turkey. Leadership passes to the pro-European secularist Kemal Ataturk.

1890. Shi'ah agitation against the granting of trade monopolies to British companies as part of the division of Persia into Russian and British spheres of influence with the acceptance of the hereditary Persian Sunni monarchs, the Shahs.

c1900. Islamic Jihad movement founded in northern India (now Pakistan) by followers of Wali-Allah. Aim is purification of Islam in preparation for Qur'anic law after British have been defeated as colonial power.

1900. Influential Egyptian nationalist Qasim Amin publishes *Women's Emancipation* arguing that women should simultaneously return to the role prescribed for them by the *shari'ah*, but at the same time play a prominent and militant role in national liberation movements.

1901. Muhammad ibn Sa'ud, a British-supported Wahhabi, captures Ottoman fortress of Masmak, near Riyadh in Arabia. Sa'ud clan are henceforth the de facto rulers of the area despite continuing nominal Ottoman rule.

1905. Formation of the Young Turk Party in Damascus as a secret association amongst reformist military officers of the Ottoman army.

4.8 RISE OF ARAB NATIONALISM and ISLAMIC FUNDAMENTALISM

1906. Constitutional revolution in Iran forces the Shahs to establish a national assembly on European parliamentary lines.

1906. Muslim League, a group of Egyptian-style modernists and reformers, formed in Delhi.

1908. Military uprising against the despotic Ottoman Sultan

Abdul Hamid II led by Enva Pasha and the garrison of Salonika. Abdul Hamid II is overthrown and replaced by Sultan Muhammad V who promises to abide by the 1876 constitution and support the reforming efforts of the Young Turk Party.

1914–18 War. Ottomans allied with Germany and Austria. British and French support Arab nationalist and Islamic fundamentalists such as the Wahhabis of Saudi Arabia against the Ottomans.

1921. Egypt becomes a sovereign nation under rule of British-type constitutional Monarch King Farouk who continues the Anglo-Muhammadan legal tradition in the teeth of opposition from traditionalists and modernists demanding a return to the primacy of Islamic *shari'ah* law.

1922. Formal abolition of the Ottoman Sultanate and formation of the modern secular state of Turkey by Kemal Ataturk.

1925. Reza Shah Pahlavi gains power in Persia from the last of the hereditary Sunni Shahs of the Qajar dynasty in a military coup. An admirer of Hitler, he renames the country Iran (land of Aryan race) in 1935. (Later the Shah allied Iran with Germany during the 1939–45 war, claiming Azerbaijan and much other territory in Soviet central Asia.)

1928. Muslim Brotherhood founded in Egypt.

1932. Wahhabi-Sa'ud clan proclaim themselves Monarchs of the new kingdom of Saudi Arabia.

1932. Foundation of the Ja'mat-i-Islami Party in British India by Sayyid Abu Ala Mawdudi.

1933. Constitution adopted in Afghanistan limiting absolute power of the king, establishing a tribal parliament with limited powers and enshrining the *shari'ah* as the country's fundamental law.

1940. Ali Jinnah's Muslim League declares aim of establishing Pakistan as a homeland for Indian Muslims after end of British rule. Wartime links with the Japanese.

1941. Muhammad Reza Pahlavi becomes Shah of Iran and follows firstly pro-German and then pro-western foreign policy combined with western-type modernisation and repression of the majority Shi'ite population.

1945. Independent republic of Kurdistan briefly proclaimed before being crushed by the combined armed forces of Iran, Iraq and Turkey, between whom the Sunni Muslim Kurds, with much justice, claim their country was divided by the Ottoman and, later, European Imperialists.

1945. Arab League founded (result of Saudi-British diplomacy).

1946. Britain recognises Transjordan as a Monarchy under King Abdullah, a Hashemite (direct descendant from Muhammad), who seeks Sunni leadership with British support. British military aid including creation of Jordanian army under British General Glubb 'Glubb Pasha'.

1947. Pakistan becomes independent.

1948. End of British Mandate in Palestine leads to division of territory between British 'puppet' King Abdullah of Jordan and the new state of Israel. Abdullah is ostracised for his involvement in the plan and forced to join war of all Arab states against Israel.

1948. The Muslim Brotherhood assassinates Egyptian Prime Minister Nuqurashi Pasha following Egypt's defeat in the war against the new state of Israel.

1951. British and French install King Idris as Sunni ruler of Libya.

1952. Yasser Arafat becomes a member of the Muslim Brotherhood whilst a student at Cairo University.

1952. King Abdullah of Jordan assassinated by pro-Nasser Sunni fundamentalists because of cooperation in creation of state of Israel.

1953. Muslim Brotherhood instrumental in the overthrow of British-backed King Farouk of Egypt and establishment of Egyptian Arab Republic.

1954. Nasser becomes President of Egypt. Expels British and German military advisers.

1954. Guerilla forces of the Algerian National Liberation Front declare all-out war on France.

1954. An attempt on Egyptian President Nasser's life provides the pretext for hanging six leaders of the Muslim Brotherhood and driving hundreds of others into exile in Sudan, Saudi Arabia and Pakistan. Whilst in prison Brotherhood leader Sayyid Qutab formulates the post-war version of modern Sunni fundamentalism which amounts to nothing less than a united Islamic republic based on the *shari'ah*.

1956. Sudan, Tunisia and Morocco become independent.

1956. Pakistan declared the world's first Islamic Republic.

1958. Nasser proposes federation of Egypt, Syria and Iraq. Only Syria agrees and forms the United Arab Republic with Egypt.

1960s. 'Black Muslim' movement founded by Elijah Muhammad in United States.

c1960. Yasser Arafat begins recruiting militant young

Palestinians who are willing to take up arms against Israel for his organisation al-Fetah. (By 1965 he was in effective political control of the Palestinian refugee camps in Jordan and Lebanon.)

1961. Nasser's United Arab Republic plan collapses when Syria withdraws. Egypt retains the title until 1970.

1962. Independent Algerian Republic recognised by France after a bitter eight-year guerilla war.

1964. Formation of the Palestine Liberation Organisation (PLO) as an umbrella organisation for Palestinian refugee welfare and guerilla organisations, chief amongst them the al-Fetah guerilla movement started in the Palestinian refugee camps by Yasser Arafat. The organisation's formation is sponsored by President Nasser of Egypt.

1965. First Indo-Pakistani war.

1965. Indonesian coup brings General Suharto to power with the active support of the *santri* councils of *shari'ah* jurists. After the coup 500,000 Communists are executed over a period of years.

1966. Military coup in Syria brings Alawite (militant Shi'ite subsect) General Salah Jedid to power. In keeping with Alawite tradition Jedid appointed the leader of the strongest Alawite clan. Hafez al-Assad President of the country.

1967. Six Day War of Arab nations against Israel.

1967. Communist government of Albania closes all mosques in an anti-religion drive (about 70% of Albanians are Muslims).

1967. Mu'ammar al-Qaddafi overthrows the pro-British King Idris of Libya in favour of his own 'divinely guided' dictatorship.

1969. President Numiery of Sudan introduces *shari'ah* law.

1969. Saudi Arabians found the World Muslim League Secretariat to finance Muslim causes with new-found oil wealth and assert their claim to leadership of the Sunni Muslim nations.

1970. Under the leadership of Yasser Arafat the Palestine Liberation Organisation, with Arafat's al-Fetah guerillas at its core, attempts a military coup to establish a Palestinian state in Jordan.

1971. Pakistan defeated in second Indo-Pakistani war over possession of the Muslim majority state of Kashmir. Bangladesh breaks away from West Pakistan citing discrimination against East Pakistanis, corruption and abuse of the *shari'ah* law for political purposes. New republic declares itself secular and socialist.

1971. Bahrain given independence by Britain.

1972. Islamic constitution adopted in Morocco, allowing King Hassan II to dissolve parliament and rule by decree at any time.

1973. Death of Elijah Muhammad, founder of the Black Muslims of America and Nation of Islam movements.

1973. Republic declared in Afghanistan after overthrow of King Zahir Shah, a Sunni Monarch. Muhammad Doud, the King's cousin, takes over as President.

4.9 PRESENT DAY FUNDAMENTALIST MOVEMENTS

1973. Ramadan war of Arab nations against Israel. Arabs use 'oil weapon' against west.

1974. Ahmadiyah sect officially declared non-Islamic by Pakistan government.

1974. PLO leader Yasser Arafat addresses the United Nations General Assembly, speaking as a 'head of state'.

1975. King Faisal of Saudi Arabia assassinated.

1977. Coup in Bangladesh brings the military to power and a new constitution which abolishes secularism and enshrines elements of *shari'ah* law.

1977. Military coup in Pakistan brings General Zia ul-Haq to power. Introduction of full *shari'ah* legal code and start of Islamisation campaign.

1977. President Sadat of Egypt signs treaty of mutual recognition and peace with Israel causing consternation in the entire Arab and Muslim world.

1977. Mu'ammar al-Qaddafi of Libya pronounces his 'third universal theory' including the theoretical abolition of the Libyan state in favour of a 'state of the people' (*Jamahirya*) where, according to the slogans, 'the people are the Caliph' and 'parliaments are now defunct'.

1977. The small Muslim state of Djibouti in the horn of Africa is granted independence by France.

1978. President Daoud of Afghanistan overthrown by a coup. His rule is replaced by the pro-Soviet People's Democratic Party of Afghanistan which embarks on a radical programme of land reform and modernisation.

1979. Islamic revolution in Iran.

1979. Iranian Shi'ite fundamentalists attack the great Mosque in Mecca during *Hajj*. Saudi Arabian government executes 73 conspirators. In keeping with the *shari'ah* they are beheaded in public.

1980. New 'basic law' is added to the Israeli constitution stating

111

that Jerusalem will remain Israel's capital 'eternally'. The Saudi Arabians officially rededicate *jihad* in response.

1980. Start of Iran-Iraq war.

1980. Military coup in Turkey.

1980. Mauritania declared an Islamic republic.

1981. Louis Farrakhan becomes leader of US Nation of Islam Movement (in 1985 confirms receipt of $5 million from Colonel al-Qaddafi).

1981. President Sadat of Egypt assassinated by a Muslim Brotherhood splinter group after recognising Israel and signing a peace treaty.

1981. Egypt expelled from Arab League.

1982. Serious fundamentalist rioting in all Algerian towns and cities leads to the fall of President Hourai Boumédienne and the emergence of President Chadli who embarks on a policy of limited Islamisation of the law and government.

1982. Polisario guerillas proclaim the independent Saharan Arab Democratic Republic (SADR) in Moroccan occupied territory of Western Sahara. SADR supported by Algeria and recognised by the Organisation of African Unity and most Third World governments.

1982. President Assad of Syria puts down an attempted Muslim Brotherhood uprising with the death of 10,000 people in the city of Hama.

1982. Fundamentalist riots in Asyut, Egypt, put down by the army.

1983. General Ershad becomes President of Bangladesh following military coup.

1983. In just five weeks the Islamic authorities of Iran announce over 300 public executions for heresy and crimes against *shari'ah* law.

1983. Right-wing Motherland Party wins Turkish elections. Pledges to take secular Turkey into the EEC.

1983. Palestinians expelled from Lebanon. Start of Lebanese civil war.

1984. Libya and France come to the point of war over the Chadian civil war.

1984. Fundamentalist riots against secularising policies in Indonesia.

1984. Serious drought and famine hit parts of Chad, Sudan, Mali, Niger and Mauritania.

1985. Sultanate of Brunei becomes independent from Britain.

1986. Martial law lifted in Pakistan.

1986. Algeria adopts new Political Charter to guide the future development of 'Islamic Socialism' which introduces *shura* (religiously guided councils) in the running of the state and the nationalised industries.

1988. Benazir Bhutto's Pakistan People's Party wins first elections after end of military rule. Bhutto maintains Pakistan's status as an Islamic Republic based on *shari'ah* law.

1988. President Zia of Pakistan dies in mystery plane crash.

1988. Riots in Soviet Tadjikstan after earthquake victims are buried in mass graves without due observance of Muslim funeral rites.

1988. Start of serious rioting between Muslims and Christians in Soviet Armenia.

1989. Chinese Muslims demonstrate in Beijing for greater religious freedom.

1989. Hojatoleslam Hashemi-Rafsanjani announces sentence of death on Salman Rushdie, British author of *The Satanic Verses*.

1989. 600th anniversary of the Battle of the Field of Blackbirds (establishing Ottoman rule in the Balkans) causes Muslim-Christian riots in Yugoslavia.

1989. Death of Imam Khomeini. Hojatoleslam Hashemi-Rafsanjani becomes President of Iran.

1989. Saudi Arabians behead 16 pro-Iranian Kuwaitis after an attempt to plant bombs in the Great Mosque during *hajj* (pilgrimage to Mecca).

PART THREE

ISLAMIC SECTS

Islam can seem very baffling to outsiders because of its division into so many rival sects. Most people in the West know of the division between the dominant Sunni and the minority Shi'ah sects — the main sectarian divide. But beyond this there are dozens of sub-divisions which have shaped the development of the religion and continue to profoundly influence the politics of the Muslim world.

Distribution of Muslim Sects and Law Schools

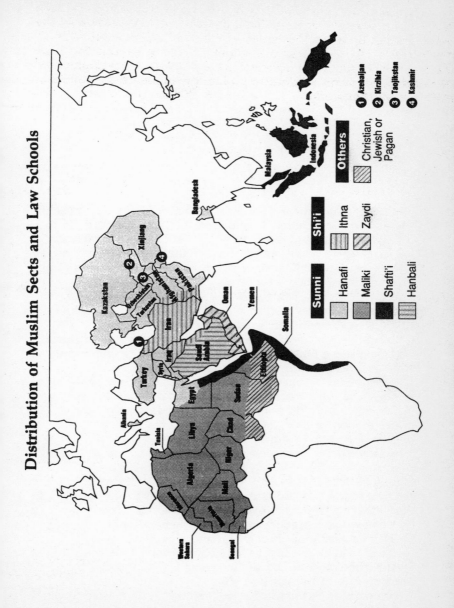

Sunni
Hanafi
Maliki
Shafi'i
Hanbali

Shi'i
Ithna
Zaydi

Others
Christian, Jewish or Pagan

1 Azerbaijan
2 Kirzhia
3 Taojiktstan
4 Kashmir

Kazakstan
Xinjiang
Uzbekistan
Turkmenistan
Turkey
Albania
Tunisia
Algeria
Western Sahara
Mali
Niger
Chad
Libya
Egypt
Sudan
Ethiopia
Somalia
Iraq
Iran
Syria
Saudi Arabia
Oman
Yemen
Senegal
Bangladesh
Malaysia
Indonesia

1.0 SUNNI ISLAM

The vast majority of Muslims in the world today describe themselves as *Sunni* ('followers of the Smooth Path').

The Sunnis take their name from the *Sunnah*, a collection of six 'authentic' (*sahih*) books of *hadith* attributed to Muhammad and his earliest followers, known as the Companions of the Prophet (*Sahabah Muhammadon*).

About 80% of the Muslim world population is Sunni and every Muslim nation has a clear Sunni majority except Iran, Iraq, Azerbaijan, Yemen and some of the Gulf States.

Sunni theology and law are based on the Qur'an, the Sunnah and, to a more limited extent, consensus of the community of believers (*ijma*). There are four main sub-divisions, all of which accept the Sunnah and vary only in the relative importance given to *ijma*. The most traditionalist, or 'fundamentalist', reject *ijma* completely but others accept a considerable degree of interpretation of Qur'anic law based on it.

Sunni law evolved during the Golden Age of the early Abbasid Empire with the first works of recognisably 'Sunni' theology produced by Abu-I-Hasan 'Ali ibn Isma'il al-Ash'ari (died 935). Above all else al-Ash'ari was concerned with supporting the political status quo and uniting all Muslims into one state to end the damaging civil wars over the succession to Muhammad. To do this he fused Arab traditionalism, demanding a legal regime based exclusively on the Qur'an and concept of predestination by Allah, with the wishes of 'rationalists' wanting a sophisticated legal regime more suited to governing an Empire and based on the principle of human free will.

According to Sunni teaching a potential Muslim ruler need not prove descent from Muhammad as long as he can gain the consent of the community of the faithful (the *umma*). Once a ruler has proved his effectiveness – by military success and upholding the Sunni version of the *shari'ah* – Sunni Muslims are obliged to follow him unquestioningly as 'viceregent of the prophecy' (*khilafat al-nubu'n*), regardless of whether he is just or oppressive, moral or immoral.

Sunni law does not recognise the right of the faithful to overthrow a bad or unjust ruler, as long as he nominally upholds the *shari'ah* and is prepared to wage *jihad* if Islam is attacked. Sunni'ism teaches that as no man except Muhammad is free from sin all rulers will be flawed and that this must be accepted by the faithful. The only exception is the Mahdi, a divinely-guided political ruler Sunnis believe Allah will deliver to them shortly before the end of time.

Apart from occasional bouts of 'Mahdi'ism' (Colonel Qaddafi of Libya is the latest to be widely thought of as the Sunni Mahdi) Sunni Islam is a deeply conservative political creed. The early revolutionary tradition of Islam is only upheld today by various Shi'ah factions believing their leaders to be both divinely guided and 'mystically' descended from Muhammad. A central part of the mission of Shi'i Islam is the overthrow of unjust Sunni rulers, and the two branches of the religion are therefore bitterly opposed.

All Sunni Muslims belong to one of four classical schools of Islamic law – the *Maliki, Shafi, Hanafi* and *Hanbali* – named after the lawyers commissioned by early Abbasid Emperors to clarify and set down the law.

According to Sunni law an Islamic ruler is free to select the school of his choice as the orthodoxy within his domain. But at the same time individual Sunnis have the right to be tried according to the school of their choice. They generally adopt the same school as their father, which has led to fairly stable judicial regimes in various Sunni Muslim states.

1.1 The Maliki and Shafi

The oldest Sunni legal school is the Maliki, founded by Malik ibn-Anas of Medina (died 795). Ibn-Anas successfully overturned the right claimed by the 'Umayyad Caliphs to make laws without reference to the Qur'an by re-emphasising the importance of *hadith*.

The Maliki school was based in Medina rather than the Abbasid capital of Baghdad, and was therefore highly Arab traditionalist. In addition Malik ibn-Anas possessed a great many *hadith* dating from the Prophet's time as ruler of Medina, when many of the more legalistic surahs of the Qur'an were revealed.

The largest and most important legal school during the Abbasid period was founded by his student Idris al-Shafi (died 820) who brought the Maliki doctrines from the backwater of Medina to Baghdad, where he founded his own Shafi school.

This attracted a great many Persian scholars who in general were more sophisticated than the Maliki lawyers and gave more scope to the concept of free will and *ijma* (reasoning by jurists backed by the consensus of believers).

The great Abbasid jurist al-Ash'ari, for example, was a Shafi. The essentials of al-Ash'ari's teaching are accepted today by all four schools who tend to define themselves by their degree of variation from Shafi law. In al-Ash'ari's time the Shafi legal school became the official law school of the late Abbasid Islamic Empire and remained the most important until Baghdad fell to the Mongals in the 13th century.

The Abbasid's successors as leaders of the Muslim world, the Ottomans, adopted the Hanafi school and both the Shafi and Maliki were pushed to the fringes of the Islamic world. Shafi became dominant amongst the merchant classes and the Maliki was re-established in Morocco.

Today the Shafi school is only dominant along the old trade routes and the majority school only amongst Sunnis in the East Indies, East Africa and the islands of the Indian Ocean. The Maliki school is dominant throughout most of Muslim Africa.

1.2 The Hanafi

The Hanafi school was founded in Baghdad by Abu al-Hanafah (died 767) to defend the more rationalist wing of legal thinking against the traditionalism of the Maliki Arabs. Al-Hanafah attached great importance to systematic consistency in application of the law, upheld the principle of the *ijma*, and used legal precedents other than those found in the *hadith* to expand the body of Islamic law and theology.

The Hanafi school greatly developed court procedure and rules of evidence and advised that extreme Qur'anic (*hadd*) punishments were to be used very rarely, and then only by way of example.

Hanafi doctrines were more suited to the smooth administration of the large and complex Abbasid Empire and the Caliphs at first favoured them over the Shafi. But they were extremely unpopular with the traditionalist masses and sparked numerous revolts. In this unsteady political climate the Abbasids tried to remove the focus of Arab and Shi'ah unrest by switching their sponsorship to al-Ash'ari's Shafi school, which took a middle course between the Hanafi and Maliki.

The Hanafi jurist Hasan al-Maturidi, a contemporary of al-Ash'ari, likewise modified Hanafi doctrines, accepting many of the traditionalists' demands for greater reliance on *hadith*. Al-Maturidi's legal compromises involved acceptance of additional *hadith*, especially the Sunnah, and less reliance on judicial independence and *ijma*.

After the fall of the Abbasid Empire the Arabs became politically powerless and their traditionalist creed was ignored by the new power in the Islamic world, the Ottoman Turks. The Ottomans, unable to claim legitimacy on even the most remote descent from Muhammad, were naturally hostile to the traditionalist Arab Maliki and Persian Shafi schools, and instead adopted Hanafi'ism. Ottoman sponsorship ensured that the Hanafi became the dominant Sunni law school throughout most of the Muslim world.

The Hanafi are the least 'fundamentalist' of the four Sunni schools and less inclined to accept legal regimes based entirely on the Qur'an and *hadith*. For this reason Hanafi Sunnis tend to be the most acceptable of all Muslims to the West, and during the colonial period Hanafi rulers in countries such as Egypt and India showed a marked affinity for Western customs and accepted hybrid Muslim-European legal codes.

Modern Turkey, the heartland of Ottoman Hanafi'ism, has now adopted an entirely secular legal system, which would be out of the question in any country where one of the other legal schools was dominant.

1.3 The Hanbali

The Hanbali Sunni law school is by far the most fundamentalist of the four. Today it is not found outside Saudi Arabia, where it is the official state creed. The school was founded by Ahmad ibn Hanbal (died 850), an extreme Arab traditionalist who broke away from the Maliki.

Hanbal entirely rejected the use of reasoning by jurists and *ijma*, and insisted that the *shari'ah* was to be based exclusively on the Qur'an. He was prepared to accept the use of *hadith*, but only reluctantly as he believed the collection which made up the Sunnah was not complete.

Hanbali'ism is thus the most puritanical version of Qur'anic law. It became virtually extinct during the Ottoman period, but was revived by the fundamentalist Arabian Wahhabi movement at the end of the 18th century.

1.4 Mahdi'ist Movements

Sunni Islam is far less prone to schisms than Shi'i Islam and there have been no significant new Sunni sub-sects since the division into the four schools.

Splinter groups are usually short-lived and based around claims of 'Mahdi' status by particular political leaders or religious scholars. The Mahdi ('chosen one'), according to Sunni theology, will be a divinely guided political leader whom Allah will send to Earth to unite all Muslims into a single political state shortly before the end of the world.

Over the centuries dozens of tiny Mahdi'ist sects based around individual teachers, 'Holy Men', or tribal and village leaders have been proclaimed – only to disappear just as quickly when the Mahdi in question dies.

Colonel al-Qaddafi of Libya, a Sunni of the Maliki school, currently believed by many of his followers to be al-Mahdi, has devised his own version of Sunni law and theology, based on both Islam and Socialism. Al-Qaddafi's so-called 'Third Universal Theory' is not, however, usually regarded as a separate sect within Sunni Islam. In 1981 a Sunni theological commission in Mecca found al-Qaddafi guilty of apostophy (reversion from Islam) and rejected his theories as non-Islamic.

The largest modern Mahdi'ist sect to both survive the death of its founder and gain some currency both in the Muslim and Western worlds is the Ahmadiyah, based in Pakistan. Founded by Mirza Ghulam Ahmad (died 1908) of Qadiyan in East Punjab in the 1880s, the sect now claims one million followers, mostly in Pakistan, West Africa and the United States.

Ahmad claimed to be not only the Muslim Mahdi but the re-incarnation of Jesus and an avatar (manifestation) of the Hindu god, Krishna. He proclaimed his mission as the unification of Islam and the incorporation of Christianity and Hinduism within it. After his death his followers formed themselves into an independent community within Islam, generally accepting Sunni teaching and law, and electing a Caliph in the manner of the four 'rightly guided' Caliphs who came after Muhammad.

When the first Ahmadiyah Caliph died in 1911 the sect split. The main group continued to teach that Ahmad was the Mahdi, whilst the smaller group, based in Lahore, claimed that instead of being the re-born Prophet, he was simply a 'renovator' or 'cleanser' of Islam (*mujaddid*). Both groups developed some highly heterodox ideas, often tinged with anti-Semitism and casting the Jews in the role of murderers of Jesus and persecutors of Muhammad.

The 'Black Muslim' Movement

Throughout the middle part of the 20th century the Ahmadiyah carried out successful missionary activity especially in Muslim West Africa, with elaborate 'conversion rituals' similar to both Christian baptism and pagan tribal initiation rites. From the 1930s onwards, from their base in West Africa, the Ahmadiyah began missionary work in the West Indies and amongst black people in the United States.

In the 1940s small communities of Ahmadiyah were established in the black ghettos of major American cities, and as they grew they slowly broke free of doctrinal guidance from Pakistan, developing a separate identity as the Black Muslims of America.

The growth of the American 'black consciousness' movement in the 1960s brought their message to a much wider audience. The group had considerable appeal to highly religious American blacks, claiming, with some justification, that their traditional religion of Christianity was essentially a creed for whites.

The most important Black Muslim leader during the 1960s was Elijah Wallace of Chicago, who took the name Elijah Muhammad on conversion, and built a large mosque bearing his name. Elijah Muhammad's version of Islam was tinged with both anti-Semitism and anti-white racial doctrines. His more idiosyncratic theories included a claim that ancient Black Islamic scientists created the moon, and that an evil Arab scientist called Yakud had created the original race of white people as a disastrous experiment in the days before Muhammad.

Despite Elijah's eccentricity the movement attracted a considerable following amongst black political activists and celebrities. The best known convert was the boxer Cassius Clay, who adopted the name Muhammad 'Ali on joining the movement. The leading civil rights activist Malcolm X also joined and took part in *hajj* to Mecca.

After Elijah's death in 1973 leadership passed to his son, Wallace Muhammad, who purged the more extreme racialist ideas and reformed the sect as a fairly orthodox Sunni community known as the Sunni American Muslim Mission. Today Muhammad Wallace is the resident Imam of the Chicago mosque built by his father.

While most of the original 'Black Muslims' followed Wallace Muhammad into Sunni orthodoxy, about 10,000 split from the movement to form the 'Nation of Islam', which retains much of Elijah's racialist outlook. It is led by Louis Farrakhan, a messianic figure who calls for the establishment of an entirely Black Muslim state within the United States. In 1985 Farrakhan received a $5 million loan from Colonel al-Qaddafi of Libya.

Although Farrakhan's following is small it is growing, especially amongst poor young urban blacks, and his influence extends far beyond actual converts as the only black American leader prepared to openly express the anti-white and anti-Jewish feeling latent amongst some American blacks. Some of Farrakhan's followers form the 'bodyguard' of the Reverend Jesse Jackson, America's leading black politician, and there was controversy during the 1984 and 1988 presidential election campaigns over allegations of anti-Semitism in the Jackson campaign.

The original Ahmadiyah group in Pakistan was officially declared 'non-Muslim' in 1980 as part of the Government's Islamisation campaign and the imposition of Sunni orthodoxy on the country as a whole. The group remains active but its followers are targets for both Sunni and Ismaelite Shi'i missionary drives.

2.0 SHI'I (SHI'ITE) ISLAM

Modern Shi'ah, in their various sub-sects, make up about 20% of the total population of the Muslim world, though the proportion rises to about 40% in the Middle East (including Iran) where they are concentrated. The Shi'ah form the clear majority of the populations of Iran, Yemen and Azerbaijan, about half the population of Iraq and there are significant minorities throughout Arabia.

The Shi'ah's title dates back to the first decades of the Islamic era when they formed the army, or 'partisans', of 'Ali ibn Abi Talib, the fourth and last 'rightly guided' Caliph to follow Muhammad. In 661 AD 'Ali was murdered and the Caliphship passed to the 'Umayyads, who were not directly descended from the Prophet. The Shi'ah have since waged an intermittent 1,300 year war to overthrow the 'usurper' 'Umayyad dynasty and the Sunni rulers who followed them and place 'Ali's descendants back on the throne of a united Islamic Empire.

Shi'i Islam is therefore older in origin than Sunni'ism and modelled much more closely on the political practices of Muhammad and the original four Caliphs. It is also predominantly a creed of martyrdom and revolution, the result of centuries of uprisings and civil wars, and is therefore often seen in the West as typifying the unacceptable medieval and warlike aspect of Islam.

2.1 The Twelvers (*Ithna-'Ashariyah*)

The 'Twelvers' (Ithna-'Ashariyah, usually shortened to Ithna) are by far the largest group of Shi'ah and their doctrines may be regarded as the 'orthodox' version of Shi'i Islam. They form the vast majority of the population of Iran and about half the population of Iraq, where they are in the majority in the eastern provinces bordering Iran. They also form the majority in the Soviet republic of Azerbaijan, which also borders Iran. There are large Twelver minorities in the eastern part of Saudi Arabia and the Gulf states, but they are found in the rest of the Muslim world only in small, scattered communities.

Like all Shi'ah the Twelvers believe that the direct descendants of the Prophet, via his daughter Fatima and son-in-law 'Ali, are the rightful rulers of the Muslim world. The line of 'Ali's offspring is held to be divinely guided, immune from sin and error and is accorded the same authority as the Prophet himself. Ignorance or disobedience to the word of any of the Shi'i Imams is heresy.

The Twelvers take their name from Muhammad ibn al-'Askari, the twelfth Imam in the line of 'Ali. On the death of his father Hasan in 873, al-'Askari became Imam at the age of four. But within days he mysteriously disappeared in the cellar of his house in Samara, Iraq, and was never found. As he had no brothers the line became extinct.

The Shi'ah, however, refuse to accept that al-'Askari died. They believe he is still at large in the world in a miraculously 'concealed' form invisible to sinners (in practice all humans). One day he will make himself visible to sinners again as al-Mahdi, the 'chosen one' mentioned in the Qur'an, who will appear shortly before the end of the world. The mystical 'concealed' twelfth Imam therefore has the title *al-Mahdi-I-Muntzar* – 'the Awaited Mahdi'.

The early Muslims, including Muhammad, believed that the world was scheduled to come an end by the year 1100 AD at the latest, and possibly earlier. The Shi'ah at the end of the 9th century almost certainly expected al-'Askari to reappear as Mahdi within the coming century.

When al-Mahdi failed to appear in the 12th century leadership of the Twelver sect passed to the *ulama* – the council of twelve Shi'ah elders selected on the basis of Qur'anic study and scholarship. The *ulama* claimed to be guided by the concealed 'Twelfth' Imam and elected a human Imam from among their number to rule on earth until the 'given time' (*gahybah*) of al-Mahdi's return.

Over the centuries as al-Mahdi failed to reveal himself the *ulama* and the human Imams gained more authority. The *ulama* began to teach that its Imam was divinely guided, incapable of error, sin-free and able to converse directly with al-Mahdi in dreams. The *ulama* also became the central political and legal institution of the Shi'ah, during the period when Twelver Shi'i was the official creed of the Persian Safavid state. At first its members tried all cases in person, but as their authority grew they devolved power to a ramified structure of clerics and judges under their control.

The leading *ulama*-appointed judges eventually became known as *Ayatollahs* and formed their own courts. The Ayatollahs (both those of the *ulama* and those lower down the hierarchy) were held to be divinely guided and were allowed to apply their own judgement without reference, in all cases, to the Qur'an.

In present day Iran the *ulama* is the supreme governing body and court of appeal both for the Twelver faithful and for the state. It collectively fulfils all the duties of the Imam, from directing *jihad* to enforcing the *shari'ah* law and *hadd* punishments. It also appoints from within its number a mortal Imam to serve as al-Mahdi's deputy on Earth.

The *ulama*'s medieval belief that al-Mahdi intervenes directly to guide their choice of Imam is unchanged even today. The Twelver Imam is held to be the wisest and least sinful man on Earth, immune from error and the only man to have a perfect understanding of both the inner (esoteric, religious) and outer (political, legal) meaning of the Qur'an.

In addition Twelver Imams are given sole access to sacred books containing knowledge given by Allah to the 12 mortal Shi'i Imams in the line of 'Ali. No other human is allowed to read these books which are believed to contain awesome and terrible guidance on interpretation of the Qur'an. They include the *Sahifah*, *Jaf'r*, *Jami'ah*, and the *Mushaf*, attributed to Fatima, the daughter of Muhammad and wife of 'Ali.

In the past popular Twelver Imams were worshipped as god-like figures even though such ideas commit the unforgivable sin of *shirk* (polytheistic 'association' of Allah with another). Many individual Imams have encouraged the idea that they are the personification of the long-awaited al-Mahdi. It is certain that many contemporary Iranians – especially at the mass level of illiterate and superstitious villagers – believed that Imam Khomeini was al-Mahdi. Khomeini quietly denied Mahdi status, but did nothing to dispel the cult which grew up around him.

2.2 The Seveners (*Isma'iliyah* or Isma'ilites)

The Isma'ilites are the second largest Shi'i sect, spread thinly throughout the Muslim world, with concentrations in Egypt, Syria, Pakistan, Bangladesh and India. There are about five million Seveners in the world, following their own line of hereditary rulers, the Aga Khans.

The Isma'ilites take their name from Isma'il, the eldest son of the sixth Shi'ah Imam Ja'far as-Sadiq. In 762 Isma'il died before his father, causing a succession crisis within Shi'ism. The main body of Shi'ah, the Twelvers, supported Isma'il's younger brother Musa-'l-Kazim, as the seventh Imam. But the Isma'ilites refused to recognise him, proclaimed the original line of Imams extinct, and adopted Isma'il's descendants as their new dynasty of Imams.

This dynastic dispute gave expression to a pre-Islamic cult of 'the sacred number seven' which had reasserted itself during the doctrinal chaos and confusion in Islam before the Abbasid Emperors laid down the doctrines of Sunni 'orthodoxy' in the 9th and 10th centuries AD.

The number seven had particular significance amongst early monotheists such as the Jews and Persian Zoroastrians, as the number of days in which the world was created. A number of esoteric doctrines had developed around this article of faith, including the idea that Allah was the 'seventh dimension' of the universe holding the other six – left, right, forward, backward, up and down – in balance. It was also believed there were seven degrees of both heaven and hell, that the Earth rested on seven plates, the stars on seven veils and that the world would last for 'seven Divine days' (of a thousand years each).

Most importantly, the Shi'ah believed the Prophethood was also governed by the number seven. There would be seven major *rasul* Prophets before the end of the world, of which Muhammad was the sixth. Muhammad had completed the Prophecy, but also foretold of a 'seventh' – al-Mahdi – who would arrive on earth as a political leader shortly before the end of time, but would bring no further revelations.

The Isma'ilites began to teach that the Shi'i Imamate also moved in cycles of seven. 'Ali had been the first, and Isma'il the seventh of the first cycle and therefore an entirely new cycle of Imams descended from Isma'il was about to begin.

The Isma'ilites took Isma'il's descendants as their Imams and named the dynasty Fatimid after 'Ali's wife Fatima, the daughter of the Prophet. They predicted that the last of the seven Fatimid Imams would be al-Mahdi or, failing this, would bring a new dynasty and a new cycle of seven Imams. The cycles would, in this way, continue until al-Mahdi finally arrived, possibly after seven cycles of seven or some other multiple of the number.

This highly metaphysical doctrine was codified in the *Rasa'il ikhwan al-safa* (Epistles of the Brethren of Purity), published by an Isma'ilite secret society in the middle of the 9th century. The Epistles are highly esoteric and densely packed with a bewildering array of philosophical and mystical ideas borrowed from Judaism, early Christian sects such as the Gnostics, ancient Babylonian astrology, and Arabian pagan number cults. As a whole it is barely intelligible, but clearly owes much to Muslim contact with superior traditions of Greek learning encountered in the contemporary conquest of North Africa.

Despite the incoherence of The Epistles, the book nevertheless marks the start of the impressive tradition of medieval Islamic scholarship in which the Isma'ilites played a very large part. The sect was, however, ruthlessly repressed and persecuted by both the 'orthodox' Abbasid Caliphs and the main body of the Shi'ah.

In order to survive, the Isma'ilites formed an underground network of guerilla fighters and missionaries (the *du'ad*) and at first hid their Imams in great secrecy. Members of the sect often posed as Christians or Jews in order to gain *dhimmi* (protected) status within the Empire. Recruits from amongst the orthodox Muslims and Shi'ah were encouraged to break the *shari'ah* (by for example drinking wine) partly as a method of disguise and partly to break down allegiance to Muslim orthodoxy in order to fully accept the developing Isma'ilite creed.

By the middle of the 10th century the sect had grown considerably and was able to mount a successful rebellion against the Abbasid Empire in Egypt. In 969 a Fatimid Isma'ilite Imam was established as the Anti-Caliph in Cairo and, after a brief civil war, gained recognition of an independent Egyptian state from Baghdad.

The Fatimid state, using the growing Isma'ilite mastery of the sciences and a trading and diplomatic network based on the widely dispersed network of *du'ad* underground cells, quickly prospered. Cairo, little more than a village at the start of the Fatimid epoch, grew into the greatest city of the Muslim world after Baghdad itself. The city's al-Azhar university became one of the great centres of learning, a position it maintains today.

The Fatimids pursued less hostile policies towards Christian Europe than Baghdad and sometimes effectively allied with Byzantium against Abbasid expansion. At the peak of their powers in the late 11th century their state extended from Tunis in the west to Palestine in the east, controlling most of the territory of modern Egypt and Libya.

The Fatimid state was destroyed as an indirect result of the Christian Crusades. Fatimid rulers had sometimes cooperated with the Crusaders against the Abbasids, but in the 12th century the Crusaders turned on them and inflicted several debilitating defeats. At the same time the Crusades had galvanised the military power of the Abbasids and in 1171 an Iraqi Abbasid force led by Sal'had-din (Saladin the Great) conquered Cairo and deposed the Fatimids. Thereafter the Isma'ilites resumed their underground guerilla existence and became notorious as the ferocious *Assassin* warriors.

2.3 Assassins (*Isma'iliyah Tayyibiyah* and *Niziriyah*)

After the destruction of the Fatimid dynasty the Isma'ilites split into two further sub-factions – the Niziriyah and the Tayyibiyah, both aiming to restore rival Fatimid princes to the Caliphship of Egypt.

The Tayyibiyah, the lesser of the two, supported the infant Fatimid prince al-Tayyib as the seventh Imam descended from Isma'il and therefore the awaited Mahdi. When the attempt to restore him to the throne failed the doctrine was discredited as, according to all schools of Islamic thought, al-Mahdi will be an invincible military leader.

The Tayyibiyah rationalised this problem by developing the doctrine of the Temple of Light of the Ten Intellects – a highly esoteric and metaphysical creed, even by Isma'ilite standards. According to the new doctrine, al-Tayyib was indeed held to be al-Mahdi, but only one tenth of him. Nine other 'tenth-part' Imams would be born and, after their deaths, their spirits would stay in the world as an increasingly bright spiritual 'Temple of Light'.

This light, which is taken to mean greater knowledge and understanding, will illuminate all Muslims immediately prior to

130

the end of the world, enabling them to recognise al-Mahdi when he arrives. The doctrine is thus similar to the Shi'ah Twelver idea that al-Mahdi ('the Twelfth Imam') is already in the world in concealed form invisible to sinners.

The larger Niziriyah faction supported the claim of al-Tayyib's older brother Nizir. Since Nizir was only the sixth Imam descended from Isma'il he could not, strictly speaking, be al-Mahdi. Instead the Niziriyah proclaimed him as the miraculous reincarnation (qiyamah) of Isma'il himself who, after an interval of 400 years, had returned to earth to rule as the seventh Imam.

When Imam Nizir also failed to recapture his father's Caliphship, the Niziriyah proclaimed him not as al-Mahdi but as the founder of a new cycle of seven Niziriyah Imams. Unlike the Tayyibiyah, who had abandoned the human Imamate in favour of pure metaphysics, the Niziriyah had established a dynastic line of rulers whom they could follow and who thereafter became the dominant Isma'ilite sect.

They also taught that their cycle of Imams would be 'repudiators' – breaking the established laws of the shari'ah in preparation for the arrival of al-Mahdi, who would restore them. The Niziriyah were thus free to drink wine and smoke hashish and, more importantly, to kill other Muslims in the course of jihad (which is forbidden by the Qur'an). The orthodox authorities, unsurprisingly, denounced them as apostates (non-Muslims) who could also be killed at will, leading to a vicious guerilla war.

The Niziriyah moved from Egypt into Syria, where they became known as the Assassins – the Arabic plural for hashish (marijuana) smokers. The Assassins revived the pre-Fatimid Isma'ilite du'ad system of underground cells and established a ramified network of agents and spies in all the cities of the Muslim world.

To try to overthrow the 'usurper' Sunni rulers they established a fortress headquarters in the Alamut valley in northern Persia, from where they mounted periodic attacks on Baghdad.

For over 200 years the Assassins were the terror of the Eastern world and the Alamut fortress itself is now the subject of many legends. But it is certain that it was a quite extraordinary place. The most reliable accounts describe it as a monastic-type institution in which young men were constantly drilled in the black arts of murder, weaponry, poisoning and disguise.

The fortress itself was enclosed on three sides by steep valley walls and according to legend – including accounts given by

Marco Polo — it was an earthly paradise based on the descriptions of Paradise in the Qur'an. Waterways carried streams of wine (Muslims believe they will be allowed to drink wine in heaven as a reward for restraint on earth), water, milk and honey through perfumed gardens of flowers and fruit trees. Hashish was in plentiful supply, and there were beautiful women, slaves and musicians.

According to legend, Assassins would be called to perform a mission with the words: 'Where do you come from?' An Assassin would reply: 'From Paradise' and be told: 'Go then and slay a man I shall name. When you return you shall again dwell in Paradise. Fear not death because the Angels of Allah will transport you nevertheless to Paradise.'

The Assassins had similar fortresses to the Alamut in Syria and Palestine and they were well known to the later Crusaders as fanatical warriors who fought both the Crusader and Muslim armies. The Assassins of Syria intermingled extensively with the local Muslim and Christian populations, and the many modern heterodox Shi'ah sects and communities of the area, such as the Alawites and the mysterious Druze, all have Assassin origins.

In 1256 the Alamut fortress fell to the Mongols and the Assassins began to disintegrate as a military force. Their last strongholds in Syria were destroyed by the Ottomans in the early 16th century.

The Assassins nevertheless maintained a discreet identity within Islam even after their destruction as a military force, with dispersed communities in Syria, Egypt, northern Persia, Afghanistan and India. The dynasty of Nizari Isma'ilite Imams has continued, via various complications, right through into the present time. In 1818 the Nizari Imam Abu-l-Hasan was given the title Aga Khan by the Shah of Persia.

The present day Isma'ilites have dropped the title Assassin and are now reconciled with the Tayyibiyah faction (now more commonly called the Musta'liyah and found mainly in the area around Bombay). The current Aga Khan, Karim II, is the 49th descended from Nizar and the seventh Imam of the seven cycles of Imams descended from 'Ali.

Despite this portentous arithmetic, Karim II has made no claim to be al-Mahdi. He is a highly Westernised individual educated at Harvard and residing in some splendour in Paris. Karim II has modernised Isma'ilite doctrines, which he now describes as the

132

tariqah 'l-Islami (spiritualist pathway of Islam).

Modern Isma'ilites sincerely accept the Qur'an's message of the equality of all races, and tend to be internationalist and charitable in outlook. Karim II administers several large charitable foundations established by his grandfather and is increasingly involved in the work of conservation organisations.

2.4 Alawites (*Isma'iliyah Alawiyun*) and Druze

Of the many Isma'ilite Assassin sub-sects which once existed in Syria only two – the Alawites and Druze – have survived into the modern world in significant numbers. Both are exclusive to Syria and Lebanon and now function as the private religions of politically important tribes.

The Alawites (upholders of 'Ali) originated in the 13th century as a splinter group from the Syrian branch of the Assassins (Nizariyah Isma'ilites). Modern Alawites form about 10% of Syria's population, but nevertheless dominate the state.

The origins of the split are shrouded in mystery and legend, but the basic issue appears to have been the Alawites' refusal to accept rule by the Nizari Assassin Imams and reversion to support for the extinct line of Twelver Imams descended from 'Ali. The Alawites are therefore much closer to the 'orthodox' Twelver Shi'ah of Iran than the rest of the Isma'ilites.

The main difference between the Alawites and other groups of Muslims is their open identification with aspects of Christian theology – especially the doctrine of Christ's resurrection which is seen as parallelling Shi'ah faith in the 'second coming' of the 'concealed Twelfth Imam'. For this reason the Alawites celebrate the Christian festival of Easter.

But the sect's historical affinity with Christianity has not been as much of a moderating factor. Syrian Christianity (which is of an entirely different tradition from Western Christianity) is as theologically extreme as messianic Shi'i Islam.

The Alawites are therefore one of the most extreme groups in modern Islam, effectively mixing the militant traditions of Isma'ilite Assassins with the fanaticism of fellow Iranian Twelver Shi'ah.

The Druze are a still more heterodox Assassin-derived group. In effect their religion is entirely separate from Islam, of which the Isma'iliyah branch merely provided the long-lost foundation.

In the current Syrian-Lebanese conflict, however, they are usually counted as 'Muslims' and are closely allied with the Alawites in Syrian politics.

The sect was formed in 1021 in Cairo when a group of Isma'ilites declared the Fatimid Imam al-Hakim the reincarnation of 'Ali, the first Shi'ah Imam. They were driven from Cairo to Syria by the majority of the Isma'ilites who regarded the proclamation as premature and heretical. The original Druze leader was al-Dazari ('the cobbler'), who was a Turk.

At the beginning of the 13th century the Druze sect was declared 'closed' to anyone other than direct descendants of the original Druze faithful, who thus became a distinct tribe as well as a religious group. At the same time the Druze retreated to the mountains of Syria and Lebanon, where they have remained to this day.

The theological content of the Druze religion was declared a secret at about the time of their emigration to the mountains and so virtually nothing is known of their beliefs other than their description of themselves as 'Unitarian'.

This probably means that, like orthodox Muslims, they worship the one god Allah, and accept much of the Qur'an. At the same time they have undoubtedly adopted the Jewish belief that Allah is the god of their tribe alone and, like the Alawites whom they most resemble, they probably also accept the doctrine of the reincarnation of Jesus. Beyond this the faith of the Druze will probably remain a mystery.

2.5 The Zaydis (*Shi'i Zaydiyah*)

The Zaydis are the most conservative Shi'i sect and closest to the Sunnis, particularly in application of Islamic law (*shari'ah*). They are mostly Bedouin Arabs and are only rarely found outside of the Yemen in southern Arabia, though there are small concentrations in northern Iran and Azerbaijan.

The sect was founded by the fifth Shi'ah Imam Zayd ibn 'Abidin (died 738), a rationalist who renounced his own Divine status and that of the line of Shi'ah Imams descended from 'Ali. After this renunciation Zayd was deposed by the majority of the Shi'ah who proclaimed his brother Muhammad al-Baqir the fifth Imam. Because of these events the Zaydis are sometimes known as the Fivers.

The Zaydi Imam is selected entirely on the basis of military skill. According to their doctrines Allah chooses the true Imam by ensuring his success in battle and by the death of all rival claimants.

Unlike the Iranian Twelvers, the Zaydi Shi'ah do not believe their Imams are either divinely guided or free from sin. In this respect their version of the Imamate closely resembles that of the Sunnis. But the Zaydis fiercely reject any attempt to establish dynasties of rulers whereas, as in the cases of Morocco, Jordan and Saudi Arabia, the Sunnis accept monarchical rule.

The result has been that Zaydi Imams have often been pious 'outsiders', often obscure desert Bedouin chieftains (*shayks*), qualified by a reputation for wise and rational settlements of legal disputes and, above all, success in battle.

The Zaydi Imamate becomes binding on the pronouncement of a simple declaration of allegiance (*da'wah*), usually on the eve of war. After that no man may oppose the Imam on pain of death until the war is concluded by either victory or defeat.

If two or more declare themselves Imam they are obliged to fight to the death. In practice rival claims to the Zaydi Imamate have often resulted in short-lived schisms with two or more 'partial Imams' being recognised until one emerges triumphant. These 'partial' Imams are known as 'summoners' (*du'at*) and have only limited jurisdiction.

Imam 'Alid, the ruler in North Yemen before the British and Saudi Arabians installed a rival Sunni ruler, was a recent example of *du'at*. The position regarding the current Zaydi Imam is unclear, partly because of the secrecy of the South Yemeni regime and the diffuse, tribal existence of the Bedouins. The appearance of a new full Imam will only become apparent when the next Zaydi uprising against either the regimes of North or South Yemen — or both — takes place.

2.6 Other Shi'i sects

In Islam there are dozens of sub-sects resulting from dynastic disputes and periodic attempts to cleanse and re-unify the religion.

Within the Shi'ah there are estimated to be over 70 identifiable groups, some with only a few hundred followers, and all organised around rival proclamations of the arrival of the 'concealed Twelfth' Imam.

135

The 'Sevener' Isma'ilites are in general even more given to schism, with countless sects emerging around competing esoteric explanations of the non-appearance of al-Mahdi (now almost 900 years overdue).

Contact with Christianity, often seen as the more effective religion of a superior colonising European culture, has influenced modern Islam far more than Islam has influenced modern Christianity. (In the Middle Ages the relationship was perhaps the opposite.) The result has been further schisms with Islamic sects adopting Christian-type beliefs, briefly flourishing, and then disappearing.

Isma'ilite Baktashis of Turkey, for example, have adopted the Christian doctrine of the Holy Trinity in the form of Allah (the Father), Muhammad (the Son) and the line of mystical Shi'i Imams (the Holy Spirit).

Shi'ah Twelver sub-sects are also scattered throughout remote tribal lands in Soviet central Asia and the North African desert. They often reflect the resurgence of tribal paganism and shamanism (worship of faith-healers) practised in desert areas for millennia before the sudden mass conversion to Islam. Dozens of other sub-sects are based on the worship of the shrines of individual Shi'i martyrs who, despite strict Qur'anic injunctions to the contrary, have been granted effective sainthood.

One of the most widespread Christian-style sub-sects in central Asia, Iran and the Shi'i area of Iraq is the 'Ali Ilahiyah ('Ali worshippers) who have deified the first Shi'i Imam 'Ali as the human manifestation of Allah – an almost identical principle to the Christian view of Jesus Christ as the Son of God.

Recent research, however, has discovered that the roots of this and similar groups in the Levant (such as the Druze) are very old. Rather than representing a recent Christianising influence on Islam, they appear to be the remnants of an ancient Persian religion based on worship of a God-King and the ability of God (or Gods) to take human form.

It appears that this extinct Babylonian religion survives in the modern world as 'Ali-worship within Islam and Christ-worship within Judaism, since Christianity is sometimes described as a Jewish sub-sect. This ancient Persian tradition certainly seems to be one source of both the Christian and Shi'i idea of a divinely guided religious leader (respectively Jesus and the concealed 12th Imam) who is also a political leader.

The real significance of the continued existence of such groups as the 'Ali Ilahiyahs is the way in which they demonstrate how Islam absorbed practitioners of earlier religions to a far greater extent than is conceded by contemporary Muslim authorities. Although deeply heretical, this unofficial religious flexibility is today expressed in a strong syncretic impulse within the religion, marked by repeated attempts by Muslim scholars to unite all world religions into one.

The most important syncretic group with Shi'i religious roots in recent times is the Baha'i religion which originated amongst Shi'i Iranians in the 19th century. Since then the Baha'is have broken completely with Islam and have become an entirely separate religion which is based on the promotion of world peace and the 'oneness of humanity' and the 'oneness of religion'.

The Baha'is claim that their faith is one of the fastest growing religions in the world and many Baha'i Houses of Worship – appropriately drawing on a mixture of religious architectural traditions – have been built in Europe and America in recent years. The most rapid expansion, however, has been in the Third World and the largest national group of Baha'is is still to be found in Iran where they are severely persecuted by the orthodox Shi'i religious authorities.

3.0 OTHER ISLAMIC SECTS

3.1 The Ibadiyah (Ibadites)

Only one group of Muslims, the Ibadites, have managed to preserve a faith strictly based on the original precepts outlined by Muhammad. They originated before the split between Sunni and Shi'ah Muslims, and date back to the first decades after Muhammad's death.

The Ibadites are direct descendants of the Khariji ('successionists') – a group of close companions of the Prophet himself, including his wife Khadijah, who is by tradition the first convert to Islam.

Small numbers of Ibadites are found in the deserts of Arabia, Iraq and North Africa. They are almost entirely nomadic Bedouin Arabs, recognise no state or clerical authorities, and organise their own affairs in complete isolation from official Islam and modern Islamic states.

'Ibadite' translates from Arabic as 'upholders of the *Ibadah*' – the basic religious law of Islam (see Part One – Faith). The Ibadites recognise no other laws and have no system of justice or permanent forms of state organisation. Like their Khariji ancestors, they believe that it is not possible for sincere Muslims to sin or break the *Ibadah* and that if they do so they commit apostophy. The Ibadites punish any crime not only with the draconian punishments prescribed in the Qur'an but also with expulsion from the religion and, therefore, also the tribe.

3.2 The Sufis

Sufi'ism is the intellectual cutting edge of Islam, organised in a series of monastic orders which have both enriched Islamic theology and repeatedly saved the religion from doctrinal disintegration or destruction at the hands of pagan conquerors.

The essence of Sufi'ism is 'spiritual detachment' from the pleasures (*zudd*) of mortal life in preparation for death and 'obliteration' (*fana*) of the self into the mind of Allah. The earliest Islamic tract on this theme is 'The Seal of the Saints' (*Khatm al-awliya*) written by Hakim al-Tirmidhi (died 898), a Baghdad mystic who was clearly influenced by the vulgarised Greek philosophy popular during the time of the early Abbasid Caliphs.

About 100 years later, Sufi tracts began to be marked by a belief in philosophical dualism – that there was a human self and a separate divine self. This doctrine contends that all humans are born with two souls, the human and divine. The human soul is at first dominant, as the 'midwife' of the divine soul. But it is the duty of Muslims to ensure their divine soul grows during their lifetime as the human soul steadily perishes.

This teaching meant that a Sufi had to follow a highly moral, preferably saintly, life on earth, as his Divine and human souls were in direct competition for spiritual nourishment. The more the human spirit was indulged through pleasures of this life, the more the divine soul would be weakened. If the Divine soul was insufficiently nourished it would die along with the human soul and the entire person would be obliterated.

The 'Whirling Dervishes'

Sufi teaching went on to enumerate four separate states (*maqamat*) which had to be simultaneously attained to ensure the rebirth of the divine soul – detachment from worldly affairs, including politics (*zuhd*); patience (*sabr*); gratitude for whatever Allah does to one – including disease, disasters and other misfortunes (*shukr*); and love (*hubb*), not merely acceptance, of what Allah commands through the Prophets.

Various exercises were prescribed to help Sufis achieve the *maqamat*. These included intense prayer, isolation in the desert, prolonged fasting, self-inflicted pain and wearing uncomfortable clothes. The actual origin of the term Sufi is unknown, but the best explanation is a translation based on the Arabic term for 'one who wears a hair shirt'.

Sufis also developed the concept that it was possible to become one with Allah whilst still alive by inducing a condition of 'holy intoxication'. In order to achieve 'intoxication' they developed extraordinary practices such as spinning for hours on the same spot and ritual trance dancing which earned the Mevlevi Order of Ottoman Sufis the title 'Whirling Dervishes'.

Other Sufi groups, particularly in North Africa, developed customs of walking on hot coals or lying on beds of nails. Still others spent hours chanting ritual incantations to induce a type of hypnotism. Qwaali, the repetitive popular folk music of modern Pakistan, is directly dervived from Sufi chanting, as are some forms of traditional rhythmic African music.

Several early Sufis were crucified by the Abbasids for proclaiming themselves to be 'Allah' whilst in a condition of 'intoxication', and in general Sufi'ism remained highly heterodox and subject to persecution until the middle years of the Abbasid Golden Age.

The first attempt to integrate it into the emerging body of 'orthodox' Sunni theology was made by the great Abbasid jurist of the Shafi school, Abu Hamid Muhammad al-Ghazali (died 1111). Al-Ghazali's book *The Revivification of the Science of the Faith* (*Ihya ulum al-din*) reconciles Sufi'ism and Sunni'ism and remains one of the seminal works of Islamic theology to this day.

Sufi Science and Medicine

Al-Ghazali injected self-denying Sufi morality into orthodox Sunni teaching, rescuing it from the extreme permissiveness and decadence of the late Abbasid period. At the same time he simplified Sufi theology by pronouncing invalid the Prophet-like pronouncements of the Sufi 'saints' made in an intoxicated state. After being given a solid and coherent theological basis by al-Ghazali the Sufis formed themselves into monastic orders to evangelise for Islam and develop its theology and related sciences.

These orders were circles of pious scholars, usually based around college-hospices (*zawiyahs*), for dying Sufis deemed to be in transition from the dominance of the human soul to the divine soul. The *zawiyah* became the basic unit of Sufi organisation and their growing mastery of medicine and related sciences was developed within them.

In the last two centuries of the Abbasid Empire the Sufis made outstanding progress in philosophy, medicine, and sciences such as chemistry, and the Sufi orders became the engines of Islamic learning, culture and external influence. Eventually the larger *zawiyah* developed associated universities (*madrasahs*) where religious subjects such as the Islamic sciences of chemistry, astronomy and 'sacred arithmetic' – essentially mathematics and architecture – were taught to large numbers of students.

The leading *madrasah* in the early 13th century was at Granada in southern Spain, under the Grand Mastership of Iban al-'Arabi (died 1240). Building on the reforming al-Ghazali tradition, he helped to steer the Sufi away from pantheism (acceptance of the gods of other religions) and saint-worship, back to the original Islamic path of strict monotheism.

Al-Arabi's theory, the 'Unity of Being' (*wahdat al-wujud*), maintained the universe was ruled by Allah, only in conjunction with mankind. Neither could exist without the other. This made him a radical humanist and rationalist almost three full centuries before similar advanced thinking was established in Europe during the peak of the Renaissance.

In al-Arabi's time Spain became the centre of the Sufi Renaissance and the period between the 12th and 14th century is now known as the *Alhambra* ('Age of Brilliance'). After the conquest of Granada in 1492 by the Catholic armies of Queen Isabella of Castille, Sufi learning was incorporated into Spanish culture by maintenance of the *madrasah* (Sufi university). Despite the loss of Spain, al-Arabi's school of thought became the Sufi orthodoxy in the Muslim world and remained the dominant influence on Islamic intellectual life until the early 17th century.

Modern Sufi'ism

In the early 17th century Sufi'ism was again reformed, this time by the Indian Sufi Ahmad Sirhindi (died 1624). Sirhindi accepted most of al-Arabi's teachings but reverted to the earlier Sufi tradition of firm belief that the world and man were essentially evil, and that the force of goodness was unique to Allah.

This meant that Sufis could no longer simply retreat from the world, but brought them much more into line with all other Muslims in their obligation to wage *jihad* (Holy War) to overcome evil. Allah demanded struggle against evil – not merely saintly avoidance of it.

Sirhindi's 'activist' version of Sufi'ism was to provide the backbone for the 18th and 19th century Muslim modernising and reformist movements which began with the Ottoman Empire and spread to all the nations of the Muslim world in the form of Islamic fundamentalist and anti-colonialist movements.

Modern Sufi Orders are organised in *tariqah* ('pathways') which link the current members of the Order spiritually to the founder. The Orders are named after their founders and the current master of an Order is called *al-Qutb* ('the axis') which may or may not feature in his name as an honorary title according to circumstance.

The method of organisation is similar to Freemasonry in the Western world – combining public charitable and educational work with a type of secret society. Acceptance into a *tariqah* is usually by invitation and is accompanied by the swearing of oaths of brotherhood and the acceptance of the various items of esoteric wisdom peculiar to the particular order.

Sufi influence is greatest in those areas of the world where Islam has been threatened by outside forces. The Orders are very widespread in Africa, especially in the Negro countries such as Nigeria, where the Muslim community itself is in a minority. And in many countries admission to the *tariqah* of the ruling group is essential for commercial or political success.

There are dozens of Sufi Orders spread throughout all the Muslim countries. Some, such as the *Chistiyah* of India and the *Salihiyah* of West Africa, are purely local. The five main international Orders – in rough order of size and importance – are the *Qadiriyah, Naqshbandiyah, Daraqwiyah, Tijaniyah* and *Khalwatiyah*.

The Qadiriyah

The oldest, largest and most globally dispersed Order is the Qadiriyah, founded by 'Abd al-Qadir al-Jilani (died 1166) in Baghdad.

The Qadiriyah are particularly important in Muslim Africa where, by becoming advisers to the courts of local kings, they laid the foundation for the spread of Islam throughout the northern half of the continent. Today the order is based in Egypt.

There are Qadiriyah *tariqahs* in most Muslim countries but they are particularly widespread in Pakistan, Egypt and North Africa. In the Maghreb desert (Libya, Algeria and Morocco), Qadiriyah are noted for trance dancing (hence Whirling Dervishes) and feats of endurance such as walking on hot coals.

The Naqshbandiyah

Founded by Muhammad ibn Muhammad Baha' as-Din Naqshband (died 1389), a noted philosopher and poet from Bukhara, the Naqshbandiyah are widespread throughout the Caucasus and central Asia where they have repeatedly organised guerilla movements against Russian and Communist rule. The Order is now based in Pakistan where it is closely associated with the movement for continuing Islamisation of the country and support for the rebels in Afghanistan.

The Naqshbandiyah Order is the most politically active of the global Orders, with close ties to ruling Sunni establishments throughout the world.

The Daraqwiyah

An Order founded in the early 19th century by Mulay-I-'Arabi Daraqwi (died 1823) in Fez, Morocco. The Order promotes an extremely conservative version of Maliki Sunni'ism and was the driving force behind the Jihad Movement which secured mass conversions throughout the mixed Berber-Arab and Negro lands of sub-Saharan Africa.

Today the order is influential in countries such as Mali, Niger and Chad where it works to maintain the purity of official Maliki Islam against the incursions of African paganism and European modernism. It is especially widespread in Morocco where the founder's birthday is celebrated as a national holiday.

The Tijaniyah

The Daraqwiyah are rivalled throughout Africa by the more moderate Tijaniyah *tariqahs*. The Order was founded by Abu-I-Abbas Ahmad at-Tijani (died 1815) and was, like the Daraqwiyah, important in the Jihad Movement. The Order took a more compromising attitude towards the French colonialists and often provided them with administrators and judges.

Cooperation with the French ensured the Order spread throughout North and Central Africa. Today it is associated with conservative businessmen in the region and membership often overlaps with the Muslim Brotherhood, a conservative pro-Saudi Arabian group.

The Khalwatiyah

The Khalwatiyah originated in 13th century Persia and Azerbaijan and quickly spread to the Caucasus and Turkey. The Khalwatiyah later became closely associated with the Ottoman Sultans, established headquarters in Istanbul and spread to Balkan Europe.

Although the Order was banned by the new secular government of Turkey in 1923 and its funds confiscated, it has nevertheless survived and has *tariqah* as far apart as North America, Egypt and Indonesia.

Sufi influence today

The influence of the Sufi Orders within the Muslim nations remains enormous. It is rare to find a Sunni Muslim ruler who is not affiliated to one or other of the Orders. In addition, education within many Muslim countries – both religious and secular – is carried out under Sufi auspices.

Ironically for a movement which played such a huge role in the advancement of human learning and culture, Sufi insistence on the unity of science and religion must now be regarded as one of the causes of the relative backwardness of the Muslim nations.

The great Sufi achievements were made within an entirely religious framework, based on the assumption that Allah existed and that the universe had a purpose. Therefore great discoveries in mathematics – such as the use of the number zero – were based on investigation of such esoteric religious questions as the exact size of Allah and how He keeps the stars from colliding with each other.

Modern science makes no such assumptions and its achievements are instead based on the application of the questioning human intellect. Modern scientists may believe in God or Allah – and may even be practising Muslims. But, unlike Sufi'ism, modern science does not take the limited view of the universe given in the Qur'an as its starting point.

PART FOUR

THE MUSLIM WORLD

The exact number of Muslims in the world today is difficult to estimate accurately. Statistics from vast and remote Muslim countries such as Indonesia and Pakistan are unreliable and, while there are tens of millions of Muslims in the Soviet Union, China and India, exact totals are politically sensitive. Numbers in these countries are almost certainly underestimated by the state and overestimated by Islamic sources. The claimed Muslim population of central Africa is enormous, but here it is not obvious how many are genuine Muslims rather than merely nominal, as many may have reverted in practice to tribal paganism. Despite these difficulties it is clear there will be at least 1,000,000,000 Muslims by the year 2000.

This vast community is concentrated in between 45 and 50 nations, according to conflicting sources, where Muslims form an overwhelming majority of the population. In theory all these nations form one united entity − Dar al-Islam ('the lands of Islam'). The non-Muslim world was designated as Dar al-Harb ('the lands of war') by Muhammad himself.

In reality, however, there are numerous identifiable 'Muslim Worlds', each corresponding to a phase in the religion's development and sectarian division. The original Muslim World was the Arabian peninsula, the birthplace of the Prophet and the land he ruled as Islam's supreme political and spiritual leader. Islam as practised here harks back to the days of the Prophet as though the intervening 1300 years of history had not taken place.

The Islam of the Arabian peninsula is very different to the religion's second great heartland − northern Arabia − where it clashed with Christianity, became heterodox and founded a great world Empire administered from cities such as Damascus, Cairo and Baghdad, which were wonders of the medieval world.

After the collapse of the north Arabian Empire in the middle of the 13th century Islam began to diverge into several separate 'worlds' − North Africa (and, for a time, Spain), the Muslim east (India and Indonesia), Iran and the Ottoman heartlands of Turkey, and the Balkans.

Still more divergence took place within the 'further lands of Islam' in distant Africa, central Asia, China and the Philippines.

Islam as it is practised today within these 'worlds' remains united in adherence to the Five Pillars. Beyond this, differences are so great that they make a nonsense of the concept of a single united world Muslim community.

The Muslim World – Africa

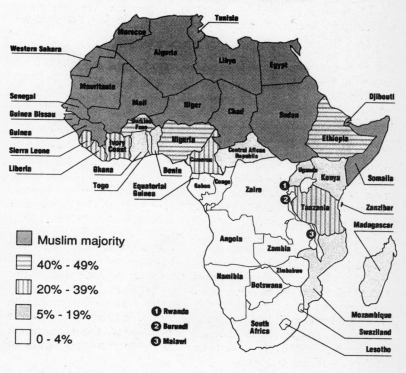

Tunisia
Morocco
Western Sahara
Algeria
Libya
Egypt
Mauritania
Senegal
Guinea Bissau
Mali
Niger
Chad
Sudan
Djibouti
Guinea
Burkina Faso
Sierra Leone
Ivory Coast
Nigeria
Ethiopia
Liberia
Central African Republic
Ghana
Benin
Uganda
Kenya
Somalia
Togo
Equatorial Guinea
Gabon
Congo
Zaire
Zanzibar
Madagascar
Angola
Zambia
Tanzania
Namibia
Zimbabwe
Botswana
Mozambique
Swaziland
South Africa
Lesotho

Muslim majority
40% - 49%
20% - 39%
5% - 19%
0 - 4%

1 Rwanda
2 Burundi
3 Malawi

The Muslim World – Eurasia

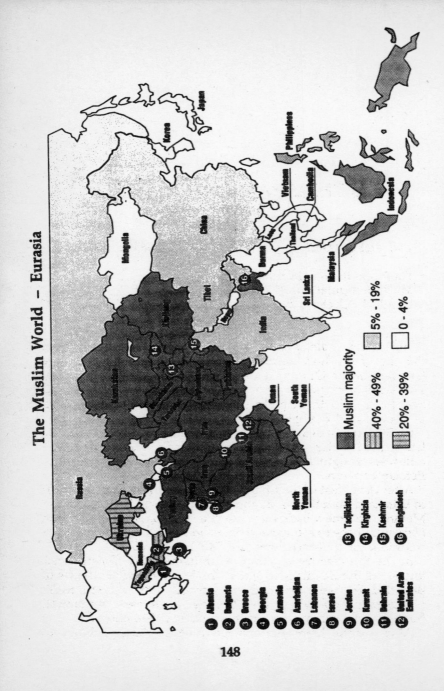

Legend:

- Muslim majority
- 40% – 49%
- 20% – 39%
- 5% – 19%
- 0 – 4%

1. Albania
2. Bulgaria
3. Greece
4. Georgia
5. Armenia
6. Azerbaijan
7. Lebanon
8. Israel
9. Jordan
10. Kuwait
11. Bahrain
12. United Arab Emirates
13. Tadjikistan
14. Kirghizia
15. Kashmir
16. Bangladesh

Labels on map: Japan, Korea, Philippines, Vietnam, Cambodia, Indonesia, Thailand, Burma, Malaysia, Sri Lanka, China, Mongolia, Tibet, India, Russia, Kazakhstan, Iran, Iraq, Turkey, Syria, Saudi Arabia, Oman, South Yemen, North Yemen

1.0 THE ARABIAN PENINSULA

(Saudi Arabia, North Yemen, South Yemen and the Gulf states)

Total population: 25.5 million
Muslim population: 99%
Dominant Sects: Sunni-Hanbali (Saudi Arabia)
Zaydi Shi'i (Yemen)

Arabia is the cradle of Islam – the birthplace of the Prophet and the site of the holy cities of Mecca and Medina. Arabic, the language of the Qur'an, remains the sacred language of Islam. The Arabs of the peninsula are Muslim almost without exception and have seen themselves throughout history as traditional protectors of the religion's purity and Muhammadan origins.

In the first five decades after Muhammad's death the Arabians, led by the Kharijis, a group of Muhammad's relatives and early followers, fought a bitter civil war against newer Syrian and Persian converts.

After the defeat of the Kharijis, Islam's capital was moved first to Damascus and then to Baghdad. Arabia, including Mecca and Medina, became a backwater notable only for its importance in *hajj* (pilgrimage to Mecca) and occasional rebellions by its deeply traditionalist or 'fundamentalist' Muslim population.

In the 9th century a group of fundamentalist Shi'ah rebels known as the Zaydis rose against rule by the Sunni Caliphs of Baghdad, but were defeated and pushed to the extreme south of the peninsula where they founded their own puritanical, Bedouin-type community on the southern Yemeni coast.

After this the Arabians remained quiet for almost a thousand years and the Ottomans eventually annexed the western coastal plain, including Mecca and Medina, whilst the British established a string of tiny tribal protectorates on the Gulf coast (the Emirates) and annexed most Zaydi lands in Yemen, establishing a base at Aden. The desert interior was ignored by all the Imperial powers and the tribes allowed to continue to practise their traditionalist version of Islam unhindered.

In the early 19th century Muhammad ibn Sa'ud brought together a confederation of interior desert tribes similar to the one created by the Prophet and liberated Mecca from the Ottomans in the name of strict fundamentalist Sunni Islam. For over a hundred years the rebels kept up a guerilla war against first the Ottomans and then the British and their Arab allies before proclaiming the Kingdom of Saudi Arabia in 1932.

The new kingdom was the world's first Sunni 'fundamentalist' state and had no constitution other than the Qur'an and the absolute power of the monarch to interpret it. Saudi Arabia at first claimed the British Emirates and the Zaydi majority lands of Yemen as part of its territory but, after a short war, recognised the existence of both the Emirates and Yemen within their current borders.

1.1 SAUDI ARABIA

The Kingdom of Saudi Arabia enforces the strict Hanbali Sunni legal regime, the most conservative and Arab traditionalist of the four Sunni legal schools. The Qur'an and the absolute authority of the king to interpret it form the sole constitution of the country.

The strict *hadd* Qur'anic penal code is enforced, including hand amputation for theft, whipping to the point of death for drinking alcohol, and stoning to death for adultery. The size of the stones to be used in this form of ritual execution is strictly laid down by *hadith*. To ensure that death is slow and painful stones must be no smaller than a chickpea and no larger than a date stone.

'Abd al-Aziz ibn Sa'ud, the first King, consolidated his power by marrying widows and daughters of defeated rival tribal leaders. He had approximately 300 wives and 45 sons, whose grandchildren and great-grandchildren, all princes, form the present Saudi Arabian royal family. The Saudi princes, numbering many hundreds, occupy all-important positions in the state which is run as a private family concern.

150

Islam permeates every aspect of life. In Saudi Arabia everything comes to an absolute halt five times a day for observance of *salat* – ritual prayers at the mosque. Business ethics, banking, clothing, food, methods of address and greeting and just about every human activity are governed by religious law.

Adherence to Islam is deeply felt and religious law is devoutly upheld by most of the Saudi population. At the same time the Committee for Encouraging Virtue and Preventing Vice (*Hay'at al-Amr bi'l-Ma'ruf wa'n-Nahi an al-Munkar*) and *Mutawwah* (religious police) exist to help prevent backsliders from straying from the true path. The *Mutawwah* roam the streets meting out instant punishment to anyone found smoking, drinking, gambling, dancing, singing, playing music in public or breaking the fast of Ramadan.

Bedouin Ibadites form about 5% of the total population but have great influence as direct descendants of the Kharijis. Although they recognise no worldly authorities or state they would almost certainly lead a rebellion of desert tribesmen in the unlikely event of any move away from fundamentalism towards reformism.

The other religious minority are the Shi'ah, divided amongst Twelvers, concentrated on the Gulf coast (facing Iran) in the oil fields, and a small number of Zaydis on the southern border with Yemen. The Twelver minority are undoubtedly influenced by the Iranian Revolution and Rafsanjani's Islamic Revolutionary Party, the IRP, which is the bitter enemy of Saudi Arabia and all Islamic monarchies. In the past ten years entire Twelver villages have been transported from the eastern oil fields to the more remote and less sensitive western provinces.

Saudi Arabia's guardianship of the Holy Places together with its massive oil wealth have guaranteed the country a pivotal position in Islam. Yet the state's role in international relations is in many ways contradictory. The country is firmly in the Western camp, but at the same time remains utterly hostile to Western support for Israel. And, unlike other pro-Western oil states such as Brunei and Iran under the Shahs, Saudi Arabia has always taken an extremely hard line within OPEC.

At the same time, through sponsorship of groups such as the Muslim Brotherhood and the World Muslim League, it has funded conservative 'fundamentalist' forces throughout the world. It has also played a major and direct role in the politics of Pakistan where, under Zia ul-Haq, the Saudi-Pakistani alliance ensured conservative domination of the Islamic fundamentalist movement in most parts of the world. The only Islamic countries beyond its influence are those like Libya, Algeria, Iran and Iraq which have oil wealth of their own, or those like South Yemen, Syria, and Somalia which receive massive Soviet economic aid.

1.2 NORTH and SOUTH YEMEN

Yemen is a desert region with a small fertile coastal strip on the southern and south western coastline of Arabia. Since 1967 it has been split into two states. The larger population is in the Yemen Arab Republic (North Yemen), which is conservative and pro-Western. The smaller forms the People's Democratic Republic of Yemen (South Yemen), which is geographically larger and pro-Soviet. The population of both is overwhelmingly Muslim, but divided between the largely nomadic Zaydi Shi'ah (Zaydis) majority and the more settled followers of the Sunni Shafi sect.

For 600 years Yemen languished under the purely nominal rule of the Ottoman Emirs of Hejaz, who governed from Mecca. So slight was the contact that Yemeni Sunnis continued to practise Shafi'ism, an early form of Sunni'ism associated with traders and merchants and only found in the outlying lands of Islam such as Indonesia.

Zaydi Shi'ism is highly puritanical, warlike and Arab-traditionalist in a similar way to the Arab-traditionalist Sunni Hanbali'ism of the Saudi Arabian royal family, but the Zaydis fiercely reject the idea of dynastic monarchies. The sect's Imams are chosen on the basis of their skill in battle and in accordance with tradition laid down by Muhammad himself.

However, when the Zaydi Imam 'Ahmad died in 1962 he named his son Mansur Billah Muhammad as Imam. The tribes immediately rebelled at what they saw as the monarchical principle and deposed him. In the civil war which followed Mansur was supported by the Sunni minority with Saudi Arabian and British forces from Aden on the Yemeni coast. The rebel tribes, concentrated in the desert and coastal mountains, were in turn supported by 50,000 Egyptian troops supplied and advised by the Soviet Union.

Under Nasserite Egyptian and Soviet influence the rebels broadened their demands to include the expulsion of the British from Aden and the overthrow of the remaining Sunni Sultans ruling small fiefdoms along the south coast of Arabia. By 1967 the Yemeni rebels had overrun them all as far as Oman and achieved military deadlock with the British in Aden.

A compromise peace was agreed and the rebels formed the South Yemen People's Republic with its capital in Aden and encompassing the defeated Sultanates. Within three years the Marxist National Liberation Front had established total control and declared the country a proletarian dictatorship.

In North Yemen Mansur was established as President and 'semi-monarch' of the Yemen Arab Republic. His power was based on good relations with the West, the growing power of oil-rich Saudi Arabia and the support of the Sunni minority. At first he ruled as an autocrat on the Saudi Arabian model, with no formal constitution or permanent state structure. Law was enforced by autonomous *shari'ah* courts which the President could overrule at will.

There was, however, growing resentment from the Sunni Shafi minority on whom he depended, and in 1970 a National Assembly was formed. But this was suspended and political parties abolished after a military coup led by Colonel Ibrahim al-Hamdi and army officers supporting the Correctionist Party, a fundamentalist movement advocating a return to the autocracy of the Imamate and the full implementation of the *shari'ah*.

After al-Hamdi was assassinated in 1977 constitutional rule was re-established and the current President, Lt. Colonel Ali Abdullah Salih, elected. The National Assembly now meets only occasionally and Salih is subject to re-election by referendum every six years. He has achieved a good measure of political stability by ensuring a fair mixture of Zaydis and Shafis in the civil service and army. He now aims at re-unification with South Yemen and negotiations are at an advanced stage. In the past Salih has also advocated further federation of a united Yemen with Saudi Arabia in a unified, conservative Arab state.

In the North the idea of unification used to be attractive, as it would have led to a share of the vast Saudi oil revenues. The Sunni minority has few doctrinal reasons to oppose Saudi rule, and the most militant anti-monarchial Zaydis left the country when the Marxist South Yemen state was formed. But large oil reserves were found in North Yemen in 1986. The prospect of independent oil wealth has reduced the appeal of federation with the Saudis whilst simultaneously making the re-creation of a unified Yemen more attractive to South Yemen.

153

South Yemen

South Yemen is organised on what used to be classical East European Communist lines. The single political organisation, the Yemen Socialist Party (YSP), is in fact a Communist Party complete with a 'democratic centralist' structure – politburo, central committee and so on – extending downward into every facet of public life.

The early leaders of the PDR modelled themselves more on the Chinese than the Russian Communists and in 1970 a Maoist faction gained control, purging the party and the army of moderate and pro-Soviet elements. A Chinese-style Cultural Revolution was unleashed but the moderates regained control under Ali Nasser Muhammad in 1980 after overcoming a 'centrist' group closely allied with the Soviet Union.

Under Ali's rule relations with the country's non-Communist neighbours improved. In 1984 he began a year-long series of negotiations with North Yemen aimed at eventual reunification but the talks came to nothing and the pro-Soviet faction regained the initiative.

After the return of a number of 'centrist' leaders from self-imposed exile in Moscow, a successful coup established the current ruler, Haidar al-Attas, as President in January 1986. As a result relations with North Yemen have once again cooled.

1.3 THE GULF
(Kuwait, Oman, United Arab Emirates, Qatar, Bahrain)

The Arabian Gulf states on the eastern coast of Saudi Arabia owe their existence to 19th century British attempts to dominate the Persian Gulf and block Russian advances into Persia itself. From the 1860s onward the British agreed to support tribal rebellions against the Ottomans (and rival clans such as the Sa'udi confederacy) in return for naval bases and free access to areas liberated from Ottoman rule.

The states are ruled by *Shayks* (tribal chieftains) and Sultans who in the main subscribe to the Shafi school of Sunni law. Shafi'ism is slightly less traditionalist than Saudi Hanbali'ism, but still deeply conservative. A strict version of the *shari'ah* is theoretically enforced in all the Gulf states. But in Bahrain in particular its implementation is lax.

By the mid-1960s it became obvious that the growing oil wealth of the Emirs meant they could support themselves, and Kuwait, the most economically viable, became independent in 1961, followed by Qatar and Bahrain. A group of smaller Shaykdoms, led by Dubai, federated as the independent United Arab Emirates in 1971.

Kuwait

In 1976 Shayk Sabah, the second shayk after independence, abolished the limited consultative National Assembly and reintroduced rule by decree after the Assembly had become a platform for sympathizers with Kuwait's 300,000 exiled Palestinian residents.

Palestinian organisations were curbed and five years later new elections gave an absolute majority to the Shayk's traditional conservative Bedouin allies, with a marked decline in support for Sunni fundamentalists. Despite this the *shari'ah* is strictly enforced for Kuwaiti nationals and Islam is widely and devoutly practised. The large Western expatriate community is often allowed to break the *shari'ah* by, for example, drinking, but this must be done strictly in private.

United Arab Emirates

The six Emirs of the Federation work together only for the purpose of self-defence. Within their respective territories the Emirs are complete despots, ruling without constitutions or any legal framework other than the Qur'an, which they interpret in disputes. The Shafi version of the *shari'ah* is enforced amongst the native population and the less strict Hanafi version amongst the vast community of Pakistani guest-workers.

Strikes and riots by these workers in 1976 and 1981 were followed by mass deportations. But the downturn in oil prices, whilst it may have other adverse long term effects for the UAE, has disciplined the workforce as competition for a decreasing number of oil industry jobs intensifies.

Oman

From 1965 until the mid-1970s the Sultanate faced a full-scale Marxist insurrection which was barely kept in check by British forces. The current ruler, Sultan Qaboos bi Said bin Taimur, came to power in a coup in 1970 and encouraged the British to deploy the SAS in covert warfare, whilst he built powerful armed forces of his own using the country's new oil wealth.

By 1975 the Sultan was claiming victory, but spending over a third of the national budget (almost entirely provided by oil revenues) on his armed forces. Money was then directed away from the army to long-term economic development, but vast military spending resumed after the Iranian revolution.

Meanwhile the Sultan rules as a complete autocrat, enforcing Qur'anic law as he sees fit and trying individual cases in the fashion of a latter-day King Solomon, even dispensing with the regular meetings with tribal elders which are the traditional form of representative government in the neighbouring United Arab Emirates.

Bahrain

Bahrain is by far the most liberal of the Gulf states. In 1972 the Emir experimented with limited democracy, but the National Assembly was closed down in 1975 when it proposed legal rights for trades unions and better wages for Pakistani guest-workers. The Emir reverted to traditional autocratic rule and trades unions have been suppressed.

The *shari'ah* is enforced in Bahrain but the island has a reputation for being relatively liberal. Saudi Arabians visit in order to get away from the strict prohibition of alcohol and gambling in their own country. Bahrain is known in the Gulf as 'the pub at the end of the Causeway'.

Qatar

In just two generations the population of Qatar has rocketed from being amongst the poorest in the world to probably the richest. The delicate political balances which held this tribal community of 250,000 together have been torn apart and new centres of power have emerged with increasing wealth and self-confidence.

The Emir Shayk Khalifah bin Hamad Al Thani's reaction has been to insist on the absolute obedience of tribal leaders to his autocracy and strict adherence to Shafi Sunni Islam, whilst leaving the technical aspects of running the country to foreign advisers.

The vast majority of the native population have retired to rural

156

estates, tended by Omani and Pakistani gardeners and servants, and the tribal pattern has stayed intact. Natives have little involvement with technical or industrial activity and more than 80% of the workforce are foreigners.

2.0 NORTHERN ARABIA

(Egypt, Syria, Lebanon, Palestine-Israel, Jordan and Iraq)

Total population: 84 million
Muslim population: 85%
Dominant Sect: Sunni-Hanafi

In the 8th century Islam exploded out of its primitive origins in the Arabian peninsula and pushed north into the 'fertile crescent' linking Syria and Egypt along the eastern coast of the Mediterranean to Iraq, the 'fertile island' between the Euphrates and Tigris.

In these lands Islam flowered into a great multi-racial civilisation open to the influences of the Christian west and pagan Asiatic east. With the establishment of Damascus, Cairo and – above all – Baghdad, Islam left behind the narrow and traditionalist outlook of the peninsular Arabs and these northern Arabian lands became the true historical heartland of Islam in its Golden Age.

For 500 years the area formed the territory of the Abbasid Empire ruled from Baghdad. Islam developed a sophisticated theology and philosophy and became highly heterodox. Great advances were made in the arts and sciences centuries before the European Renaissance.

The great civilisation of northern Arabia and Iraq came to an abrupt end in 1258 with the Mongol invasion and destruction of Baghdad. In the following 600 years the region languished and became backward under the domination of the despotic Ottoman Turkish Sultans.

The region remained culturally united under the Ottomans but was divided into two main administrative areas – Egypt and Greater Syria. Egypt achieved autonomy in the 1860s following a religious revival which fused nationalism and Islam. From then on Islam was seen as a potent force for pan-Arab nationalism – the idea of uniting all the northern Arabian lands into a single powerful and modern state.

The collapse of the Ottoman Empire in 1919 brought great expectations that the pan-Arab dream was about to become a reality. Instead the region turned into a steaming cauldron of political intrigue with France, Britain, Italy, Turkey and a variety of radical and conservative Arab factions competing for influence and power.

Egypt gained independence in 1923 but the former Ottoman province of Greater Syria was divided into League of Nations mandates administered by Britain and France. The mandate territory of Syria was reduced to a rump around Damascus, ruled by the French; the area round the former Syrian trading port of Beirut became the independent French mandate territory of Lebanon; and the new mandate states of Palestine and Jordan to the south, and Iraq to the east, came under British control.

All these new states were highly unstable. Various Arab attempts were made to reunite Greater Syria as a prelude to political union with Egypt, but all fell foul of dynastic disputes and tribal feuds manipulated by astute Anglo-French diplomacy.

After the Second World War the position was transformed by the creation of the state of Israel. This was seen not only as a direct attack by the Western powers on the Arab world but an affront to Islam. In 1948 the Syrian, Egyptian, Jordanian and Iraqi monarchies jointly declared war on Israel and in so doing greatly strengthened pan-Arab feeling and fused it further with Islam.

The defeat of the Arab monarchies in the 1948 Arab-Israeli war shook the entire Arab world. The demand for pan-Arab unity became intense and there was a new factor – a growing pan-Arab 'Islamic Socialism' movement firmly rooted amongst both intellectuals and young officers of defeated Arab armies. In the two decades which followed, the pan-Arab socialist movements overthrew the monarchies in all the northern Arab countries except Jordan. Military coups brought Nasser to power in Egypt and the Ba'th (Arab Socialist Renaissance) Party to power in Syria and Iraq. Egypt and Syria federated as the United Arab Republic in 1958 but, following further coups, Iraq stayed outside the union.

159

In Jordan the Royal Family survived a Palestinian-led pan-Arabist insurrection and remained implacably hostile to the idea of union. Lebanon also refused to join. In 1961 the United Arab Republic collapsed when the Syrian Ba'th Party pulled out complaining of Egyptian domination.

Defeat for the Arab nations in the 1973 Yom Kippur war with Israel led to mutual recriminations, further coups and the complete disintegration of the pan-Arab ideal. The Ba'th Party still rules in Syria and Iraq in the name of 'Islamic Socialism', but in practice the Syrian and Iraqi wings have evolved separately and are now extremely hostile to each other.

Egypt has made peace with Israel, Jordan effectively recognises the Jewish state and Iraq is pre-occupied with its continuing 'cold war' with Iran. Only Syria keeps alive the old idea of unification – now in the form of aggressive and grandiose plans to create 'Greater Syria' by means of the destruction and military conquest of Lebanon.

The role played by Islam in the tragic conflicts of the Middle East is, in purely formal terms, slight. The Muslim regimes of the area are highly secular and Islam is entirely secondary to Arab nationalism, but beneath the surface the Islamic traditions of *jihad* (Holy War) and martyrdom play a crucial role in Arab intransigence towards both Israel and rival Arab states who are seen as insufficiently hostile to the Jewish state.

Jerusalem, currently under Israeli administration, is Islam's third Holy City after Mecca and Medina. The Dome of the Rock mosque in the centre of the city is a Muslim shrine second only in importance to the Holy Ka'bah in Mecca. Still further beneath the surface is traditional Muslim antipathy towards the Jews. Popular accounts of Muhammad's life cast the Jews as evil, greedy and scheming allies of pagan foes who attempted to destroy the religion at its inception.

2.1 EGYPT

Egypt is by far the largest and fastest-growing Arab nation, with twice the population of the next largest Arab country, Morocco, and approximately a quarter of the total population of all the Arab nations put together. Of all the Arab Islamic nations it has the longest tradition of effective modern nationhood and is the home of both Arab nationalism and modernising 'secularist' Islam.

The Islamic modernist movement began in Egypt in the 1860s with the first systematic revision of the *shari'ah* legal code, by Muhammad Abduh (died 1905), the chief legal officer (*mufti*) of the British colonial administration.

Abduh cut out many of the mystical, irrational and authority-worshipping customs which had been absorbed into the *shari'ah* during centuries of Ottoman despotism and Sufi sophistry. Instead he produced a simplified version of Islamic theology, developed a secular penal code to replace the draconian *hadd* punishments of the Qur'an, and relegated religious law to control of family and private matters.

Contemporary Islam in Egypt is still officially based on Abduh's approach, but since the 1920s there has been growing pressure from fundamentalists for full implementation of the *shari'ah*. The fundamentalist Muslim Brotherhood was formed in 1928 and – despite being officially banned – is still the main focus of fundamentalist agitation.

The Brotherhood enjoys close relations with the Saudi Arabian government and, since the Saudis repeatedly bail out the bankrupt Egyptian economy, this gives them considerable protection and freedom to operate within the country.

Secular Egyptian 'Islamic Socialism' reached its peak in the 1960s during the Presidency of Gamal Nasser. Following Nasser's death in 1970 his successor, Anwar Sadat, leant on external Saudi and internal fundamentalist support to reverse the leftist domestic policies of the Nasser years and steer Egypt from the Soviet into the Western camp. The process culminated in the US-sponsored Camp David peace accords with Israel and the recognition of Israel's right to exist in a treaty signed in 1980.

Following Camp David, Egypt was thrown out of the Arab League and Sadat was assassinated in 1981 by members of his own guard acting under the influence of a militant splinter group from the Muslim Brotherhood. His death was met with general rejoicing by 'hard line' Arab leaders like Colonel al-Qaddafi of Libya, who declared a public holiday to mark the event.

Sadat's successor, President Muhammad Hosni Mubarak, has built a cordial relationship with the United States and is rebuilding bridges to the Arab world through increasing unofficial diplomatic contacts with Saudi Arabia, often carried out under the auspices of the Muslim Brotherhood. Internally, Mubarak has continued Sadat's policy of reversing Nasserite 'Arab Socialism' by introducing free markets and encouraging foreign investment and tourism. At the same time he has granted various token concessions to the fundamentalists whilst maintaining a ban on their overt political activities.

Mubarak has also reduced the repression of other political parties and relatively free elections were held in 1984 and 1987. The Egyptian parliament is nevertheless dominated by the state- and army-sponsored National Democratic Party. The only significant opposition parties are the Socialist Labour Party and the Wafd Party. The SLP is ultra-nationalist and the Wafd effectively a 'front' organisation for the technically illegal Muslim Brotherhood.

The extra-parliamentary fundamentalists have considerable support amongst the urban poor of Cairo and have gained in influence through attempts by both Sadat and Mubarak to use them as a counterbalance to what remains of the radical Nasserite Left.

Fundamentalist groups led an open insurrection in the southern city of Asyut in 1982 and have been involved in isolated terrorist incidents and occasional riots against Cairo's soaring food prices (a consequence of Mubarak's World Bank-directed free market policies), but the fundamentalists lack organisation or mass support amongst the peasants, who constitute 65% of the population. In the countryside strict observance of Islamic rituals and the *shari'ah* has declined under the influence of secularist policies pursued by the central government and it is likely many peasants are now no more than nominal Muslims.

2.2 SYRIA and LEBANON

Until the 1970s Syria was subject to chronic political instability, with coup and counter-coup establishing and deposing governments in an endless series of faction fights between the different wings of the Ba'th Party, its allies and opponents.

The current ruler, Ba'thist President Lt General Hafez al-Assad, came to power in a coup in 1970. Assad has imposed a measure of stability by ruthlessly eliminating opponents and staffing the top levels of the army, civil service and largely nationalised industries with members of his own clan, who all subscribe to the minority *Aluwyin* ('Upholders of 'Ali' or Alawite) Shi'i sub-sect.

The current Syrian constitution dates from 1973 and declares the country 'a democratic Arab nation' with government based on the principles of 'Socialism, Freedom, Economic Justice, Arab Unity and Islam'. There were riots when the first draft failed to mention Islam and it was duly amended, along with the provision that the President must be a Muslim (there are sizeable Christian and Oriental Jewish minorities in Syria) and legislation based on *shari'ah* law. But Islam is mainly a political – or tribal – creed in Syria, manipulated as a support for the all-important concept of Syrian nationalism and its mission to unite the Arab lands.

Assad uses the tightly-knit structure of the Alawite sect to maintain control of the Ba'thist power structure which in turn permeates every sphere of public life. The sect dominates the economy and government whilst constituting only 10% of the mainly Sunni-Hanafi population. Alawite power is concentrated in the Special Defence Units (SDUs) which are effectively above the law and used to terrorise the population and police the army and Ba'thist structure.

The SDU executed at least 300 members of the Muslim Brotherhood following an assassination attempt on Assad in 1980 and shortly afterwards, according to press reports, 200 more were buried alive in the compounds of the SDU's Tadmor prison in Palmyra, central Syria. In 1982 the Syrian Army, led by the SDU, occupied the town of Hama and slaughtered the entire population of about 15,000, including women and children, as a reprisal against an attempted insurrection allegedly started by the Brotherhood.

The regime is extremely hostile to all its Arab neighbours. Israel, Jordan and Lebanon to the south are regarded as occupying the historic lands of Greater Syria, which must be reconquered. Jordan is particularly despised on religious-doctrinal grounds because the 'usurper' Jordanian kings have 'collaborated' with Israel, Britain and the USA against the Palestinians who are seen as Greater Syrian nationals.

Syria invaded Lebanon in 1976, reducing the once prosperous multi-ethnic and multi-religious state to its current condition of anarchy. Now 30,000 Syrian troops dominate the north of the country, though they have suffered serious and repeated defeats at the hands of the Israelis and their Maronite Christian allies.

As part of the war Syria has sponsored a variety of Lebanese terrorist groups, including the Lebanese Arab Army, the Lebanese National Front (which grew out of the Lebanese wing branch of the Ba'th Party), and the dissident Maronite Marad Brigades. It is also the only Arab country to unite with Iran to co-sponsor the suicidal Shi'i Amal and Hozbullah terrorist-martyr groups.

There is a bitter feud with the fellow Ba'thist leadership of neighbouring Iraq which purged its left-wing, pro-Syrian faction in the 1960s. Assad was the only Arab leader to support Ayatollah Khomeini (a fellow Shi'ah, though of a different sect) during the Iran-Iraq war. Syria and Iraq are now fighting a proxy war in Lebanon with Iraq supplying arms to the Maronite Christians.

2.3 JORDAN and PALESTINE

The Hashemite Kingdom of Jordan was created by British diplomacy as a model secular, conservative and pro-Western Arab state. The country's ruling royal family, the Hashemites, claim direct descent from Muhammad and have enshrined Islam in the country's constitution as a means of legitimising their rule.

The first Hashemite ruler, King Abdulah, had plans to extend his rule throughout northern Arabia and thus became the direct and bitter opponent of radical republican pan-Arabists. His power was largely based on the British who trained his army and made it the most effective in the Arab world, but he was badly let down in 1948 when his British allies allowed the state of Israel to be established in Palestine – previously claimed as part of the Hashemite Kingdom. Jordanian participation in the 1948 Arab-Israeli War was only lukewarm, and after the Arab defeat Abdulah was accused of collaborating with the 'imperialists' to bring Israel into being.

As a result the pan-Arabists passed the death sentence on the entire Jordanian Hashemite clan and, with the support of radical Palestinians who flocked into Jordan as exiles, pledged the destruction of the Jordanian state. In 1951 Abdulah was gunned down by Nasserite pan-Arabist terrorists on the steps of the main mosque in Amman, the Jordanian capital. He was succeeded by his son Hussein, an Anglicised graduate of the British military college at Sandhurst. King Hussein's first problem was the half million or more Palestinian refugees from Israel who doubled Jordan's population.

The refugee camps were soon seething with rebellion. One of the principle agitators was Yasser Arafat, who in the late 1950s founded the main Palestinian guerilla movement *al-Fetah* (the fighters) with the aim of destroying both Israel and Jordan and creating a 'democratic secular' Palestinian state in their place. In 1964 al-Fetah launched a broadly based political wing, the Palestinian Liberation Organisation (PLO) which has since claimed to function as the Palestinian 'parliament' with Yasser Arafat being the 'President in exile' of the proposed Palestinian state.

In 1967 the Arabs were again defeated in a war against Israel, and the Israelis occupied former Jordanian territory on the West Bank of the Jordan river, including all of Jerusalem, sending more Palestinian refugees into what remained of the country.

Hussein moved against the Palestinians in 1970 and defeated them in a brief but bloody civil war. Hundreds of thousands of Palestinians fled to Iraq, Syria and the Gulf States. Another large group of Palestinians ended up in Lebanon setting off the tragic chain of events leading to the current civil war.

Minority factions of the PLO based in Syria remain implacably hostile to Jordan and there have been dozens of assassination attempts on Hussein. In response the King has developed a network of spies, informers and bodyguards legendary throughout the Middle East.

The more moderate faction of the PLO, led by Arafat himself, has adopted a conciliatory approach to Jordan and now proposes Hussein should play an important part in comprehensive peace negotiations for the region. The PLO has officially dropped its demands for the destruction of Israel and Jordan, suggesting instead the creation of Jewish, Palestinian and Jordanian states within the existing territory of Jordan and Israel. So far Israel has refused to negotiate.

2.4 IRAQ

For 500 years, from the middle of the 8th to the 13th centuries, Iraq was the centre of the greatest civilisation and Empire Islam ever produced. The capital, Baghdad, was the wonder of the world with magnificent mosques, palaces, gardens, markets, schools of law and art, universities, hospitals and libraries. In backward Europe the legend arose that the streets of Baghdad were paved with gold, and that its scientists had devised magic flying carpets and elixirs of eternal life.

Today what remains of Baghdad's former Islamic greatness is exploited not as a source of religious inspiration but as a tourist attraction. As a secular Arab state based on 'Arab Unity and Socialism', Islam plays only a small role in the official life of the country and Islamic fundamentalism or excessive religious zeal are officially discouraged.

President Saddam Hussein came to power in 1968 following a faction fight within the ruling Ba'th Party. Hussein purged the party of its Marxist wing, banned the Communist Party (which had previously ruled in coalition with the Ba'thists) and turned the country into a totalitarian one-party state based on his total power.

As in the other countries of northern Arabia the official Islam practised in Iraq is of moderate Sunni Hanafi variety. Fundamentalism is rare amongst the Hanafi and they are the Muslims most likely to accept and support secular regimes. About half the population, however, is Shi'ah – the faith of Iraq's hostile eastern neighbour, fundamentalist Iran.

The Shi'ah's holiest shrine of the martyr Imam Husayn is at Karbala in the eastern part of the country and annual Iranian Shi'ah pilgrimages have become a focus of fundamentalist opposition to the secular regime in recent years. Fear of growing Shi'ah fundamentalism was one of the main causes of Iraq's attempt to overthrow the Iranian regime with the 1980 invasion.

Hussein hoped to destroy the Iranian regime before the Shi'ah revolution could spread to his eastern provinces and in the process annexed small amounts of territory along the Iran-Iraq border which had been claimed since the 1930s. He clearly expected Iran to collapse quickly and when it did not was forced to abruptly change international alignment.

Previously the country had been closely allied with the USSR and Syria. But the Soviets remained neutral whilst Syria backed Iran. Hussein turned for help to Saudi Arabia and the West who, disturbed by the threat posed by the Iranian regime, unambiguously supported him.

During the war Iran attempted to incite the Iraqi Shi'ah to revolt and continued after peace was declared. Hozbullah, the foreign wing of the ruling Iranian Islamic Republican Party, is active in eastern Iraq and a new party, *al-Da'wah al-Islamiyyah* (Islamic Call) has been active since the mid-1980s. Neither has attracted mass support and both have been severely repressed.

As the Iraqi Shi'ah are Arabs rather than Persians, Hussein has countered Iranian propaganda with appeals to Arab nationalism and a Ba'th Party recruitment drive amongst them. Discrimination against the Shi'ah has ended and many have been rapidly promoted in the civil service, army and even the heart of Ba'thist rule, the Revolutionary Command Council itself.

The Kurds

The Kurds are a non-Arabic Muslim people forming the majority of the population in the north eastern provinces of Iraq. There are also groups of Kurds in neighbouring Turkey and Iran who, together with the main group in Iraq, proclaimed an independent state of Kurdistan in 1945. The state was crushed within weeks by the joint action of Turkey, Iran and Iraq and the Kurds have been denied statehood ever since.

Iraq's 1974 Kurdish autonomy plan did, however, grant them the right to speak their own language, but stopped short of self-government. Two Kurdish groups, the Patriotic Union and the Unified Socialist Party, have kept up a limited guerilla war ever since.

3.0 TURKEY AND THE BALKANS

(Turkey, Albania, Yugoslavia and Bulgaria)

Total population: 86 million
Muslim population: 75%
Dominant Sect: Sunni-Hanafi

From the 12th century onwards waves of pagan central Asian invaders began to sweep into the ancient Islamic heartlands, attracted by the fabulous riches of Baghdad and its Empire.

One such group of invaders, the Turks, settled in Iraq and had converted to Islam by about 1150. At first they were employed by Iraq's Arab rulers as mercenaries and palace guards but, as Arab rule became decadent, gained in power. By the start of the 13th century effective political power had passed from the Arab Emperors to the Turkish warlords.

In the middle of the 13th century AD, Genghis Khan's pagan Mongol horde swept into Iraq and Syria and put Baghdad and Damascus to the sword in an orgy of destruction. The Turks fled west to Asia Minor – the territory of modern Turkey – capturing it from the declining Christian Empire of Byzantium. Damascus and Baghdad became backwaters, Mecca and the Arabian peninsula became even further removed from the historical stage, and only Cairo survived to preserve, in a greatly weakened form, the heritage of the Golden Age.

Under the leadership of the Ottoman dynasty of Sultans the Turks developed a highly efficient military machine which became legendary for its ferocity and frequent barbarity. In a century of unrelieved warfare they captured all the lands of the Byzantine Empire, extinguishing Christianity forever in Asia Minor and established their capital Istanbul ('city of Islam') in the former Byzantine capital of Constantinople.

Under the Ottomans Islam was manipulated to serve as the ideology of an Empire otherwise based entirely on military ruthlessness and the despotic rule of the Sultans. Worship at the mosque became not a mark of free submission to Allah, but of forced submission to the Sultan.

The Ottoman conquest of Balkan Europe was achieved at the cost of much bloodshed and great cruelty was shown to the indigenous Christian populations. As a result, Ottoman rule in the Balkans linked Islam with barbarism in the European mind. The reconquest of the Balkans by the Europeans left behind large Muslim minorities in Bulgaria and Yugoslavia who are still despised by their Orthodox Christian compatriots.

By the 16th century Ottoman 'Islam' had become a stultified, backward and – above all – fatalistic dogma overlaid with primitive superstitions and arcane rituals of submission to worldly authority.

3.1 TURKEY

Modern Turkey is the least 'Islamic' of all major Muslim nations. The Turkish national state, established in 1923, was devised specifically to break the political grip of six hundred years of backward 'Islamic' Ottoman rule. *Shari'ah* courts were abolished, women were given the vote and it became illegal for members of the armed forces or the civil service to profess Islam in public by, for example, growing long beards or wearing religious dress. Islamic education was banned in schools, the Latin alphabet replaced Arabic (the sacred script of Islam), and the considerable endowments of various Islamic organisations – especially the Sufi monastic Orders which had grown rich under Ottoman patronage – were confiscated by the state. Turkish Islam was thus reduced to being a purely private religion of conscience. The Sufi orders promptly rose in revolt but were crushed and have remained banned ever since.

Religious observance has declined enormously, especially in the cities and amongst the young, and many mosques – other than those preserved for the tourist trade in Istanbul – are deserted and face dereliction (a mosque, however, may never be used for any purpose other than worship and may not be demolished – a rule upheld even in secular Turkey).

In foreign affairs a series of generally right-wing and repressive governments have steered Turkey away from the Islamic world and firmly into the Western camp. This strong pro-Western stance has often been the focus for internal unrest but opposition comes entirely from secular left-wing movements.

'Islamic' opposition is restricted to the Kurds, a Muslim ethnic minority found in eastern Turkey on the border with Iran and Iraq. But the Kurds are notably secular and socialist in their outlook and their opposition to the central state, violent in the 1940s and '70s, is based on national and ideological rather than religious grounds.

During the 1970s there were repeated clashes between an alliance of Marxist and Kurdish groups and neo-fascist 'death squads' like the paramilitary Grey Wolves organisation which, it was alleged, had the backing of factions within the Turkish army. In 1980 the army stepped in to take power, imposed martial law and banned all political parties, trades unions and other opposition groups.

After severe repression, and the arrest of 40,000 suspected 'terrorists', elections were held in 1983 and the right-wing Motherland Party came to power to carry on the army's policies of 'law and order' and free market economics backed by the World Bank and enormous US economic and military aid. The Motherland Party has developed economic links with the EEC, which it one day hopes Turkey will join (Saatchi and Saatchi has been hired to organise its PR campaign).

The country is now being promoted as a European tourist destination to rival Greece and this is as good an indicator of Islam's position within the country as any. Semi-naked sun bathing would be out of the question in a country like Saudi Arabia and has to be confined to highly segregated areas even in relatively liberal Muslim tourist destinations like Tunisia. No such provision for the sensibilities of the faithful is being made in Turkey.

3.2 ALBANIA, YUGOSLAVIA AND BULGARIA

Albania is the only European country with a Muslim majority, though there are large minorities in neighbouring Yugoslavia and nearby Bulgaria. These Balkan Muslim communities are all that remains of 600 years of Ottoman rule in the region which began with the defeat of the Serbian Orthodox Christian Empire following the Battle of the Field of Blackbirds, in the modern Yugoslavian province of Kosovo, in 1389.

All three countries became officially atheist Socialist states at the end of the Second World War. All religions, including Islam, have been officially discouraged since then though, at first, Muslims were permitted to worship both at the mosque and in private with relatively little difficulty.

In 1967 the Albanian authorities, inspired by the Chinese Cultural Revolution, closed all the country's churches and mosques and have since officially maintained that there are no practising Muslims in the country. Albania is one of the most closed and secretive countries in the world and the exact position is impossible to ascertain, but human rights groups report that various groups of Muslims have been arrested for professing the religion.

Bulgaria and Yugoslavia have more religiously liberal regimes and the problem faced by Muslims in these two countries is their status as an ethnic rather than a religious minority.

The ethnically Albanian Muslim majority in the Yugoslavian state of Kosovo has been repeatedly attacked in recent years by the state's Serbian Christian minority. Commemoration of the 600th anniversary of the Battle of the Field of Blackbirds in 1989 was marked by Christian-Muslim riots which had to be suppressed by federal Yugoslav troops.

In Bulgaria a Muslim minority making up about 15% of the total population has faced repeated harassment from the government mainly on ethnic grounds. In 1989 the Bulgarian government took legal steps to force Bulgarian Muslims to abandon their Islamic names and adopt Slavonic ones. As a result thousands of Bulgarian Muslims have fled to exile in Turkey.

4.0 IRAN

Total population: 50 million
Muslim population: 99%
Dominant Sect: Ithna Shi'i (Twelvers)

Iran, known as Persia until the 1930s, is unique amongst the Islamic nations because of its overwhelming Shi'ah, rather than Sunni, population. It is also the only modern Muslim nation apart from Afghanistan with a centuries-old tradition of national independence – gained at the cost of long and bloody struggles against both Sunni Muslim Empires and European Colonialists. Shi'ism and ancient Persian nationhood combine to make Islam in modern Iran quite different from that found in the other Muslim 'worlds'.

Shi'ism was established as the dominant form of Islam in Persia in 1500 by the Safavid dynasty of Shahs after a century of bitter guerilla war against the Sunni Ottoman Turks at the height of their military power. But as Ottoman Islam began to decline, Safavid Persia became the centre of an Islamic civilisation deeply influenced by the ancient and sophisticated culture of pre-Islamic Persia.

The Safavid capital of Isfahan became one of the greatest cities of later Islam and, in its architectural and artistic achievements (not least the living arts of poetry, cuisine, clothing and – above all – carpet making), came to rival the heyday of Baghdad.

From the 18th to 20th centuries Persia declined under the rule of Afghan dynasties with Mongol ethnic roots. For two hundred years Islam and the state were separated along the lines of the division between church and state roles in many Western countries. The Shi'ah developed a ramified religious hierarchy – the only one of its type found in Islam – which allowed the Shahs to run the state but maintained a tight grip on the religious life of the people.

In 1906 the Afghan Qajar dynasty of Shahs framed a Western-type constitution granting autonomy to the Shi'ah clergy and allowing them to run schools, charities and religious foundations. The separation was maintained by the short-lived Pahlavi dynasty of Shahs, founded by Reza Khan Pahlavi, an army officer who overthrew the pro-British Qajars in 1925 with a military coup.

After the Second World War Shah Muhammad Reza (the 'last Shah') developed the separation of state and clergy still further in the belief that if the Shi'ah authorities were granted greater control over education and the moral, religious and private lives of the population, they would leave him free to develop the country into a Western-style secular state.

But by the 1970s the Shi'ah clergy had decided that Muhammad Reza Shah had gone too far in his campaign of Westernisation. Since the 1950s rapid economic development had been threatening the grip of Shi'ism, based on the traditional peasant structure of the countryside and the bazaar economy of the cities. Eventually the governing religious body of the Shi'ah – the *ulama* (council of Divinely guided judges) – began to preach that the Shah was working to destroy Shi'i Islam through a wave of secularisation and Western permissiveness.

The Mullahs' Revolution

The *ulama* was particularly incensed by the lavish celebrations marking the 50th anniversary of the Pahlavi dynasty in 1975, which clashed with Islamic religious festivals and peaked with parades glorifying the pre-Islamic pagan gods of ancient Persia accompanied by drinking binges and Western pop music.

At first the religious opposition joined the secular left in the so-called movement of the Red Mullahs, led by Ayatollahs Kashani and Shariati, focusing on the cultural and economic effects of Western-style capitalism and the enormous American military presence within the country. This movement was crushed by SAVAK, the Shah's notorious secret police, but the conservative religious wing of the opposition, led by Ayatollah Roudollah Khomeini, was largely ignored.

Exiled to Iraq and then to Paris, Khomeini began to preach the

173

overthrow of the Shah and the imposition of rule by the *ulama* ('the rule of the jurists') under his leadership as Imam. Finally, in April 1979 an incoherent coalition of what remained of the left-wing and liberal movements, bazaar merchants threatened by the Shah's capitalist reforms, and Shi'ah clergy (mullahs) rooted in every part of the country, deposed the Shah and proclaimed an Islamic Republic.

New institutions were formed in 1980 but the real power in revolutionary Iran passed to the *ulama* and Imam Khomeini – who was officially held to be the Divinely guided representative on earth of the 'concealed' Twelfth Imam of the Shi'ah (see Part Three, Islamic Sects – the Twelvers).

The *ulama*, working through the larger 83-member Council of Experts, appoints all judges and can overturn their decisions. It also functions as the supreme command of the Iranian armed forces and revolutionary guard, ratifies the election of the Iranian President and can dismiss the Majlis (National Consultative Assembly or Parliament) or overturn its decisions. The *ulama* also directs foreign policy and may declare war or make peace.

The *ulama* is the top layer in a hierarchical clerical system similar in many ways to that of the Roman Catholic Church. Its power is based on about 100,000 mullahs (priest-teachers) who transmit its decisions and instructions to every town and village in the country. The mullahs are, in the main, 'lay' clerics who have jobs as peasant farmers or bazaar merchants and thus penetrate Iranian society far more effectively than a full-time professional clergy.

About 40,000 mullahs have the rank of *mojtahidi* – clerics sufficiently learned to give legal ruling in the local *shari'ah* courts. Above them are several thousand *hojatoleslami* (regional judges or 'deputy Ayatollahs') and about 100 Ayatollahs (national judges).

The five most senior Ayatollahs, the *Ozma* (Grand Ayatollahs), form the highest religious and judicial authority in the country. The *Ozma* sit with seven other Qur'anic scholars – who may or may not be Ayatollahs – as the *ulama*. The *ulama* in turn elects the *Imam* – the Shi'ah 'Pope' – from within its number.

The main instrument used by the *ulama* to keep Iran in a permanent state of revolutionary mobilisation is the Friday prayer meeting, held in the grounds of Tehran university and televised throughout the country in an awesome display of totalitarian unity. The message of these meetings is a mixture of religion and politics which have become inseparable since the revolution. All

174

Iranians must take part in communal Friday prayers on pain of serious punishment and the full five daily prayer cycles of the *salat* are also strongly encouraged. Observance is widespread.

Ayatollah Hossein-Ali Montazeri, leader of Friday TV prayers, was appointed by the *ulama* as Khomeini's successor in 1982 and took the post of Imam on his death in 1989. Montazeri was also a candidate for the Presidency of the Islamic Republic, but was outmanoeuvred by Hojatoleslam Hashemi-Rafsanjani, speaker of the Majlis and head of Iran's only legal political party — the Islamic Republican Party (IRP).

Islamic Republican Party (IRP)

Rafsanjani formed the IRP immediately prior to the 1979 revolution and the party is now the only source of power in the country apart from the *ulama*. The IRP controls the distribution of state oil revenues in the form of rationing as well as promotion within the civil service, army and judiciary.

The IRP has several sub-groups, the most notable of which is Hozbullah (Party of God), active amongst Shi'ah fundamentalists abroad, particularly in Syria and Lebanon where Hozbullah cells carry out terrorist, kidnapping and ransom activity on behalf of Iranian-backed causes. Hozbullah also runs the police force in Tehran which is well known for beating people with clubs for minor breaches of the *shari'ah*.

President Rafsanjani's IRP and Imam Montazeri's *ulama* define the two main factions within current Iranian politics. Rafsanjani's proclamation of the death sentence on the British author Salman Rushdie was widely interpreted as an astute political move, winning him many supporters amongst the clergy in the political manoeuvrings for the Khomeini succession.

Rafsanjani, with his power base within the Majlis parliament, is marginally more flexible than Montazeri and represents what remains of pluralism within the Iranian political system. His support in the country is based on the growing power of patronage of the IRP and the zeal of the party's paramilitary wing, the Revolutionary Guard, which enforces *shari'ah* law and the decisions of local IRP committees.

Montazeri's support on the other hand is mainly clerical and represents the strict orthodoxy of the *ulama* in the tradition of Khomeini. He is a distant and semi-Divine figure as far as the mass of Iranians are concerned, but still wields great influence through his continuing leadership of Friday prayers.

The Opposition

Both the IRP and the *ulama* have attempted to keep Iran in a state of constant revolutionary mobilisation and religious frenzy by exploiting the cult of martyrdom and *jihad* (Holy War) which is central to Shi'ism.

Originally the mullahs had been effectively allied with the secular left-wing opposition to the Shah, especially the large pro-Communist Tudeh Party and the 'Islamic Socialist' Mujahideen guerilla movement. But these left-wing allies, together with heterodox religious groups such as the Baha'is, have now been denounced in the name of Shi'ah orthodoxy and viciously persecuted.

The Mujahideen Party (*Sazman-e Mojahedin-e Khalq-e Irani* or 'Opposition Organisation of the Crusaders of the Iranian People') supported the mullahs' revolution and, despite the organisation's professed secularism, voted for the establishment of the Islamic Republic in 1980. It then attempted to function as a legitimate secularist opposition within the Majlis parliament.

In 1981 the IRP's Revolutionary Guard opened fire on a Mujahideen demonstration in Tehran, killing hundreds. The organisation went underground, was banned and thousands of its supporters have been tortured and executed. When the Mujahideen denounced the Iran-Iraq war and called for a peace settlement, death sentences were passed on their exiled leaders.

The Mujahideen now operate openly only in the far western Kurdish province, where they are allied with the only other significant opposition to the regime, the leftist Kurdish nationalists of the Iraqi and Turkish border region. The Iranian Kurds supported the Islamic Revolution as an opportunity to establish an autonomous Kurdish state, but Tehran denounced them as Iraqi collaborators and crushed Kurdish separatism by force.

It is likely that the Mujahideen still enjoy wide support in Iran as they represent the strong strand of secularist and leftist Shi'ism which has been popular amongst the workers in the oil industry and the educated middle classes throughout this century. Before being banned, the Mujahideen Party had the second largest group of representatives in the Majlis parliament and gained millions of votes. The fanaticism with which Mujahideen are hunted down by the IRP is testimony to the fact that they still have hundreds of thousands – possibly millions – of sympathisers inside the country.

Other opposition groups, such as the Communist Tudeh Party, the radical Palestinian-allied Fedayeen, the Social Democratic National Iranian Resistance Movement, and the royalists (who campaign for the return of the last Shah's son, Muhammad Reza II, currently exiled in Morocco) have all been effectively destroyed and mount no serious threat to the IRP.

With all effective internal opposition smashed, the IRP's rule is surprisingly stable. Oil wealth continues to flow into the country and is distributed through a rationing system controlled by the IRP, which thus further consolidates its power. At the same time the Ayatollahs have shown a surprising degree of flexibility and pragmatism in their dealings with the outside world demonstrated, above all, by the secret negotiation with the 'Great Satan' himself – the President of the United States – in order to obtain Western arms.

Pragmatism extends to Iran's greatly reduced foreign trade where, in theory, interest-free Islamic banking takes place. But Iranian banks – like those in Libya and Saudi Arabia – operate a fixed scale of monetary 'gifts' payable on loans which amount in practice to a form of interest. In the longer term Iran is threatened by the medievalism of the Islamic Revolution, which has led to suspicion of Western technology, irredeemably associated in the minds of the great mass of Iranians with the regime of the Shahs and the American presence.

The most likely source of political change is a rehabilitation of the Mujahideen which would steer the country towards closer relations with the Soviet Union, especially in the wake of the Soviet withdrawal from Afghanistan. A return of the Mujahideen would also result in some measure of secularisation and the withdrawal of the clergy to concentrate on education, private morality and the enforcement of the *shari'ah* on lines similar lines to Pakistan and Saudi Arabia.

The tumultuous events of the late 20th century have widened the division between Shi'i and Sunni Islam into an unbridgeable gulf. The Shi'ah see the Sunnis as religiously degenerate and unwilling to discharge their sacred duty of *jihad* against unbelievers and 'usurper' Sunni monarchies like Saudi Arabia, Jordan and Morocco.

The Sunnis, meanwhile, see the Shi'ah as heretics who have lapsed into a form of Christian-type polytheism. Shi'ah faith in

177

the Christ-like 'second coming' of the mysterious 'twelfth Imam' is dismissed as a medieval superstition and their worship at the shrines of martyrs is condemned as a form of paganism. The maintenance of a permanent clergy and obedience to the 'Shi'ah Pope' – the Imam – is also condemned as a deeply heretical breach of the Muhammadan *hadith* that Islam has no priests.

5.0 THE MUSLIM EAST

(Pakistan, Kashmir, Afghanistan, Bangladesh, Malaysia, Indonesia and Brunei)

Total population: 400 million
Muslim population: 90%
Dominant Sects: Sunni-Hanafi (Indian sub-continent)
Sunni-Shafi (East Indies)

Islam was established in north west India and Afghanistan in the 8th century AD but languished under a series of local Emirs and Sultans during the Golden Age. The lands of Islam were forever divided between west and east by the Mongol destruction of Baghdad in 1258. Thereafter the 'eastern' Islam of the sub-continent developed independently of the dominant Ottoman west.

With the Ottoman Empire entering its last phase of decline in the 16th century, Islam in India experienced a spectacular revival in the form of the heterodox, Hindu-influenced Mogul Empire. For two hundred years Muslims and Hindus cooperated to create a great civilisation, now chiefly remembered for great architectural monuments such as the Taj Mahal.

During the peak of the Mogul Empire traders and missionaries set out from western India to Bengal (part of which now forms the territory of Bangladesh) and the Malay-Indonesian archipelago. Local Hindu and pagan princes converted to Islam, creating dozens of religiously heterodox and prosperous Sultanates – later welded together by European colonialists to form the modern states of Indonesia and Malaysia.

In India itself the later Mogul emperors reversed the policy of religious toleration and embraced a narrow and sectarian version of Ottoman-type Hanafi Islam. Countless Hindu-Muslim wars sapped the power of the Empire and led to its conquest by the British. Under British rule Indian Muslims became a despised minority in a hostile Hindu-dominated nation.

Partition of the sub-continent into the states of Pakistan and India in 1947 was an unsatisfactory attempt to reconcile the rival political ambitions of Muslims and Hindus. From the beginning there were great doubts that the partition would be stable and, in practice, the new state of Pakistan quickly began to disintegrate.

In West Pakistan Islam inherited the narrow sectarian creed of the late Mogul period and the Afghan tribesmen. The elusive search for Islamic purity was expressed as an increasingly dogmatic and intolerant 'fundamentalism,' deeply hostile towards Hindu-influenced Muslim refugees from the central and southern parts of the sub-continent.

In East Pakistan (later Bangladesh) the Muslim community was based on relatively recent Bengali converts from Hinduism who had little in common with the West Pakistanis and retained ethnic, cultural and linguistic ties with the Hindus of the neighbouring Indian state of West Bengal. Islam here remains relatively heterodox, moderate and secularist in outlook.

In remote Afghanistan, meanwhile, ferocious highland tribesmen and warlords remained untouched by both Mogul civilisation and British influence. Like the Bedouins of the Arabian peninsula they preserved a highly traditionalist form of Islam, rebelling against foreign rulers and attempts to change their ancient way of life.

5.1 PAKISTAN

The state of Pakistan is a purely political invention designed as a homeland for the Muslims of the Indian sub-continent following the dissolution of the British Indian Empire.

In the last decades of British rule in India many Muslims supported Mahatma Gandhi's All-Indian Congress movement in its campaign for a secular, multi-religious Indian state free from British rule and encompassing the entire territory of the sub-continent.

But as independence grew nearer they began to fear that, as

a religious minority within India as a whole, they would become second class citizens. In 1930 Muhammad 'Ali Jinnah withdrew from the Congress and began agitation for the establishment of a Muslim 'homeland', based on the old Mogul territories in north west India and federated with distant Muslim majority territories scattered throughout the sub-continent.

In 1947 the British and the Hindus compromised with Jinnah and granted him the Muslim majority territories of Punjab and Sind, which became West Pakistan. East Bengal – separated from West Pakistan by 1,000 miles of Hindu majority territory – became East Pakistan. Amid much bloodshed millions of Hindu and Muslim refugees migrated between the two new states of Pakistan and India, the borders of which were often no more than arbitrary lines drawn on the map.

The largest group of Muslim refugees – the *Mujahdirs* (literally 'foreigners') – came from Hyderabad in the centre of India, fleeing mainly to West Pakistan. The Mujahdirs, although a minority in Hyderabad, had formed its ruling class. They were heterodox Isma'ilite Shi'ah and had absorbed many Hindu customs and religious practices including an Islamised version of the main Hindu festival of *Diwali* (known throughout the sub-continent as the festival of the Night of Forgiveness – *Shab-i-Barat*).

The Mujahdirs were not only religiously heterodox but highly educated and cultured by Pakistani standards. They soon came to dominate commerce and public life in the West Pakistan and were deeply resented by the more orthodox native Sunni Hanafi Punjabis and Sindis. The Sunni desire to sweep the Mujahdirs out of the government and civil service fuelled a campaign for 'Islamisation' of Pakistan, leading to the declaration of an Islamic republic in 1956.

Mujahdirs, Muslim secularists and modernists were hounded and a stifling Hanafi orthodoxy was imposed. Celebration of non-orthodox Muslim festivals such as Shab-i-Barat was banned, narrow 'Islamic' education was imposed in the schools and the capital was moved from cosmopolitan Karachi to the new citadel of orthodoxy – Islamabad. A paranoic desire to root out Hindu influence and Indian 'traitors' swept Pakistan setting in motion the chain of events leading to the 1971 Indo-Pakistani war over Kashmir and the secession of East Pakistan as Bangladesh.

The creation of Bangladesh disturbed the internal balance of Pakistani politics. Islamisation was blamed for the secession of

East Pakistan and a short-lived, but intense, secularist backlash took place. Zulfikar 'Ali Bhutto's secularist Pakistan People's Party won a large majority in 1972 elections on a platform of halting the Islamisation campaign.

Bhutto's new 1973 constitution gave more power to the secularising PPP-dominated parliament and limited the power of the army. During his Presidency Pakistan's endemic economic crisis worsened causing strikes, food riots and a fresh wave of anti-Mujahdir feeling. The growing unrest was exploited by the 'fundamentalist' Ja'mat-i-Islami Party which had strong support in the army. In 1977 a military junta under General Zia ul-Haq seized control, imposed martial law, executed Bhutto and revived the Islamisation campaign.

Panels of Islamic judges were attached to all higher courts, and a federal *shari'ah* court given the power to overturn the decisions of lower courts. The country adopted the *hadd* penal code of Qur'anic punishments – the first modern country, other than Saudi Arabia, to do so.

Islamisation remained largely superficial. A grandiose new mosque was built in Islamabad with Saudi finance and daily attendance at the mosque for the five prayer cycles of *salat* was imposed in the army and civil service, but the communal Friday prayers remained the main form of observance for Pakistani Muslims. As ever, the changes at the top of the country had only a limited impact on the vast mass of the illiterate Pakistani peasantry.

Military rule brought a measure of stability to the country and, with the help of massive Saudi Arabian and American aid (the US provided $3.2 billion over five years), Pakistan adopted a strongly anti-Soviet foreign policy and became the main base for the guerilla war against the neighbouring Soviet-allied state of Afghanistan.

The alliance of Saudi Arabia – an Islamic Monarchy with a tiny population but huge wealth – and Pakistan – an Islamic Republic with a huge population but little wealth – became one of the most dynamic in the Islamic world and still provides the backbone of contemporary conservative Sunni fundamentalism. It is underpinned by the presence of millions of Pakistani 'guest-workers' in oil fields of Saudi Arabia and other Gulf states whose remittances provide one of Pakistan's main sources of foreign currency.

In 1986 martial law was lifted and General Zia was killed two years later in a mystery plane crash. Soviet-sponsored terrorism was suspected, but never proved. In 1988 Bhutto's daughter Benazir returned from exile to win a general election narrowly for the Pakistan People's Party, but her room for political manoeuvre has been slight and the supreme *shari'ah* court retains power to overturn any 'non-Islamic' legislation enacted by her government.

The massive scale of continuing US and Saudi economic aid compensates for the gigantic cost imposed on the country by its sponsorship of the guerillas in the Afghan war. Five million destitute Afghan refugees have flooded into Pakistan's northern provinces causing severe economic dislocation and potential political instability. Bhutto desperately wants a negotiated settlement to the war but the USA and Saudi Arabia − who exercise an effective economic veto over the country's policies − have ruled this out.

5.2 KASHMIR

The beautiful but sparsely populated mountain state of Jammu and Kashmir on the Indo-Pakistani border has a slight Muslim majority in the state as a whole, which is concentrated in the entirely Muslim western provinces on the border with Pakistan.

Kashmir was claimed by Pakistan in the partition settlement of 1947, but invaded and annexed by India in 1948. The two countries have clashed over it many times, but an uneasy peace has been established since 1972 when it was placed under military occupation and partitioned between them.

The Hindu majority of east Kashmir is now the target of a concerted missionary campaign led by the wealthy Shi'ah Isma'ilite sect whose members are found in small concentrations throughout India. The Isma'ilites provide clinics and schools which are highly popular with low-caste 'untouchables' who are otherwise denied access to education.

In recent years entire 'untouchable' villages have converted to Islam throughout India but especially in Kashmir. As Muslims they are immediately released from their status as virtual slaves and, in east Kashmir, enjoy effective Pakistani protection as a religious minority.

Islam is growing faster in India than in any other major Muslim minority country and on present trends Muslims may well constitute the majority in Indian east Kashmir within the next few decades, with the consequent probability of reviving Indo-Pakistani conflict.

5.3 AFGHANISTAN

The inhospitable mountains of the Hindu Kush in Afghanistan, which became a province of the Arab Islamic Empire in the first century after Muhammad, have served as Islam's impregnable Asian fortress ever since. The highly traditionalist Afghan warlords have preserved an ancient and conservative form of Islam strikingly resembling that of the ungovernable Bedouin Arabs.

Afghanistan, unlike central Asia to the north and the Muslim lands of India to the south east, never came under the rule of either Imperial Russia or Britain (though in the early part of this century it did briefly become a protectorate of the British Raj as a guarantee against Russian domination).

As in Iran, the only other Muslim country to remain independent since the Middle Ages, Afghani Islam has become fused with militant nationalism and *jihad* (Holy War in defence of Islam). And at the same time Afghan independence has become a potent symbol of how 'fundamentalism' can survive European domination.

For centuries dynasties of Turkic, Iranian, Mongol and indigenous Pashtan Afghani rulers have attempted to limit the power of the chieftains and impose centralised rule on the country, but have failed without exception. In this century a limited amount of economic development based on tourism and mining opened the country to foreign influences and the small educated middle class began to blame the power of the chiefs for the backwardness and dire poverty of the country.

In the early 1960s a student-based radical movement began agitating for land reform and other modernising policies. The movement culminated in the overthrow of the king who had hitherto maintained his power by manipulating a fragile alliance of tribal chiefs and regional warlords.

The new secular republic which was established was popular with the urban population of Kabul and with the poorer peasants, who were promised land of their own and freedom from virtual slave status in the service of the chiefs, but the pace of change was slow and fiercely opposed by traditionalist Muslim groups led by the Muslim Brotherhood.

In 1977 a further coup brought a Marxist government to power, proposing the immediate collectivisation of agriculture and other measures such as education for women, bitterly opposed by the chiefs. Uniting under the title *Mujahideen* (literally 'fighters' or 'Crusaders'), the chiefs declared *jihad* on the government.

The Marxist government came under Soviet influence and, after early Mujahideen successes, a pro-Soviet faction widely seen as a Soviet 'puppet' came to power and requested Soviet military assistance. The Muslim and Western worlds have since regarded Afghanistan as under Soviet occupation and have supplied the Mujahideen (more commonly known in Afghanistan as *Basmachi* – literally 'Bandits') with increasingly amounts of sophisticated modern weaponry. Western and Soviet involvement led to a bitter military stalemate which ruined the country's economy and caused five million refugees to flee to neighbouring Pakistan.

Predictions that the Mujahideen would quickly overthrow the Afghan government following the withdrawal of Soviet troops in 1988 were premature. But they currently control large parts of the country, imposing a crude form of Islamic rule based partly on the *shari'ah* and tribal customs such as 'removing the shirt' – skinning alive from the waist up – a form of punishment reserved for supporters of the government.

What sort of government the Mujahideen might form if they ever do come to power is impossible to predict. The guerilla leaders are divided amongst themselves along tribal and regional lines and the most likely outcome would be collapse into warring tribal fiefdoms.

The current government's original fundamentalist opponents, the Muslim Brotherhood, has split into two tribal based groups – *Hizb-e Islami* (roughly 'victorious Islam'), based amongst the tribes of minority ethnic groups, and the larger and better organised *Jamiat-e Islami* (roughly 'Islamic regroupment'), based amongst the majority Pashtans. Both groups want to make Afghanistan an Islamic Republic based on a puritanical version of the *shari'ah* and are formally committed to expanding the war into the Muslim countries of Soviet central Asia.

Two other armed groups, *Jabha'ye Nejat-e Milli-ye Afghani* (Afghan National Liberation Front) and *Mahaze-e Milli-ye Islami-ye Afghani* (National Islamic Liberation Front of Afghanistan) are also divided along tribal lines. They are more moderate than the two Brotherhood derived groups and led by chiefs who played an important role in the old monarchy.

The Soviet Union and the government have proposed a negotiated settlement with the rebels and put the restoration of the monarchy on the table as one possible solution to the war. The new, and more moderate, government of Benazir Bhutto in Pakistan has welcomed the idea, but negotiations have foundered on Mujahideen intransigence and internal rivalries.

The chaos in Afghanistan − whether the current government is overthrown or not − is certain to continue for many more years yet and, as millions more refugees flood across the border, Pakistan faces the danger of further serious economic disruption and internal instability.

5.4 BANGLADESH

Bangladesh comprises the territory of the eastern part of the old Mogul outpost of Bengal, a densely populated peasant province based on the fertile Ganges delta. Islam in Bengal is a comparatively recent addition to the religious landscape which, for a thousand years, was dominated by Hinduism and Buddhism.

The ancestors of today's Bangladeshi Muslims were mostly low-caste Hindus who escaped from their status by converting to Islam during the Mogul heyday 300 years ago. As a far-flung outpost of Islam they escaped much of the sectarianism of the late Mogul years and today have strong linguistic and cultural ties to the Hindus of Indian West Bengal.

Bangladeshi Islam, in stark contrast to the version dominant in Pakistan, is mainly secular in outlook and highly tolerant of other religions including the large Hindu minority (12%) within the country.

The incorporation of the Muslims of Bengal into the state of Pakistan in 1947 must now be judged as one of the greatest political and economic disasters of the century. The new province of East Pakistan was denied access to its traditional markets in Calcutta 80 km across the new border and was instead put under the control of Karachi, 2,400 km away in West Pakistan. As well as economic unviability the partition brought chronic political instability as West Pakistan attempted to force 'Islamisation' on the reluctant Bengalis. In 1971 East Pakistan declared itself neutral in the Indo-Pakistani war over distant Kashmir and, after a nine month civil war, became the independent state of Bangladesh.

In December 1972 a secular constitution was brought in which, in contrast to West Pakistan's status as an Islamic Republic, proclaimed Bangladesh a secular, socialist and non-aligned People's Republic, with no legal status for the *shari'ah*.

Hopes of a new beginning were quickly dashed. The economic plight of the country worsened as Bangladesh moved towards the Soviet Union and India in Asian affairs and thus, unlike Pakistan, cut itself off from US and Saudi Arabian aid. And from the late 1970s onwards the low-lying delta – home to the vast majority of the poverty-stricken population – began to be hit by a series of increasingly disastrous floods.

Political instability continued as factions accused each other variously of pro-Indian, pro-Pakistani, pro-Chinese or pro-Western treachery. Between 1973 and 1977 three civilian Presidents were assassinated in a series of coups. Reaction against the left-wing secular political parties brought the Bangladesh Nationalist Party to power under the leadership of Hossain Muhammad Ershad on a platform of mild Islamisation which was designed to rebuild bridges to Pakistan and Saudi Arabia.

In 1983 Ershad seized total power in a military coup, banned the opposition and reorganised the judiciary and local government. Islam was enshrined as the state religion and the Islamisation campaign was begun. In 1986 martial law was lifted and new elections were held in 1988, which Ershad's Nationalist Party won on a very low turn-out amid accusations of ballot-rigging.

Since then events have been dominated by continuing floods, crop failures and famine, provoking fears that Bangladesh may never become economically or even ecologically viable. There are signs that the course of the Ganges has been irreparably altered by erosion and irrigation schemes in the Indian Himalayas and, combined with the phenomenon of rising sea-levels, this may mean that within the near future the fertile Ganges delta may disappear under water. If the worst forecasts are correct then almost the entire population of Bangladesh – perhaps 100 million people – will be forced to evacuate.

Having penned themselves into the sectarian Muslim enclave of East Pakistan it is unlikely they would be welcomed in neighbouring Indian West Bengal, where they would swamp the local Hindu population. And having fought a bloody civil war to gain independence from Pakistan it is unlikely that they would accepted there even in small numbers.

5.5 THE EAST INDIES (*Indonesia, Malaysia and Brunei*)

The East Indian archipelago is made up of 13,000 islands stretching nearly 5,000 km from Sumatra and the Indian Ocean in the west to New Guinea and the Pacific in the east. The 150 million inhabitants speak over 300 different languages and belong to many different tribal groups.

Islam was first established as a major force in the early 16th century when Hindu-influenced Muslim merchants and missionaries from Mogul India clashed with the Chinese for control of the declining indigenous Hindu and pagan tribal civilisations.

Fearful of growing Chinese power, the Hindu princes turned to the Hindu-influenced Mogul Empire for help. In the century that followed dozens of Hindu princes converted to heterodox Mogul forms of Islam, mainly under the influence of Sufi missionaries who established themselves as physicians and advisers in Hindu courts.

By the middle of the 17th century most of the islands were under the rule of indigenous Muslim Sultans and the southward spread of the Chinese religions of Buddhism and Confucianism was halted and confined to the mainland of south east Asia.

The Sultans adopted the Shafi school of Sunni Islam, a variant of the *shari'ah* which has always been associated with Muslim traders and explorers, because it is particularly forgiving of non-performance of the pilgrimage (*hajj*) to Mecca.

Hajj is a subject of some importance for distant Muslim communities such as these. Performance of the pilgrimage is one of the Five Pillars but is obligatory only for those who can 'find their way' (3:97). Despite this many early East Indian Muslims made the trip on foot – a journey of at least 8,000 km each way through jungles and across mountain ranges and deserts.

Over the past 200 years hundreds of poorer East Indian Muslims have settled in Mecca and Medina rather than attempt the return journey. Together with other long-distance *Hajji*, such as the Chinese and West Africans, the East Indians now form a distinct ethnic minority in the Holy Cities. Many have sold themselves into slavery (which is still unofficially sanctioned in Saudi Arabia) and sent a large remittance home to meet the Qur'anic obligation to care for families placed on *Hajji*).

Apart from Shafi Islam's special approach to the problem of long-distance *hajj* it is otherwise slightly more traditionalist than the Hanafi'ism practised in Pakistan and Bangladesh. The early Muslim Sultans nevertheless pursued a policy of religious toleration towards the indigenous Hindu population. Conversion of the mass of the population from Hinduism to Islam was a slow process and the full Islamisation of the archipelago has not been completed even today.

By the 18th century about 75% of the population had been Islamised when the process was frozen by the arrival of the European colonialists. The Sultanates fell increasingly under European control and their territories were divided by rival British, Dutch, Portuguese and German rulers.

The division of the Sultanates between the British and Dutch Empires, the two largest powers in the region, resulted in the eventual creation of the states of Malaysia (a federation of formerly British controlled Sultanates) and Indonesia (the former Dutch Sultanates) after the Second World War.

The Sultanate of Brunei, although controlled by the British, was left out of Malaya and is now a tiny — but extremely rich — independent Muslim state.

Indonesia

Islam in Indonesia is moderate and influenced by Hinduism, Buddhism and heterodox Sufi'ism. Since the formation of the country in 1945 most Indonesian Muslims have been happy to live under a secular, nationalist government and to tolerate large Hindu and other religious minorities. Although about 80% of the 150 million Indonesians are Muslims, Islam is only one of five state-recognised religions alongside Christianity, Confucianism, Buddhism and Hinduism.

After promoting Islam as an anti-Communist force in the 1960s and 1970s, the right-wing Nationalist regime of President Suharto is now attempting to reduce the role of the religion in the country and introduce even greater secularism.

Since 1969 Indonesian politics has been dominated by Suharto's attempt to forge 'New Indonesian Man' from the bewildering ethnic patchwork of islands. A highly secularised version of Islam has been included in the official make-up of 'New Indonesian Man' but his first allegiance must be not to religion but to 'Indonesia-ism'.

The main effects of the New Order campaign have been felt in remote eastern islands such as Timor and West Irian (the Indonesian half of New Guinea) where Stone Age tribes have been exterminated or transported to make room for 'New Man' settlements of Javanese Muslims. Large areas of tropical rain forest in this area are now under threat from Javanese developers using Japanese and American multinational capital.

Opposition in Indonesia – both religious and secular – is severely repressed by Suharto's New Order Party (The Golkar) and is confined to state controlled official opposition parties. One of these, the Development Unity Party, is in favour of introduction of *shari'ah* law and other conservative pro-Islamic reforms. But the main function of the DUP is to institutionalise and confine Islam as a political force, and the party's demands have generally been ignored by the secularist government.

However, further secularisation campaigns in 1984 and 1985 provoked rioting by Muslim youths in urban areas, campaigning against a ban on 'Islamic ideology' in public life and the allegedly privileged status of Christian and Chinese Confucians in the civil service and army. The rioters were suppressed, but the government was badly shaken and further secularisation measures have now been shelved.

Malaysia

Islam in Malaysia is very similar to that found in Indonesia but is marginally more sectarian, feeling more threatened by the larger and more confident Buddhist and Chinese religious minorities who constitute about a quarter of the population.

During World War Two the Chinese Malaysians fought a guerilla war against the Japanese, whilst the Muslim majority either acquiesced or actively collaborated. After the war the guerillas, under the influence of the new Communist Peoples' Republic of China, continued their war against the British.

By the early 1960s the British had put down the pro-Communist rebellion with great barbarity and in 1963, underwritten by a large continuing British military presence in the country, Malaysia was granted independence as a secular Muslim majority federation. In 1966 the Malaysian government recognised Islam as the official religion of state but did not apply the *shari'ah* for fear of upsetting the fragile balance of ethnic and religious groups in the community.

Brunei

The independent Sultanate of Brunei, a tiny enclave on the Malaysian north coast of Borneo island, is all that remains of the powerful Muslim Sultanate of Borneo which, at the height of its power in the 15th century, dominated the East Indian islands as far as the Philippines and the South China Sea. The ancestors of the large Muslim minority now found in the Philippines were merchants and settlers from Muslim Borneo.

In 1888, reduced to an 80 km strip of coastline, the Sultanate became the British protectorate of Brunei within its present borders. The Sultanate would probably have been included in the Federation of Malaysia if it had not been for the discovery of commercial quantities of oil. The Sultan was determined to keep this new source of wealth for himself and his subjects.

Sultan Hassanal Bolkiah has ruled the 250,000 population – mostly Malay Muslims with a large Chinese minority – as an absolute autocrat since independence from Britain in 1985. The *shari'ah* is strictly enforced and all political opposition is illegal.

The Sultan's rule is underpinned by massive oil wealth, passed on to the small population through free education, medical care, state loans and padded civil service salaries (GNP per head in 1989 was $16,000 per capita, the highest in Asia outside the Gulf). The Sultan also rents a force of 800 British Gurkha troops.

6.0 NORTH AFRICA (The Maghreb)

(Morocco, Algeria, Libya, Mauritania and Tunisia)

Total population: 58.5 million
Muslim population: 99%
Dominant Sect: Sunni-Maliki

The coastal fringe of North Africa was conquered by the Islamic Army at the end of the 7th century at the same time as the centre of the Muslim world moved from Mecca and Medina to the north Arabian lands and Iraq. The indigenous population of Berbers or 'Moors' – an ancient Mediterranean people similar but ethnically distinct from the Arabs – retreated to the inland Maghreb desert and resisted Arab rule.

In the 8th century the Meccan traditionalists defeated in the civil wars over the Muhammadan succession were also forced into exile in the Maghreb, mingled with the Moors and converted them to a traditionalist version of 'pristine' Islam hostile to the Arab aristocracy of the coast.

The Moors and their new Meccan allies, known as the Ibadites ('upholders of religious law'), founded cities like Fez and Marrakech, deep in the Maghreb beyond the control of the heterodox Emperors of Baghdad and their Arab governors on the North African coast.

By the 10th century the Ibadites and Moors had swept the Arabs out of North Africa and replaced them with a series of states ruled (unlike the 'usurper' Emperors in Baghdad) by descendants of the Prophet via his daughter Fatima. The Moors also conquered Spain from its Arab Muslim rulers (Spain was conquered by the

Arabs in 711 and became an Emirate under the overall rule of Baghdad) and held parts of it for two hundred years before the Christian reconquest.

The Moorish rulers of the Maghreb adopted the strictly conservative Maliki school of Sunni law which today is the official doctrine of most of Muslim Africa. For 600 years Moorish descendants of Muhammad ruled most of the territory of modern Morocco, Algeria, Libya, Mauritania and western Egypt before slowly falling under Ottoman and then French colonial rule.

The influence of these Imperial powers − like that of the Arabs a thousand years before − did not penetrate much further than the coastal strip where, especially in Algeria, there was considerable French settlement. The Maghreb desert preserved a simple and highly traditional form of Islam tightly closed to outside influences. Today the Muslim regimes in the region − from the bizarre, messianic form of Islam adopted in radical Libya to the grandiose Imperial schemes of conservative Morocco − share the same tendency to act as though the rest of the world did not − or ought not to − exist.

6.1 MOROCCO

Morocco's official title is Kingdom of the Maghreb and the state still claims sovereignty in theory over all the lands ruled by the 15th century ancestors of the current ruler King Hassan al-Sharif, a direct descendant of the Prophet. The claimed territory includes all of Morocco's southern neighbour Mauritania, most of Mali, the southern half of Algeria, most of Libya, part of Sudan and Egypt as far east as the Nile.

Until 1956 Morocco formed part of the French North African Empire which encompassed most of the Maghreb except Libya. After the Second World War King Hassan's father Muhammad al-Sharif tried to persuade the French to make him king of all their North African possessions. The French at first refused but in 1956, following the Anglo-French defeat at the hands of Colonel Nasser of Egypt and the start of the Algerian war of independence, they changed their mind. Muhammad was given the territory of the former French protectorate of Morocco and proclaimed King of the Maghreb as a conservative, pro-French alternative to the radical anti-Western Arab independence movements active in virtually every French colony.

King Muhammad purged the more radical nationalist element amongst his own supporters and the French built up his Royal Armed Forces in preparation for the day when, following the expected French victory in Algeria, he would annex it to the Kingdom.

Muhammad died in 1961 and was succeeded by his son Hassan. When the Algerians finally won their own independence in 1962 the plan to annex the territory was effectively shelved and a constitution adopted for the state of Morocco alone. The new constitution established a limited parliament which could be dissolved at will by the king and enshrined Islam as the state religion. A hybrid legal system was developed using both the Maliki version of the *shari'ah* and French criminal law.

In 1965 Hassan dissolved parliament, claiming that the Kingdom was threatened by Algerian-backed Communist subversion, and ruled by personal decree. During these years the King repeatedly recognised and then challenged the boundaries of the neighbouring countries of the Maghreb and appeared confused about his territorial demands in the region.

The confusion prompted two botched coups by the army and Hassan's conservative supporters who clung to their Imperial dreams. In 1972 Hassan re-established the parliament, packed it with supporters of his own Royalist Party and has since ignored it.

In 1975 he restored much of his popularity with the army by annexing the newly independent territory of Western Sahara – a stretch of barren, inhospitable desert which nevertheless formed part of the Maghreb Kingdoms of the Middle Ages. Hassan personally led the so-called 'Green March' – a mass exodus of Moroccan settlers into Western Sahara, forcing the indigenous population to flee across the border into neighbouring Algeria. Settled in camps in eastern Algeria the refugees have formed an effective guerilla army called the Polisario Liberation Front which is armed by Algeria and Libya and diplomatically supported by the majority of African and Arab countries.

To keep the Polisario guerillas out the Moroccan army has built a high wall and earth embankment fifty times longer than the Berlin Wall along the entire length of the Algerian-West Saharan border. The wall and the cost of the continuing war and occupation has hit the already weak Moroccan economy and, worst of all, the initial enthusiasm of the Green March has dried up and the Moroccans are drifting back north or have to be paid large sums by local standards to stay or move to the occupied zone.

The problems caused by the faltering war in Western Sahara contributed to a wave of internal unrest in the early 1980s led by the secular left-wing political opposition and the Communist-influenced trades union movement. After serious urban rioting against food price increases in 1981 the trades unions and leftist parties were utterly crushed by the army. Over 600 leading leftists are believed to have been killed and more than 2,000 were sent to jail, where many still remain.

There have been further riots sparked by food prices, notably in Marrakech in 1984, but these have tended to be leaderless and the disgruntled urban poor, deprived of their former Socialist Party and trades union representatives, may well drift in the direction of Sunni fundamentalism in the future.

Even after dismembering the opposition, Hassan retains the right to overturn legislation and dissolve parliament at any time. He retains immense personal power as commander-in-chief of the armed forces and director of the national TV and radio service. As the country's supreme religious authority he also dictates what is taught in schools and what is preached in the mosques.

The King remains popular with the illiterate peasants of the countryside – who vaguely link him with dimly-remembered former Imperial glories – but his support in the towns is far less certain.

The 'King of the Maghreb', has managed only to annex a useless strip of coastal desert. His latest scheme is the construction of a gigantic mosque on the coast at Casablanca to function as a dynastic mausoleum intended to rival the triumphs of the Abbasids and Moguls in its scale and splendour.

6.2 ALGERIA

Algeria became a French colony in 1830 and there was extensive settlement by French nationals in the large coastal cities. This large scale foreign presence was something entirely new in the thousand year history of the Maghreb's isolation and was to profoundly influence the post-independence development of Islam in the country.

A significant number of ethnically Moorish (or Berber) Algerians became Westernised, adopted French habits, received French education and came into contact with the European political idea of socialism. In the early years of this century ethnically Algerian socialists – often lawyers or other professionals – began agitating for national independence.

But these Westernised Algerians were politically isolated. In 1945 there was a 'conventional' socialist-inspired uprising based around demands for nationalisation of French-owned agricultural estates. This was easily put down by the authorities with heavy loss of Algerian lives.

In the late 1940s a younger generation of Algerian nationalists became convinced that the traditional insularity and puritanism of Islam in the Maghreb interior was the only force powerful enough to overthrow French rule. Whilst the older generation of radicals had encouraged secularism and appealed to the Muslim population as 'workers', the new radicals, the National Liberation Front (NLF), adopted Islamic customs and traditional dress. They began to agitate against the flagrant breaches of the *shari'ah* – such as drinking, gambling, the display of female bodies – taking place in the French quarters of Algerian cities.

By the mid-1950s law and order had collapsed in the cities. Drinking clubs and casinos were bombed and French colonial restrictions on religious dress and practice were openly flouted. The inevitable French backlash produced a steady supply of martyrs whose deaths in defence of Islam caused the tribesmen of the interior to join the revolt.

By 1958 isolated terrorist outrages had escalated into a full-scale civil war with half a million French troops deployed against an almost completely united Muslim Algerian population. Appalling massacres were committed on both sides and by the end of the war in 1962 France had lost more soldiers in Algeria than they had in World War Two, the mainland had been brought to the brink of civil war, and General de Gaulle had become President of France with dictatorial powers.

The new Algerian NLF government, headed by the wartime guerilla leader Ben Bella, enshrined Islam as the national religion but at the same time retained a largely secular legal system. Most of the economy was nationalised along socialist lines and simultaneously 'Islamised'.

Banks were forbidden to charge interest in line with the Qur'anic injunction against 'usury' and the joint capital venture method of finance – where a proportion of the profit went to the capital lender or bank – was substituted.

Wages and prices were fixed by central government according to the classic socialist model, but the Qur'anic reference to 'moral contracts' was also invoked. The second surah states: 'When you [trade] with each other in contracting a debt for a fixed time, then write it down; and let a scribe write it down in fairness' (2:282). Measures like these, which upheld the *shari'ah* and fitted well with centralised socialist economic planning, became known as 'Islamic Socialism' and Algeria quickly became the archetypal Islamic socialist state.

In 1965 Ben Bella was replaced as NLF leader by his former assistant Colonel Houari Boumédienne in a bloodless coup. On the pretext of the continuing 'Imperialist' threat, Boumédienne abolished the Constituent Assembly and replaced it with a military junta constituted as the Revolutionary Command Council.

The NLF under Boumédienne built a prosperous state by Third World standards based on the export of oil and minerals. Internationally Algeria became an important backer of the non-aligned 'Tricontinental Movement', also sponsored by Cuba and Burma. Within the Muslim world this meant supporting Nasserism, nascent guerilla movements like the Palestine Liberation Organisation and the Fedayeen guerillas active against the Shah of Iran.

Since 1976 Algeria has recognised the Saharan Arab Democratic Republic declared within Western Sahara by the tiny indigenous population in opposition to Moroccan rule. The majority of the Western Saharan population, facing the possibility of genocide, has fled across the border to Algeria where the NLF has been more than ready to feed and shelter them and provide arms and training for the 40,000 guerillas of the Polisario Liberation Front.

In 1986 Algeria adopted a new Political Charter to guide the future development of 'Islamic Socialism' which elevated the importance of the *shura* (religiously guided councils) in the running of the state and the nationalised industries. At the same time greater freedom for private enterprise was granted within an overall framework of state control.

But unrest caused by growing corruption and nepotism within the NLF, along with falling oil revenues, have found expression in Islamic opposition to the reforms of the *shari'ah* in the early 1980s. These reforms abolished polygamy (already rare in practice) and granted formal equality to women.

Algeria, nevertheless, remains essentially stable and, with the more liberal atmosphere in the country following the adoption of the Charter, is likely to remain so. It continues to be important in international affairs because of its leading role in the non-aligned movement and as a mediator between various factions of the PLO and warring Lebanese factions.

6.3 LIBYA

From the 19th century onwards the Berber-Moors of the Libyan desert became the most extreme adherents to the highly traditionalist and insular form of Maliki Islam found throughout the Maghreb.

The cause of this renewed bout of extremism, which still profoundly marks Islam in Libya today, was the Sanusi movement launched by Zayid Muhammad 'Ali as-Sanusi (died 1859). Sanusi was an Algerian Berber who studied theology in Fez and Mecca and became a dedicated follower of the Wahhabi movement in the Arabian peninsula, the first group of modern Muslim fundamentalists. He returned to the Maghreb, settled in Libya and began propagating the Wahhabi message.

Sanusi attempted to rally the Berber tribes of the Maghreb to overthrow Ottoman Egypt in the way Wahhab and his followers had attacked the Ottoman authorities in the peninsula. The Libyan Berbers were enthusiastic. Contemporary Egypt was the centre of despised Muslim heterodoxy and the old enemy from dozens of Berber-Arab wars in the Middle Ages.

Sanusi died before he could unleash the rebellion and leadership of the movement passed to his son Sayyid al-Mahdi (the apocalyptic 'chosen one'). Al-Mahdi fought the Egyptians in Sudan and assisted in the establishment of the short-lived Mahdi'ist Republic in Khartoum. In Libya al-Mahdi set up a network of hundreds of secret Sanusi lodges (zawiyah) giving the movement a permanent structure – rare for a Sunni Muslim sect of this type.

Muhammad Idris, Sanusi's grandson, allied with the Italians in a short war against Ottoman Egypt, establishing himself as Emir of an independent Libya under Italian protection. Idris allowed himself to fall more and more under Italian control during the middle years of this century but, after the Italian defeat in the Second World War, emerged as King of an Independent Libya in 1951 with British and French support.

He had strengthened the grip of the Sanusi sect on the country and by 1951 at least one third of the population had joined local

Sanusi *zawiyah*. As King, he tried to use the Sanusi network to establish a conservative fundamentalist regime friendly to the Western powers along the lines of Saudi Arabia. But lower down the Sanusi structure younger members grew frustrated with his conservatism and especially his failure to support the radical Nasserite regime in Egypt over Suez.

Nasser was greatly admired by the radical Sanusi as the man who had overthrown the despised British-backed Farouk monarchy and championed the cause of war against Israel. In 1969 a group of young Sanusi army officers formed themselves as the Free Unionist Officers Movement (MLCU), overthrew the monarchy, and pledged to root out foreign influence and impose Sanusi-influenced Muslim rule in the country.

Twelve leaders of the MLCU formed themselves into a Revolutionary Command Council military junta under the chairmanship of Colonel Mu'ammar al-Qaddafi, who quickly emerged as the dominant figure in the new regime. In 1977, having reduced the RCC from twelve to six people and established complete personal control of the regime, al-Qaddafi published his 'Green Book' outlining the Colonel's 'Third Universal Theory' – the official ideology of the country.

The Book is a bizarre collection of traditionalist Berber, Sanusi and extremist socialist thinking. It calls for the revolutionary overthrow of all the governments of the world and their replacement with the direct rule of Allah by obedience to Qur'anic law (the *shari'ah*) and al-Qaddafi's own Divinely-inspired Green Ideology.

Where the *shari'ah* is inadequate to deal with modern problems, as al-Qaddafi concedes is often the case, he believes that laws can only be made by a gathering of the entire people of the country (in Libya's case some two million adults) through a series of People's Assemblies and local committees.

In line with these ideas he 'dissolved' the Libyan state in 1977 and replaced it with a 'state of the masses' (*Jamahiriya*) composed of local committees dispensing the functions of the state and judiciary. The committees are also responsible for implementation of the *shari'ah*, though there is a national court of appeal and a supreme court in Tripoli. The personnel of the appeal and supreme courts are selected by the People's General Congress which carries out the functions of central government. The General Congress meets from time to time to decide matters such as the national budget and is composed of up to 1,000 delegates from local committees, trades unions, women's organisations and the like. These gatherings are reportedly chaotic and in practice controlled by the Congress Secretariat composed of 19 regional representatives.

In 1979 al-Qaddafi resigned as General Secretary of the Congress Secretariat and retired to a tent in the Libyan desert. Moving about to avoid possible assassination he directs a parallel national structure of Revolutionary Committees whose cell-like structure extends into every corner of Libyan society. The Revolutionary Committees from a tightly-knit and fanatical elite, based in turn on the secretive structure of the Sanusi *zawiyah*, which polices the whole committee system.

In 1980 a Sunni theological commission in Mecca accused al-Qaddafi of apostophy – reversion from Islam – and the Colonel is now widely described by other Islamic rulers as a non-Muslim (*kafir*). Despite this, he is widely regarded by his followers as al-Mahdi and uses his position as head of the armed forces to rule the country. Conscription is enforced and Libya is one of the most militarised nations in the world, with reportedly more aircraft, guns and tanks than it has people able to operate them.

The 1985 American air strike against Libyan targets was a response to Libyan sponsorship of international terrorist groups. According to Western intelligence, al-Qaddafi has at one time or another financed, trained or supplied arms to various factions of the PLO, the Red Brigades, the Baader-Meinhof group, the American Black Panthers and the Provisional IRA. He is also accused of sponsoring coup attempts or other forms of subversion in Egypt, Niger, Chad, Sudan, Mali, Tunisia, Saudi Arabia, Lebanon, Jordan, Guinea and The Gambia. He came to the brink of all-out war with France in 1984 over his role in Chad and, in addition, is accused of masterminding the secret export of Niger uranium to Iraq as part of a plan to build an 'Islamic Bomb'.

Although Western leaders would dearly like to see him deposed, al-Qaddafi's Revolutionary Committee structure maintains a tight grip on every institution in the country where opposition might develop. As part of his security mania al-Qaddafi keeps a heavily armed team of female bodyguards permanently at his side, and his security police, often posing as students, go to enormous lengths to keep tabs on tiny groups of dissident exiles who present no possible threat. Nevertheless 'hit squads' have been dispatched on occasions to kill them.

Islam in Libya today is a strange cocktail of traditional Maghreb 'other-worldliness', paranoia-ridden Middle Eastern politics, messianism, Maoism and a rag-bag of puritanical Muslim ideas gathered from the most diverse Islamic sources imaginable. The undoubtedly strange personality of al-Qaddafi adds another explosive ingredient to the mix.

6.4 MAURITANIA

The Islamic Republic of Mauritania is a remote, vast, inaccessible desert nation divided into three distinct ethnic groups. The 1.5 million population is united only in adherence to a narrow version of traditionalist Maliki Islam now enshrined as the basic constitution of the country.

In Mauritania ancient Berber-Moorish Islam begins to give way to the more heterodox and recent Islam of Negro sub-Sahara. The dominant ethnic group, making up only about 25% of the population, is known as the White Moors and forms the ruling class of the country. The White Moors are linked by clan ties to the Moroccan aristocracy.

The remaining 75% of the population is divided between the Negro Hausa, concentrated on the southern border with Mali and Senegal, and the so-called Black Moors – descendants of Arabised Negro slaves who are ethnically Negro but culturally Moorish. The slave trade was made illegal under French rule but resumed after independence in 1960.

The Mauritanian state was at first secular but highly traditionalist. The government was dominated by the White Moor ruling class, many of whom favoured the immediate incorporation of Mauritania into Morocco as part of a revived Maghreb Empire. The country's first President Moktar Ould Daddah, rejected this idea as impossible because of the overwhelming size of the non-Moorish ethnic majority. Daddah nevertheless followed strongly pro-Moroccan policies culminating in 1975 with the joint occupation of the former Spanish colony of Western Sahara which neighbours both countries.

The occupation was unpopular with the majority non-Moorish population. If it was a success it would give the Moroccans a common border with Mauritania for the first time, across which, it was feared, they might invade in order to add yet more territory to the Moroccan 'Kingdom of the Maghreb'.

In the event the war was a disaster for Mauritania. The native

West Saharan population resisted the occupation and in 1976 declared the independent Saharan Arab Democratic Republic. Mauritania suffered heavy losses and the guerillas became active in the northern provinces of the country itself.

In 1978 a coup led by the Negro Hausa tribe brought down the Daddah government and ended the war. Mauritania's foreign policy moved sharply against Morocco and evolved into diplomatic support for the Polisario guerillas. The war and the coup had brought the Hausa population of the south and the Moorish population of the north close to civil war.

The new Hausa regime sought to broaden its base amongst the Moors and found an ally in the form of the Muslim Brotherhood. The regime accepted a Brotherhood proposal to turn the country into an Islamic Republic based on full implementation of the *shari'ah* law as the price of continuing Moorish support.

The Islamic Republic of Mauritania was proclaimed in 1980 and the first public hand amputations for theft took place in September of that year. At the same time, slavery was abolished and many Black Moors were freed. Since then the country has been stable by the standards of the region and has avoided disintegration into civil war between northern Berbers and southern Negroes.

The Mauritanian economy, based on copper mining, has suffered from the decline in world commodity prices since their peak in the 1970s, but economic disruption is slight in comparison with the neighbouring southern and eastern agricultural states badly hit by the changing climate and the gradual southward shift of the Sahara.

6.5 TUNISIA

Tunisia is too far north and too narrowly coastal to have been permanently included in any of the inland Berber-Moorish Maghreb Empires of the past. It has thus remained predominantly Arab both in population and culture and therefore slightly more open to outside influences. And the country does not feature in the Imperial schemes of the Moroccan royal family.

The Tunisian Arabs nevertheless share the highly conservative Maliki version of Sunni Islam found in the neighbouring Berber-Moorish states. The country is also home to many small pockets of extreme fundamentalist Ibadites. The offshore island of DJerba – about the size of the Isle of Wight – is home to 50,000 fanatical

Ibadites who live more or less as their ancestors did when they fled there from Mecca 1,300 years ago.

Tunisian independence was granted by France in 1955 without a fight, mainly because the country was an economic liability and had no large indigenous French population. Most of the rural population was scarcely touched by French rule and completely unexcited by its passing.

Post-independence politics have been dominated by the tiny French-educated middle class, rural estate owners (many of whom are French) and the small urban working class. The secular state is dominated by the Constitutional Socialist Party (PSD) led by the octogenarian Habib Bourguiba.

The PSD came to power with the support of the French government but relations deteriorated during the Algerian war. After Algerian independence Bourguiba attempted to copy the far-reaching socialisation of agriculture and industry implemented by the Algerians but the population did not display sufficient revolutionary zeal to overcome opposition from the landowners.

In the early 1970s Bourguiba abandoned socialism in favour of free market economic policies promoted by the World Bank, to which Tunisia is heavily in debt as a result of the high-spending socialist policies of the past. Through the 1970s food subsidies were steadily withdrawn and the economy was progressively denationalised. Service industries – particularly tourism – were encouraged.

In 1981 the pace of economic liberalisation increased and there were strikes and protests against unemployment and high food prices. The trade unions, traditional allies of the government, were placed under severe legal restraint and became largely ineffective. Left-wing opponents within the government party were expelled and independent left-wing groups curbed.

The repression is mild by the standards of nearby Morocco where similar economic and political action has been taken and has failed to stop the periodic unrest. In recent years anti-government demonstrations have become incoherent and violent and, as in Morocco, increasingly 'Islamic'.

Rising prices and falling wages are linked in the minds of many Tunisians with the arrival of foreign tourists and their shockingly un-Islamic behaviour. Measures have been taken to strictly segregate the alcohol-swilling, sun-bathing tourists but the impact on this highly traditionalist society has been profound.

The Islamic Tendency Movement, widely believed to be a 'front'

203

organisation for the illegal pro-Saudi Arabian Muslim Brotherhood, emerged for the first time as an active force during the 1984 food riots. The Movement links popularist demands for lower food prices with demands for full implementation of *shari'ah* law, at present restricted to the personal affairs of practising Muslims. The Tendency also wants a ban on permissive activities by tourists – particularly female nakedness.

7.0 CENTRAL AFRICA

(Sudan, Mali, Chad, Niger, Senegal, The Gambia and Guinea)

Total population: 57.5 million
Muslim population: 85%
Dominant Sect: Sunni-Maliki

Islam on the southern fringes of the Sahara is the result of contact between the Berber-Arab Muslim civilisation of the Maghreb and the indigenous pagan religions of great pre-Islamic Negro Empires such as Malinke (Mali) and Ghana. For 800 years Muslims and pagans alternately cooperated and fought and the result is two very different trends within Islam as practised in the region.

At the official level sub-Saharan Islam is highly political and often used as a focus for national unity in countries such as Chad, where there are great ethnic differences between the Arab-Berber population in the north and the Negro population in the south. This 'official Islam' is close to the orthodoxy and austerity of the Muslim nations of the Maghreb to the north.

In the south the Negro population has developed an idiosyncratic form of 'African Islam' which becomes steadily more heterodox as the semi-desert and grassland gives way to the Negro heartlands. Magic, idol worship and ancient pre-Islamic customs such as 'female circumcision' (removal of the clitoris) are all practised in the name of Islam.

The most widespread form of magic is fortune telling based on the *mandalah* — a five pointed star with an ink blot at the centre, usually drawn on the palm of a virgin boy. A Qur'anic verse is inscribed at each point of the star and the verse: 'Yea! we have removed your veil and today your sight is penetrating' (50:22) is chanted as an incantation. The boy is then believed to be capable of having visions by concentrating on the ink blot.

The *mandalah*-palm design is also worn as a piece of metallic jewellery known as the 'Hand of Fatima' – a reference to the daughter of the Prophet who is repeatedly described in Muhammadan *hadith* as knowing the 'right way'. These objects are thought to have originated as crude 'lodestone' compasses used for divining the direction of Mecca and are now used for casting spells and divining water.

Many African Muslims fear the continuing power of the surrounding tribal religions and protect themselves from spells with *gri-gri* – leather amulets worn around the neck. These amulets contain inscriptions from the Qur'anic 'verses of refuge' which describe how Muhammad was protected from Arabian black magic. A typical *gri-gri* verse is: 'And we have guarded [the Prophet] from every outcast devil' (15:17).

The continuing influence of pre-Islamic traditions is one reason for African Islam's extreme heterodoxy. The other is the all-pervasive influence of heterodox Sufi orders often sharing the indigenous population's enthusiasm for magic and mysticism.

Islam was first carried across the Sahara in the mid-11th century by Berber-Arab traders who dominated the gold trade between Negro Africa and the rest of the world. These merchants established ghettos within the cities of the great pre-Islamic Negro Empire such as Ghana and Malinke (Mali) but made no attempt to convert the local population.

By the late 13th century these Muslim trading communities were wealthy enough to support Sufi *madrasahs* (college-hospitals) which were to be the key to converting the region to Islam. Under the rule of the great Malian King Sundiata in the 13th century AD the Sufis (known as *karamoro* in the Malian language) replaced the traditional witch doctors and magicians as advisers to the Malian court. Some of Sundiata's many sons converted to Islam and ruled in the name of the religion following his death. But there was no attempt to convert the Malian tribesmen, who clung to their pagan religions, treating Islam as an auxiliary religion of state.

The Malian Empire reached the peak of its power in the 14th century under Emperor Mansa Musas, who established Sufi institutions in Timbuktu run by Negroes independently of the Arab and Moorish Sufi orders. In the middle of the 15th century

Muslim Mali was conquered by surrounding Songhay pagan tribes. Sufi'ism preserved a core of believers who eventually converted the Songhays, but Islam in the region diverged from the strict orthodoxy of the Berber-Arab Maghreb for 200 years, taking on its distinctively Sufi-magical form.

Following the Islamic millennium in 1622 AD (1000 AH) a wave of religious fervour swept all branches of Islam and was expressed in the Maghreb as the 'Jihad Movement'. Waves of Berber-Arab invaders swept across the Sahara determined to convert the entire population by force. A hundred years of Berber-Arab war on the pagan Negro tribes to the south followed. Defeated tribes who would not submit to the Berber version of orthodox Islam were taken as slaves and sold to the European powers.

Sufi-influenced 'African Islam' was only one of many religions in the region before the Jihad Movement but by the end of the 17th century it became dominant. Almost all the population of the present day states of Mali, Mauritania, Niger and Chad converted to Islam during the early stage of the Movement.

However, the spread of the religion was bitterly resisted further south in the present day countries of the African coast such as Nigeria, Togo and Ghana. For two centuries the Negroes of the far south held out against repeated Berber invasions from the north until the process of forced conversion (or slavery for those who would not) was arrested by the arrival of the European colonialists. Islam never managed to convert the majority of the population in any significant area south of the 16°N line of latitude.

The French colonised sub-Saharan Africa, which by that time overwhelmingly subscribed to the Maliki Sunni'ism of the Maghreb whilst the British took most of the west coast, which remained pagan with Muslim minorities in the north. (Later, owing to British missionary activity, many of these countries also became largely Christianised).

During the half century of French rule the sub-Saharan Muslim countries generally stagnated and the religion began to diverge into the southern Negro heterodoxy and northern Berber-Arab orthodoxy found before the Jihad movement. The influence of Sufi'ism in the south, however, remained all-important and it is rare these days to find a Negro Muslim who is not affiliated to one or other of the Sufi orders.

Since independence all the sub-Saharan countries have experienced tension between the Berber-Arab north and Negro

Muslim or pagan south. As a result the various regimes have, unlike the Maghrebian countries to the north, followed secularist policies designed to prevent power struggles between different Islamic factions.

7.1 MALI

Independent Mali was established as a democratic secular republic with the multi-party National Assembly dominated by the left-wing African Democratic Party of Modibo Keita. His government followed 'anti-Imperialist' policies aimed at rooting out French influence and naively trying to create a viable Malian national economy free from dependence on France by refusing French economic aid.

The economic policy was a disaster and reduced Mali to one of the poorest countries on the continent. In 1968, in an attempt to smother growing opposition, Keita dissolved the National Assembly and declared a socialist one-party state.

He was immediately overthrown by a military coup led by Brigadier General Moussa Traore, who ruled as the head of a military junta until 1979 when a limited National Assembly was re-established. Traore was elected President, Prime Minister, Commander in Chief of the Armed Forces, Foreign Minister and Minister without Portfolio by an unlikely 95% of votes in an equally unlikely 99% turnout.

His party, the Democratic Union of the Malian People (UDPM), won all the seats in the National Assembly, again with a suspiciously huge majority, and declared itself henceforth the only legal party. Traore has remained in power ever since, presiding over a mixed military and civilian cabinet.

As an agricultural country Mali's economy has been devastated by two major droughts in the last fifteen years and the country is entirely dependent on foreign food aid. At first this was distributed by the government, which helped political stability, but in recent years, despite protests from Traore, food supplies have by-passed it.

The only political opposition has come from the ruling UDPM's student wing, which has held demonstrations against the abandonment of socialist policies and the introduction of competitive examinations for entry into the civil service. But this opposition is secular. Islamic opposition has not surfaced.

7.2 CHAD

Chad is divided between a Muslim majority region in the north and a large pagan and Christian African minority in the south. The northern Muslim majority has been unable to assert its control over the south at any time.

At independence in 1960 the northern Muslim provinces remained under French military occupation and politics was dominated by the non-Muslim south where a process of de-Islamisation and reversion to paganism was already under way.

The re-unification of north and south in 1965 immediately resulted in a debilitating civil war which continues today. The degree of violence, fuelled by *jihad*-type feelings in the north, and hateful memories of Muslim slave trading and persecution in the south, has few parallels anywhere in the world and sickening massacres have taken place on both sides.

At first the civil war ran along the simple north-south religious fault on the 16°N line of latitude roughly marking the southern extent of Muslim settlement in Africa. The southern borders of the Muslim countries of Senegal, Mali and Niger run roughly along this line, but Chad extends another 950 km south, deep into the non-Muslim belt. N'Djamena, 320 km south of 16°N, is the furthest south of any major Muslim settlement in central West Africa. Since the 1960s the region south of N'Djamena has been in the hands of an anarchic collection of armed tribal groups controlling dozens of small fiefdoms at war with each other as well as N'Djamena itself. These groups, known collectively as the *Codos*, are held together only by their hatred of Islam.

Since 1969, when Colonel al-Qaddafi seized power in Libya, as Chad's northern neighbour, he has provided military support for President Goukouni Oueddi. As a result Oueddi made substantial military progress in the south in the late 1970s. By 1981 the Libyans were effectively occupying Chad and conducting the war in the south independently of the small Chadian army. But in 1982 Col Hissene Habre, a Muslim, led a French-backed military coup and with at least 2,000 French paratroopers secured control of N'Djamena from Oueddi and the Libyans, who retreated north of the 16°N line.

Oueddi declared himself President of a Transitional Government of National Unity (GUNT) and by 1984, with the support of some 7,000 Libyan troops, controlled all the north except a small area around N'Djamena, which remained under Habre and the French.

In 1984 the Libyans and the French agreed a joint withdrawal of forces and effective partition of the country along the 16°N line. But the Libyans have not withdrawn from the north as agreed and instead they have effectively annexed the area. Libya could attack N'Djamena at any time to overthrow Habre who only remains in power because of French support.

The south of the country remains in rebel hands and so Habre, the internationally-recognised President, rules only the immediate vicinity of N'Djamena and a small strip of territory to the west. The state is effectively bankrupt and Habre faces the constant threat of mass defection to the better paid Libyan army of the north or the rebels of the south, to whom many of his soldiers are related.

Chad is thus in a crippling deadlock and faces several more decades of starvation and decline until a southern tribal confederation strong enough to take N'Djamena emerges. Then, if the French consented, a southern tribal state could be formed, with the north either incorporated into Libya or declared independent under effective Libyan control. Much will depend on the attitude of the French government which, in turn, will be decided by developments within Libya.

7.3 SENEGAL and THE GAMBIA

Senegal is the most developed of the Muslim countries of the former French African Empire, but still has a mainly agricultural economy based on exporting peanuts, a crop which has been badly hit by droughts in recent years. But the country still has a remarkably stable and democratic political constitution based on moderate secularism, free elections and an independent judiciary.

The country was ruled by President Sedar Senghor from independence in 1960 until his retirement twenty years later, making him the first African head of state to retire voluntarily and then be replaced by free elections without military supervision.

His successor, Adbou Diouf, also represents the Senegalese Socialist Party (PS) which dominates the national assembly after winning 111 of the 120 seats in the 1983 election.

The pattern of Senegalese politics has been similar to that of many Third World countries. Socialist measures, including large scale nationalisation, were adopted in the 1960s to break the influence of the former colonial power, but disillusionment and a growing external threat, accompanied by mild political repression as the ruling party rid itself of its Marxist wing, mounted in the 1970s. Free-market policies dictated by the IMF and major French and other Western aid donors have followed in the 1980s.

The main threat to Senegalese political stability has been the former British enclave of The Gambia, a tiny country with narrow strips of territory along the banks of the Gambia river flowing through central Senegal. The Gambia, with a population of only 700,000, is a curiosity left over from Anglo-Franco political intrigues of a hundred years ago and made independent by Britain in 1970.

In its first decade it was far less stable than Senegal and in 1981 the pro-Western government had to call on Senegalese troops and, it is widely accepted, the British SAS, to put down a Libyan-inspired leftist uprising. Since then it has stabilised and there is a faltering plan for the two countries to merge as the federation of Senegambia.

Senegal's main problems are economic rather than political. The free market policies adopted in the 1980s have proved as ineffective as the state control of the previous two decades. The population barely clings to existence and another serious drought like the one in 1984–85 would create problems similar in scale to those of Ethiopia and Sudan.

7.4 NIGER

Niger's economy is one of the weakest in the world, with most of the population scraping a living farming the poor semi-desert scrub lands of the vast territory. Almost all the population is in the western part of the country on the thin strip of land irrigated by the Niger river. The east and north of the country is mostly desert which is slowly spreading. The population faced famine in 1984–86 because of drought.

The pattern of Niger politics is similar to that of neighbouring Mali, with a democratic, elected government following policies of non-alignment and moderate state socialism which tried to

211

diminish French influence in the first two decades of independence.

Islamic organisations appear to play a only a very limited role in the life the country and religious observance has declined markedly from the high point of the later Jihad Movements which swept Niger and the surrounding countries in the 17th–19th centuries.

Leftist, pro-Libyan opposition to IMF-directed austerity measures has been ruthlessly crushed.

7.5 GUINEA

Guinea is the only African Muslim state where the vast majority of the population is Negro rather than Berber-Arab.

From 1958 to 1984 Guinea was ruled by President Ahmad Sekou Touré, a moderate socialist and secularist, and his Guinea Democratic Party (PDG). Although democratically elected, the PDG dominated the small National Assembly and, on the well-established African pattern, began to move towards a one-party state. Touré's regime became increasingly repressive and more than a million Guineans − 20% of the population − fled into exile in neighbouring countries and France.

Touré was overthrown by a military coup in 1984 and a junta under the control of Colonels Lansana Conte and Diarra Traore set up. In 1985 Traore launched a coup against his partner but failed, thereby firmly establishing Conte as President. His rule has been more liberal than Touré's and many exiles have returned. But the country faces a grave economic crisis despite the adoption of IMF-approved free market policies, and supporters of the more leftist Traore present a constant threat.

The economy is dependent on the export of bauxite, the raw material for aluminium. The world price was high in the 1970s, enabling Touré to consolidate his rule through extensive bribery, but a slump since then has created great economic difficulties.

Another source of political instability is the tiny neighbouring country of Guinea-Bissau, a former Portuguese, rather than French, colony. Bissau became independent in 1974 and followed Marxist policies until 1980, when a military coup led to a more pro-Western stance. Bissau, however, sees itself as part of the Portuguese African world and therefore has closer links to Angola than to Guinea.

212

Islam plays a limited role in life in Guinea and is far less important politically than tribal divisions. The religion is less well established than in the neighbouring Islamic countries of Mali and Mauritania – an official Islamic republic – and a third of the population cling to pre-Islamic tribal religions like ancestor worship, voodoo and witchcraft. These people still associate Islam with distant memories of the slave trade.

It is likely many nominal Guinean Muslims in actual fact practise traditional religions and the official figure of a 69% Muslim proportion of the population is almost certainly an overestimate.

7.6 SUDAN

Official Islam in Sudan is Sunni Maliki – as in the rest of the region – but its development has been shaped by contact with the Hanafi'ism of Cairo and Egypt which borders the country to the north.

There have been backlashes against Hanafi influence throughout the history of Sudan. The most important Maliki rebellion took place in the last two decades of the 19th century AD in the form of the Mahdist revolt – the high point of the late Maliki Jihad Movements.

In 1881, with Egypt under the effective control of the British, the Sudanese Muslims declared their leader al-Mahd – the long-awaited 'chosen one' who will cleanse and re-unite Islam – and proclaimed a Mahdist state independent from Egypt and their British overlords.

The Mahdists practised a fundamentalist version of Islam purged both of Hanafi modernism and pagan-influenced Negro 'African Islam'. Britain declared war on them and after bitter fighting, including the celebrated loss of a British force under General Gordon, recaptured Khartoum in 1898.

The Mahdists were crushed and Hanafi-based secular Anglo-Muhammadan law was re-established, administered from Cairo. But, as in Libya, the spirit of Mahdi'ism lives on in the form of bouts of religious extremism and sectarianism.

These days Sudanese Muslim sectarianism is mainly directed against the sizeable Christian and pagan minority left in the south by arbitrary borders drawn up by the British when the country became a part of their African Empire.

213

During the Mahdist revolt the French claimed the territory of what is now southern Sudan for their African empire, which would have given them control of an uninterrupted chain of possessions stretching across the entire continent from west to east and cutting off British Egypt from the British colonies of East Africa. The British fought the claim, defeated the French in minor skirmishes, and annexed the southern and Negro part of the country. The annexation created a nonsensical hybrid nation which was immediately plunged into a smouldering civil war as soon as modern Sudan became independent in 1956.

There was a brief respite in 1969 when the army under the skilful leadership of General Ja'far Muhammad Numiery seized power in Khartoum. Numiery tried to appease the southerners by granting them religious freedom and political self-rule, but when he attempted to retain 'Islamic' support by introducing and strictly enforcing *shari'ah* law in the north, sometimes with great brutality, he provoked a renewed flare-up of the civil war.

The rebels quickly gained ground and the Sudan People's Liberation Army, led by John Garang, became the dominant and most effective southern rebel force after a series of military successes. In the face of the worsening military situation Numiery was deposed in 1985 by a bloodless coup and power passed to the Transitional Military Council under the leadership of General Siwar al-Dahab, who offered talks with the SPLA. The rebels refused to cooperate until *shari'ah* law was revoked in the south.

Al-Dahab abolished much of the *hadd* penal code, but was unable to lift *shari'ah* rule in its entirety for fear of provoking a fundamentalist revolt and counter-coup. The result was deadlock, with the framework of moderated *shari'ah* law in force throughout the whole country and continued rebel activity in the south.

In 1986 the Sudanese government sponsored multi-party elections after abolishing the one party state machinery of Numiery's Sudanese Socialist Union. But there was no voting in most of the southern provinces because of the civil war. The election was won by a coalition of two moderate parties, the secular conservative Democratic Unionists and the moderately Islamising Muslim People's Party (The Umma Party). The National Islamic Front, a creation of the Sudanese Muslim Brotherhood, formed the opposition.

The democratically elected government under the Prime Ministership of Sadiq al-Mahdi faced formidable economic problems caused by the decline in world commodity prices, a

214

reduction in Saudi Arabian aid, and the burden of hundreds of thousands of refugees from its own civil war, aggravated by refugees from the wars and famines in neighbouring Uganda, Ethiopia and Chad. On top of this the country was hit by a series of alternating floods and droughts, which left at least half the population homeless and a quarter at starvation level.

In 1989 a military coup brought a new regime to power which has sought to maintain the status quo over implementation of the *shari'ah* whilst abolishing democracy and attempting to restore order.

8.0 EAST AFRICA

(Somalia, Djibouti and the Indian Ocean Islands)

Total population: 8 million
Muslim population: 95%
Dominant Sect: Sunni-Shafi

Islam in East Africa is older than in the African interior. It was founded by small enclaves of Arab merchants shortly after the death of Muhammad but was never able to penetrate beyond a thin coastal strip because of the power of the ancient Christian Abyssinian Empire (now reduced to the modern state of Ethiopia).

Instead Islam spread down a series of merchant towns on the east coast of the continent such as Dar es-Salam (in modern Tanzania), and onwards to hundreds of tiny islands in the Indian Ocean. Islam in this region is almost entirely of the Sunni Shafi variety – the traditionalist law school most closely associated with the merchant class of the Abbasid Empire during its Golden Age.

The only major East African country to have a Muslim majority is Somalia, a coastal strip bordering Ethiopia in the Horn of Africa. In the countries to the south, all of which have large amounts of inland territory, the coastal Muslims form a minority.

As in other regions where Islam has come into contact with heterodox foreign influences, the Sufi Orders are important and widespread. In Somalia, for example, rival tribes are these days identified mainly by the Sufi Orders to which they belong.

8.1 SOMALIA

Two of the three largest ancient Arab cities – Mogadishu and Djibouti – are found on the Somalian coast. Djibouti now forms a separate city state. The third of these centres, Zanzibar, is in modern Tanzania, 800 km to the south.

From the 12th century onwards the Arab cities developed into independent Sultanates free from African rule. By the late 19th century Somalia had been divided between the Italian and British, with a French colony in the Sultanate of Djibouti in the north.

The independent Somalian Republic was proclaimed in 1960 while Djibouti remained under French administration until 1977 when it also became an independent republic.

In 1969 the head of the Somali armed forces, General Muhammad Siyad Barre, took power in a coup and dissolved the National Assembly, which had previously been dominated by the feuding chieftains affiliated to rival Sufi orders. Although Islam was declared the official state religion, *shari'ah* law was not introduced and the legal system continued to be modelled on European lines. The new junta was secular and Marxist in outlook and the administration of Islam was placed under state-directed Spiritual Boards similar to the ones which administer the religion in the Muslim Soviet Republics.

Barre espoused a version of Islamic socialism similar to that found in Algeria. He also moved the country firmly into the Soviet orbit by accepting large scale military and economic aid. In 1975, prompted by a law granting formal equality to women, the feuding chieftains united against him and rebelled in the name of Islam.

The revolt had a tribal as well as a political dimension. It was easily crushed with Soviet military help and Barre, himself the head of the third largest tribe in the country, was able to establish himself as unchallenged tribal leader by executing the ten most important rival chiefs.

In 1977 he invaded neighbouring Ethiopia, claiming the province of Ogaden belonged to his tribe and therefore to his country. When the Soviet Union refused to help him he moved to the Western camp and accepted French military aid. The Soviet Union backed the new Marxist leadership in Ethiopia, which repulsed the Somali invasion with the help of Cuban forces.

In 1986 the Soviets finally engineered a settlement, forcing Barre to accept Ethiopia's borders. He continues, however, to support secessionist guerillas in the Ogaden. The 1986 settlement was a military defeat for him which may encourage what remains of the tribal opposition to challenge his rule once again.

For the time being, however, his position looks secure. The economic crisis in Somalia is less severe than in the rest of Africa thanks to generous interest-free Soviet aid during the 1970s. As East-West relations improve and the Soviet Union attempts to reform its economy, the level of aid is likely to fall off, seriously threatening Barre's position for the first time in 20 years.

8.2 DJIBOUTI

The Republic of Djibouti consists of the ancient Arab fortress town of Djibouti and a tiny strip of adjacent coastline. Since independence 4,000 French troops have remained to guard it against possible invasion from both Somalia and Ethiopia.

The Republic's politics are dominated by two main clans – the Muslim Somalian Issas and the Muslim Ethiopian Afars. Neither clan favours union with its respective homeland. The Somali Issas are a minority tribe in Somalia itself and hostile to Barre; the Afars are likewise fearful of becoming a minority in Christian Ethiopia.

The two tribes have thus been forced together to defend Djibouti and now carve up political power between them.

The President, Hassan Gouled Aptidon, is an Issa, but he has made sure that a fair share of government posts have gone to the Afars, including the Prime Ministership.

8.3 THE INDIAN OCEAN ISLANDS

All these islands have sizeable Muslim communities founded by merchants who converted the population. They tend to have Arab Muslim aristocracies, descended from the original traders and explorers, and indigenous Bantu-related lower classes who converted to Islam much later.

Generally the smaller the island the more complete was the conversion, and Muslims of all classes speak Swahili, the East African Arab-African trading language.

Comoros Islands

This former French colony was declared an Islamic Republic in

1975 by President Ahmad Abdullah. But within a month he was overthrown by a Maoist-type secularising movement, before later regaining control with the aid of the French.

Abdullah re-declared the Islamic Republic in 1978 and with the support of French mercenaries and the ruling Arab clans has tightened his grip, surviving periodic assassination attempts, and turning himself into a Muslim Sultan on the classic Arab Imperial model. The *shari'ah* is enforced by a seven member supreme court which can, however, be overruled by him.

Zanzibar

The island of Zanzibar and the associated mainland port of Dar es-Salam are ancient centres of Muslim and Arab civilisation. The island is currently federated with the Republic of Tanzania. Zanzibar is almost entirely Muslim and much wealthier than the Christian and pagan African mainland.

Generally the union of these two very different countries has been surprisingly successful. The current President of Tanzania, Ndugu Ali Hassan Mwinyi, is a Zanzibar Muslim.

The Maldive Islands

This chain of two hundred islands, scattered across eight hundred kilometres of Indian Ocean, were ruled by a Muslim Sultan for 700 years before the British placed the Maldives under joint British and Hindu-Buddhist rule from Sri Lanka.

The islands have now reverted to a Sultanate-type of rule with a series of Presidents and Prime Ministers drawn entirely from the traditional Arab ruling class. The *shari'ah* is enforced but the penal regime is liberal and women have many formal civil rights.

The majority of the islands remain extremely orthodox Muslim, and Islam dominates everyday life. The islands, which are extremely beautiful, have been developed as a tourist destination, but tourists are strictly segregated and allowed little contact with the islanders.

The Laccadive Islands

The Laccadive Muslims are a stranded community, arbitrarily incorporated into the state of India in 1948 and constituted as

Union Territory in 1956. The small population is packed on to the habitable surface at a density of 1,300 per sq km. The population is entirely Muslim.

9.0 THE CAUCASUS AND VOLGA REGION

(Azerbaijan, the Tartar and Checo-Ingush regions of the USSR)

Total population: 12 million
Muslim population: 55%
Dominant Sects: Twelver Shi'i
　　　　　　　　Sunni-Shafi

There are an estimated 40 million Muslims in the USSR as a whole, comprising about 12% of the total population and forming the largest religious minority.

Soviet Muslims are divided into three main groups. The largest, numbering about 20m, is the Turkic Muslims of central Asia (see – 10.0 Transoxia and China). The other two, which are both much smaller, are the Azeris of the Caucasus region and the Tartars, a large minority in the Volga valley.

The history of the Caucasus and Volga regions, which border each other, is intertwined with two thousand years of war and continuous migration by tribal peoples from the east. The area has been ruled at various times by an extraordinary collection of Armenian and Byzantine Christians, Jewish Khazar Khans, Pagan and Islamic Bulgar Kings, Pagan Persians, Mongol Khans, Ottoman Sultans, Tartar chieftains, Sufi saint-princes, Ukrainian Cossacks, Russian Tzars, German Nazis and Soviet Communists. As a result the region is a dense patchwork of ethnically and linguistically distinct Christian and Islamic peoples. They are organised firstly into four Soviet Republics and then 13 autonomous areas within them. The total number of nationalities and sub-linguistic groups in estimated at over fifty. About half of the population in the region as a whole is Muslim. But Muslims only form the clear majority in Azerbaijan. The Azerbaijani, or Azeri, Muslims belong to the Shi'i Ithna ('Twelver') sect.

The rest of the Muslims in the region are Sunnis and are only slightly in the minority in the Tartar, Dagestan, Checho-Ingush and Kalmyk Autonomous Republics – countries which form a chain of historically Muslim lands down the length of the Volga Valley from Kazan in the north to the Caspian and Black Seas in the south.

Muslims lost their majority status in the Volga region after World War Two, partly because of increasing settlement by ethnic Russians and Ukrainians and partly because of mass deportation of the indigenous populations to central Asia (particularly the Tartars and Ingush). They may, however, now be moving back into the majority as the Muslim birth rate is higher than that of the Europeans.

9.1 Azerbaijan

Of all the Muslim, and former Muslim, lands of the Volga and Caucasus, Azerbaijan is of the greatest strategic and economic importance to the USSR. Most of the Soviet Union's oilfields are within it and it is rich in other minerals. Over a third of the population is directly involved in heavy industry, making it one of the most heavily industrialised and technically advanced countries in the Islamic world.

Azerbaijan forms the Soviet border with Iran and there is a large Azeri minority in the north of Iran. Soviet and Iranian Azeris are directly related, speak the same language and subscribe to the same Islamic sect – Ithna 'Twelver' Shi'ism, dominant in Iran as a whole.

In theory, Azeri Muslims are subject to the religious authority of the Shi'i Ayatollahs of the *ulama* in Tehran. But the federal Soviet government has established a local Shi'i hierarchy, the Muslim Spiritual Board of Transcaucasia under the leadership of the Shayk al-Islami.

The Russian Empire conquered the region in the early 19th century. The Imperial administration attempted to introduce backward Ottoman Sunni Islam by placing Imams imported from Balkan territories captured from the Ottoman Empire. However, this tactic backfired. Sunni rule was deeply resented by the Shi'ah and became a focus for discontent. Furthermore, some of the Sunni Imams were members of clandestine Sufi Orders who, regardless of doctrinal differences, led Azeri rebellions against the Russians.

The Naqshbandi Sufi Order provided the backbone for a guerilla movement based in the Caucasus mountains, and therefore known as the Mountaineer Movement. The mountains remained outside Russian control until 1859, when the local leader of the order, Muhammad Sham'ail, was captured and executed. Many of the Naqshbandi were deported to Siberia and central Asia where they unsuccessfully attempted a fundamentalist reformation and also founded the guerilla movement in Transoxia known as the *Basmachi* (Bandits).

The Naqshbandi were replaced in the forefront of the anti-Russian movement by the Qadiriyah Sufis, who originated in Persia. Following the execution of Sham'ail the Qadiriyah declared a military *jihad* against the Russians.

Meanwhile in 1878 the Ingush Muslims of the Volga had declared their own anti-Russian *jihad* through full scale revolt which the Russians ruthlessly crushed, executing hundreds of village leaders and transporting hundreds to Siberia and central Asia.

The events of 1878 turned many Ingush and Chechos into fanatical anti-Russian nationalists and they remained in a continuous state of revolt until the 1940s when the bulk of the population, about two million people, was transported to central Asia by Stalin.

With the collapse of the Russian Empire in 1917 the Qadiriyah rose in open revolt in Azerbaijan and the Volga where, as the Mussavat (Tartar Nationalist) Party, they dominated the Baku Soviet (revolutionary national committee). By 1920 the Red Army had occupied Azerbaijan and the neighbouring Christian republics of Armenia and Georgia in the name of defending them against Kemal Ataturk's new Turkish national army which occupied part of Armenia and was threatening Azerbaijan.

The Red Army backed successful coups by Bolshevik minorities in the Soviets of each of the three Republics, securing their federation as the Transcaucasian Socialist Federal Soviet Republic (TSFSR) in 1922. The TSFSR then federated with the Ukrainian and Russian Soviet Republics in the same year to form the Union of Soviet Socialist Republics (USSR).

Whilst Azerbaijan remained passive, there were major Sufi-inspired revolts in the Kazan area throughout the 1920s and '30s. During World War Two the Naqshbandi sided with the German invaders, helping recruit Tartars, Ingushi and Azeris into paramilitary SS 'punishment squads' and regular Waffen-SS units. Anti-semitism flared, especially amongst the Tartars and Ingush (whose conversion to Islam had been secured by the Qadiriyah on the basis of racial hatred of the Russians and Jews), and lower Volga Muslims played an important role in the Nazi 'final solution' in the area.

After the decisive battle of Stalingrad the Red Army regained control of the Volga and Azerbaijan regions and punished the collaborators severely. In 1941 two million Ingush – over half the total population – were transported to the Muslim territories of Soviet central Asia.

Hundreds of thousands of Tartars were likewise transported or executed. The Tartar and Ingush Autonomous Republics still exist but now have Russian majority populations. Islam as a publicly practised religion has all but ceased to exist.

The Soviet government also established the (Sunni) Muslim Spiritual Boards of Dagestan and the Northern Caucasus, and the separate (Shi'ah) Muslim Spiritual Board of Transcaucasia (Azerbaijan). The aim of both boards was to purge Volgan and Azeri Islam of pro-Nazi, anti-Jewish teaching and replace the anti-Russian Sufi Orders.

The Boards have substantial powers and state funds and require that Muslim clerics register with them before they can lead prayers in mosques or administer funeral rites. They also print the Qur'an and other religious publications and dispense grants for the training of clerics in conjunction with the state education system. The Sufi-based religious training colleges have been closed. Clerics are now trained in general institutes of education and must complete state-approved courses.

Public worship has declined markedly since the war – a trend well established throughout the developed world – and many mosques have closed, further reducing demand for clerics.

Pilgrimage to Mecca (*hajj*) poses particular problems for Soviet Muslims. *Hajj* is an obligation on all Muslims who are physically able to take part but in practice it is difficult to get permission to leave the country. The obligation to take part in *hajj* ensures that the Muslims remain passive in the hope they will get permission.

The most serious threat to stability is ethnic rivalries between the patchwork of autonomous ethnic regions and Republics. The boundaries of ethnic areas enclose the heartland of each linguistic group, but may contain towns and areas belonging to ethnic neighbours.

Within Azerbaijan, for example, there are 4,500 sq kms of solidly Christian Armenian territory constituted as the Autonomous Region of Nagorno-Karabakh. In 1988 and 1989 there was serious rioting by the Christian Armenians of Nagorno-Karabakh demanding elevation to the status of a full republic and the secession of the majority Muslim territory dividing it from the rest of Armenia. The Azeri minority in the region, about 20% of the total population, rioted for full incorporation into Azerbaijan and federal troops have been deployed to stop the fighting.

The Nagorno-Karabakh dispute has still not been settled and many similar ones smoulder, especially in Christian Georgia where a nationalist movement has developed in the last few years and major demonstrations have taken place. In Azerbaijan the sense of nationhood is inextricably linked to the country's Islamic history, so any Azeri or Tartar nationalist reaction to the increasingly vocal nationalism of Armenia and Georgia would almost certainly involve an Islamic revival to some degree.

An independent Azerbaijan would be one of the richest countries in the world, with oil reserves comparable to the Gulf States but a population just half the size of Saudi Arabia. With recent developments this seems to have moved from being a remote to a merely unlikely possibility.

Whether an independent Azerbaijan would follow the path of the Islamic Revolution chosen by its southern neighbour Iran is an open question. Much will depend on whether the sharp decline in Azeri religious observance is, as the Soviet government maintains, the result of greater education and social welfare, or whether it is the result of repression.

10.0 TRANSOXIA AND CHINA

(Uzbekistan, Kazakstan, Turkmenia, Tadjikstan, Kirzighia and Xinjiang)

Total population: 60 million
Muslim population: 65%
Dominant Sect: Sunni-Hanafi

The Turkic peoples of Transoxia are directly related to the Muslim populations of modern Turkey and the Balkans three thousand kilometres to the west − areas settled by Turkic tribes migrating westwards, eventually founding the Ottoman Empire. They are also indirectly related to the Muslims of Afghanistan, India and Pakistan whose Mongol ancestors they intermingled with in the Middle Ages.

Today the Muslims of central Asia are the most remote of the major Islamic communities. For centuries they were cut off from the Islamic heartlands of north Arabia by the simple facts of geography as well as pagan invasions from the east, and in this century by Communist states which have, in addition, kept the faithful tightly controlled.

They are amongst the most secularised Muslims in the world, the result of very high educational standards, relatively high living standards and eighty years of secularising, atheist Communist propaganda.

Islam was originally founded in Transoxia in 649 AD when 'Uthman, the third Caliph, crossed the river Oxus and began the rapid conversion of the Turkic peoples of 'Transoxia' to Islam. For 500 years Transoxian Turkic Islamic civilisation flourished under benign Abbasid overlordship, eventually pushing even further east to establish Islam in the northern Chinese region of Xinjiang.

In 1219 Genghis Khan's pagan Mongol Horde captured Transoxia and destroyed much of the original Abbasid civilisation. But by 1300 the Mongols had converted to Islam and in 1360 the Mongol Khan Tamberlaine established his capital in the Transoxian city of Samarkand.

Tamberlaine's 'Islamic' Horde, made up of Mongols and the indigenous Turks, quickly conquered the whole of central Asia and European Russia as far as the borders of modern Poland in the west, and China in the east. The ancient Russian cities of Kiev and Moscow both came under Muslim rule.

In the following centuries Tamberlaine's empire slowly disintegrated. The eastern part (Xinjiang) came under Chinese rule and the western part (the Volga region and Transoxia) under Russian. Thereafter Transoxian and Chinese Islam developed separately. Russian colonisation of the Islamic lands started in the 1720s with the capture of Azerbaijan in the Caucasus and the steady acquisition of the former Tartar territories in the Volga and southern Ukrainian regions from the declining Ottoman Empire.

Colonisation of Transoxia did not begin until the mid-19th century, but when it did it was achieved quickly. Kazakstan was incorporated into the Empire in 1854, followed by Turkmenia (1864), Uzbekistan (1868), Tadjikstan (1884) and Kirzighia (1895).

Under Russian rule the Muslims of Transoxian cities such as Samarkand and Tashkent were ghettoised. Muslims were not regarded as citizens but as subject colonials with no rights and were excluded from the army and police, which remained Russian or Cossack. The Russians, whilst permitting freedom of worship in the mosques, persecuted leaders of the various Islamic modernising movements of the time.

They also backed the most arcane and backward Ottoman Sunni-type trends which preached a fatalistic acceptance of rule by any power, regardless of religion, so long as the basic rules of the *ibadah* (prayer, fasting, etc) were not flouted. The only organised resistance came from Sufi orders which had preserved Transoxian Islam under pagan Mongol rule 700 years previously and now launched an intermittent guerilla war against the Russians.

The Kazakstan Soviet Socialist Republic (SSR) was established in 1920 and the Turkmenistan SSR in 1924. Kirzighia and Tadjikstan were, however, directly annexed to the territory of the

Russian Federal SSR. The Sunni establishment accepted Bolshevik rule as easily as they had accepted Russian rule, with many Sunni clerics becoming Communist Party secretaries, but the Sufi *Basmachi* rebels (from the Uzbek word 'bandit'), provoked by the introduction of atheist secular education in schools and proposals to give Muslim women civil rights for the first time, resumed their guerilla war.

The Basmachi fought bravely and viciously. But they had little support amongst the majority of the Muslim population and were easily defeated by the Red Army, ceasing to be an effective military force by 1928.

Meanwhile the central Asian republics enjoyed a national renaissance in the 1920s and the population benefited greatly from the break-up of the old feudal land-owning system and a continuous series of literacy drives. Hundreds of native languages were revived and recorded for the first time and Arabic and Russian Cyrillic script abolished in favour of the more flexible Roman alphabet. But in the 1930s this all ended when the republics were subjected to the same Stalinist terror as the rest of the Soviet Union.

In the 1920s the Communist Party had emphasised the ideological points of contact between Marxism and Islam – of which there are many. But under Stalin in the '30s all religion was denounced as backward and Islam, in addition, was said to be worse by being 'foreign'. Sufi institutions were closed as part of a campaign to root out fictitious Basmachi threats and British agents. Separate Muslim schools were abolished and religious endowments, used for missionary work, were confiscated.

Devout Muslims were denounced as fanatics, religious dress was discouraged and in the mood of terror many Muslims began to pray in private, causing the closure of many mosques. Islam declined to the status of a religion of private conscience, as in Turkey, and Russification in the name of emergency industrialisation resumed. In 1940 Cyrillic script was re-introduced and native languages downgraded in the education system.

The mood of terror increased during World War Two when many Tartar and Azeri Muslims in the territories far to the west of Transoxia collaborated on a large scale with the Germans, forming their own anti-Soviet units under German command. Partly in response to this, Stalin further tightened the Communist state's grip on Islam with the establishment of the Muslim Spiritual Board of Central Asia in 1943. The Board, which still administers Soviet Sunni Islam today, was given considerable state funds, powers of patronage and lavish headquarters in Tashkent. As in Azerbaijan Muslim clerics are required to register with the Board and only registered clerics may lead prayers in mosques or perform funeral rites.

In addition the Board controls the two *madrasahs* (Sufi centres of religious learning) expropriated in the 1930s and now used for the training of conventional Sunni clerics in Hanafi Islam (the official religion of the Ottoman Empire). The Board is also responsible for the upkeep of mosques. Those with obvious tourist potential, such as the great mosque of Samarkand, have been renovated, but the rest allowed to fall derelict. The number of functioning mosques in Transoxia is now estimated at less than 200.

Islam's decline is not only the result of state pressure but also of high levels of literacy and education. The tendency of religions of all types to decline in educated, technical societies is well established and central Asia in no exception. Central Asian Muslims are, on average, the best educated, best housed and healthiest in the world. Average incomes are also high by the standards of the Muslim world, probably the highest excluding those Muslim countries with the artificial and temporary benefit of oil exports. In addition, women have equal social status guaranteed by law and play a full part in the professions. There is also a coherent system of criminal justice and a low crime rate.

Literacy in central Asia is almost total. There are 150 Uzbek language newspapers alone, with official circulations totalling 5.5m. Uzbekistan has one doctor for every 350 people and one university or polytechnic level teacher for every 500 people. This compares with ratios of 1/8,300 for doctors and 1/6,500 for university places in neighbouring Afghanistan and 1/2,500 for doctors and 1/2,000 for university places in Pakistan.

Despite complaints about the relatively backward position of central Asia within the USSR, there is little evidence that the Muslims of central Asia wish to trade all this for the poverty and backward social life which they see in the nearby Islamic Republic of Pakistan. However there have been occasional outbursts of protest from Sunni Muslims in recent years when religious sensibilities have been offended by the state. In 1988 there were riots, for example, when Muslim victims of the Tadjikstan earthquake were buried in mass graves without due observance of Muslim funeral rites.

229

The main destabilising factor in central Asia is inter-communal strife between the different Turkic nations. The borders of the central Asian republics have been re-drawn several times since 1917 and there is continuing discontent with Uzbeks claiming Turkmenian land, and vice versa. These problems are further aggravated by the growing presence of Mongol Muslim immigrants from former Tartar territories in the Volga valley, hundreds of kilometres to the west.

This immigrant group comprises about two million Tartars from the Volga valley and about 1 million Crimean Tartars and Volga Chechen and Ingush Mongols who were forcibly deported east because they had collaborated extensively with the Germans during the Second World War. In recent years there have been serious clashes between these groups and the indigenous population.

The current Soviet reform programmes of *perestroika* and *glasnost* have already exposed large-scale corruption and nepotism within the Republics and this may become the focus for discontent in the future. The most serious medium-term problem for central Asia is the threat of the introduction of free market economics, which would expose them to international competition for the first time.

Isolation from the world's main consumer markets and economic status as primary and agricultural producers would no doubt bring a sharp drop in incomes (as experienced in China following similar reforms). In the longer term, disintegration of the USSR would mean the loss of superpower status for the central Asian Republics and expose them to military danger from Transoxia's historic enemy – China.

Other possible military threats come from fundamentalist Iran, where right-wing nationalists believe Transoxia is the historic property of greater Persia, anti-Communist Pakistan – heavily armed by the United States – and possibly the Mujahideen, who may extend their *jihad* into the region if they triumph in Afghanistan.

10.1 Xinjiang

There is a substantial Muslim minority spread throughout China, but Muslims predominate only in the north western province of Xinjiang, bordered by Muslim Transoxia to the west and Buddhist

Mongolia and Tibet to the north and south. Xinjiang is vast, sparsely populated and has a very low level of economic development, even by Chinese standards.

The first Muslims to arrive in Xinjiang were merchants from the Abbasid Persian Empire along the Silk Road through Transoxia. The growth of Muslim influence followed the same pattern as other areas remote from Islam's north Arabian heartlands. Merchants first formed themselves into autonomous settlements under local Chinese rulers and steadily converted local people. When the Muslim community was well established Sufi missionaries arrived from Baghdad and, with their mastery of science and medicine, become advisers to the courts of local pagan or Confucian Chinese chieftains.

The Chinese, reaching the height of their power under the Tang Dynasty at the time the first Muslim communities were formed, appear to have had no objection to this alien presence, regarding the Muslims as people of inferior race and culture who would eventually be assimilated.

Islam's great advance in China came with the fall of the Tang Dynasty and the conquest of northern China by the Mongol Horde. When the pagan Kublai Khan ('Khan of the East') took power in China he called upon his brother Halagu Ill-Khan ('Khan of the West') to supply thousands of literate Muslims from the territories of the conquered Persian Empire to administer China on his behalf.

From the 15th century onwards the ethnically Chinese Muslim converts in Xinjiang, known as the Hui, outnumbered the ethnically Turkic and Persian trading community and Mongol administrative class. The first settlers have been assimilated and are no longer ethnically distinct, but in modern Xinjiang there are Muslims in ethnic minority tribes such as the Turkic Tadjiks and Uighurs, who migrated east from Transoxia to escape Russian expansion in the 19th century.

With the fall of the Chinese Manchu Dynasty in 1911 Xinjiang gained autonomy under the rule of local warlords – often doubling as Sunni Imams. The local warlord, Yang Tseng-hsin, was an enlightened ruler who reduced taxation, allowed full religious freedom, and ended persecution of the minority Uighurs and Tadjiks by the majority Hui. After the Bolshevik revolution he developed relations with the new Muslim Soviet Republics of Transoxia as a further counterbalance to central Chinese influence.

The warlords who ruled after Yang's death, however, were less supportive of Islam, discouraging religious practice, resuming persecution of the Tadjiks and Uighurs, and attempting to assimilate the Hui into the dominant Han Chinese ethnic group. There were numerous revolts amongst the Muslims, especially by the Uighurs who, with Soviet backing, declared a fully independent Uighur Republic sympathetic to the Chinese Communists, who were entering the last phase of their successful civil war against the Nationalist government of Chi'ang Kai-Chek.

With the proclamation of the Communist People's Republic of China in 1949, Beijing imposed its authority over Xinjiang for the first time since 1911. Muslims were granted a degree of religious freedom and Xinjiang given limited self-government as the Xinjiang-Uighur Autonomous Region (later Republic). Imam Saifudin, an Uighur, became governor with Communist Party support. At the same time the Communist government established the Chinese Islamic Association, which was given funds to renovate mosques, print copies of the Qur'an and supervise the Muslim clergy.

Between 1966 and 1976 – the period of government-inspired atheist-Communist fanaticism which became known as the Cultural Revolution, gangs of Communist teenagers – the Red Guards – arrived in Xinjiang from other parts of China to interrupt prayer meetings, attack Imams with clubs and vandalise mosques.

Muslims who continued to worship did so in secret and the mosques which had not been actually destroyed by the Red Guard fell into disrepair. The Chinese Islamic Association ceased to print the Qur'an and delivered atheist tracts to the Imams, who were expected to distribute them to the faithful. Many thousands of Muslims, especially of Turkic ethnic minorities, fled to the relatively liberal religious regime of Transoxia to the west. Others fought back and there were serious riots and clashes between Muslims and Red Guards in cities such as Kashgar, Urumchi and Khotan.

There is little doubt that the Chinese leadership would like to destroy Islam in China or turn it into a tourist curio, just as it has ruthlessly dealt with Buddhism in Tibet. Whilst the Chinese have felt under few constraints in dealing with the Tibetans, the Muslims of Xinjiang are protected to some degree by Chinese foreign policy, which aims at leadership of the 'second world' of post-colonial countries against the USA and the USSR. Many 'second world' countries are Islamic and China has therefore developed military and diplomatic relations with several, especially Pakistan and – in the early 1970s – South Yemen.

Since the expulsion of the Maoists from the central government Beijing has tried to make amends by resuming publication of the Qur'an, reducing anti-religious propaganda and restoring desecrated mosques and Muslim monuments, such as 9th century stone tablets which record passages from the Qur'an and give instructions for building mosques.

The Chinese regime's Islamic Association attempts to gain the cooperation of Muslims but the organisation was discredited during the Cultural Revolution and has still not recovered, while continuing Muslim resentment over the aftermath of the Cultural Revolution occasionally breaks out into mass demonstrations in favour of greater national independence. Muslim demonstrations took place in Beijing in the early part of 1989 a few months before the wider 'Democracy Movement' exploded onto the streets.

11.0 SUMMARY

There are at least 45 nations in the world where Muslims form the undisputed majority, and in most of these nations the majority is overwhelming. Some Muslim sources include the three million exiled Palestinians and the Indian-occupied state of Kashmir as Muslim nations and add them to the total.

The total number of Muslims living outside Muslim majority countries is estimated at about 100 million and the vast majority of these are to be found in Nigeria, the Philippines or the Balkans where the European powers reversed the process of Islamisation in the 17th and 18th centuries before it was completed.

Some Muslim sources claim that Nigeria and several other central African nations have a Muslim majority, but this is not accepted by the countries concerned. Outside these areas the number of 'minority' Muslims never reaches much more than a few percent and communities are usually based on immigrants or guest-workers as in Britain, France and West Germany.

11.1 INDONESIA (*Republic of Indonesia/Republik Indonesia*)

Capital:	Jakarta
Population:	173m
Muslim pop:	80%
GNP per cap:	$560
Sects:	Overwhelmingly Sunni-Shafi. Sufis influential.
Islam Founded:	C16th – 17th by traders from Mogul India.

Ind. since:	17th August 1945 (Netherlands).
Constitution:	Secular unitary republic (limited democracy).
Legal system:	European secular (Dutch model). *Shari'ah* applied in religious courts only.
Int. rel'tns:	Pro-Western (ASEAN member)
Fund. Movnts:	Santari (religious councils) oppose further secularisation. Islamic opposition institutionalised and confined within the state-controlled Development Unity Party.
Comment:	Islam is politically manipulated by the regime as a focus of national unity for the diverse collection of islands.

11.2 BANGLADESH (*People's Republic of Bangladesh*)

Capital:	Dhaka
Population:	104m
Muslim pop:	80%
GNP per cap:	$130
Sects:	Sunni-Hanafi (95%), Shi'i Ismailite minority. Sufi influence widespread.
Islam Founded:	1331 local independent Deccan Sultanate. C16th Delhi rule re-imposed by Mogul Emperors until C19th.
Ind. since:	December 1st 1971 (Islamic Republic of Pakistan).
Constitution:	Sovereign republic.
Legal system:	Amended 1977 constitution established supreme court guided by 'absolute trust and faith in almighty Allah' which can overturn 'non-Islamic' judgements in lower courts.
Int. rel'tns:	Non-aligned.
Fund. Movnts:	A campaign for further Islamisation is being mounted by political parties and groups such as the Muslim Brotherhood.
Summary:	Bangladeshi Islam is tolerant and has absorbed a great deal of Hindu culture.

11.3 PAKISTAN (*Islamic Republic of Pakistan*)

Capital:	Islamabad
Population:	102.2m
Muslim pop:	95%
GNP per cap:	$390
Sects:	Sunni-Hanafi (80%), Shi'i (both Twelver and Isma'ilite). Small Ahmadiyah minority. Sufis tolerated.
Islam Founded:	711 'Umayyad Dynasty established rule from Damascus. C9th local rule by Turkic Sultanate of Delhi. Province of Indian Mogul Empire from C16th to C19th.
Ind. since:	14th August 1947 (British Empire).
Constitution:	Islamic republic since 1956. Parliament constitutionally obliged to further Islamisation.
Legal system:	Federal *shari'ah* court supervises secular-type lower courts and can overturn 'non-Islamic' laws and judgements. Both the federal and local courts operate *hadd* penal code for both Muslims and minorities.
Int. rel'tns:	Pro-Western (US bases. Sponsorship of Afghan rebels). Economically dependent on Saudi Arabia.
Fund. Movnts:	Extremist Ja'mat-i-Islami Party. Afghan rebels in border camps. Army-sponsored Islamisation campaign.
Summary:	Pakistan was the first modern nation created specifically to enshrine Islam as a political creed.

11.4 TURKEY (*Turkish National Republic/Turkiye Cümhuriyeti*)

Capital:	Ankara
Population:	50.67m
Muslim pop:	95%
GNP per cap:	$1,230
Sects:	Sunni-Hanafi (90%). Small Shi'i minority on eastern Iranian border. Sufi institutions abolished (1920s).

Islam Founded:	13th century by the Mongol-Persian Seljuk tribe. Turkic Ottoman rule from C14th (rule from Istanbul from 1453) until C20th.
Ind. since:	29th October 1923 (Ottoman Empire dissolved).
Constitution:	Sovereign secular republic. Limited democracy.
Legal system:	European secular (based on Italian model). Religious courts abolished in 1924. *Shari'ah* and *ibadah* have no legal validity.
Int. rel'tns:	Pro-Western (US bases). NATO. Seeks EEC membership.
Fund. Movnts:	Illegal and limited to small Shi'i minority. Islamic political parties and religious dress are banned.
Summary:	Islam in Turkey is declining and the country is one of the most secular in the Muslim world.

11.5 IRAN (*Islamic Republic of Iran/ Jomhori-e-Islami-e-Iran*)

Capital:	Tehran
Population:	49.86 m
Muslim pop:	99%
GNP per cap:	$2,160 (pre-revolutionary figure)
Sects:	Overwhelming majority are Twelver (Orthodox) Shi'i outside Kurdish (Sunni) ethnic territory of north west. Approx 3% of ethnic Persian-Azeri ethnic minority are Sunnis.
Islam Founded:	642 by 'Umar the second Caliph.
Ind. since:	1639 Eastern Persia (territory of modern Iran) independent from Ottoman Empire.
Constitution:	Islamic republic. Supreme legislative and judicial authority held by the *ulama* (council of wise men) who appoint a divinely guided *Imam* (supreme leader) as their spokesman. The *ulama* and Imam may overturn legislation proposed by the elected parliament.

Legal system:	The entire Shi'ite version of the *shari'ah* and *hadd* penal code is in force. 109 crimes for which *hadd* punishments such as decapitation, stoning to death and hand amputation are applicable.
Int. rel'tns:	Non-aligned and isolated.
Fund. Movnts:	Permanent revolutionary mobilisation of the Shi'ah population by the hierarchical clergy led by the *ulama*.
Summary:	Iran is the only major country where the Shi'ah form the overwhelming majority.

11.6 EGYPT (*Arab Republic of Egypt/Al-Jumhuriyat Misr al-Arabiya al-Egypt*)

Capital:	Cairo
Population:	49.28m
Muslim pop:	93%
GNP per cap:	$700
Sects:	Sunni-Hanafi (90%). Small Isma'ilite minority. Many Sufi foundations.
Islam Founded:	642 'Umayyads established rule from Damascus. (Destruction of previous Egyptian Christian Coptic civilisation). 969 local Fatimid Caliphs (sponsored Isma'ilite Shi'ah sects). Rule by Mameluke Sultans (1171-1517). Ottoman province (1517-1805).
Ind. since:	26th February 1928 (British Empire).
Constitution:	Sovereign secular republic. Limited democracy.
Legal system:	European secular (based on Anglo-Muhammadan model). *Shari'ah* has no legal validity. *Ibadah* enforced by private religious courts only.
Int. rel'tns:	Pro-Western. Expelled from Arab League (1981) for treaty with Israel. Dependent on Saudi Arabian and US aid.
Fund. Movnts:	Muslim Brotherhood originated in Egypt. Pro-Libyan terrorists include Islamic Jihad and Takfir wa'al Hijrah ('Repentance and Holy Flight' - murderers of Pres. Sadat).

	Muslim Brotherhood is influential in Wafd opposition party in parliament.
Summary:	Egyptian Islam is heterodox and Cairo is the main centre of the surviving Islamic culture of the Arabian Golden Age. In this century it has been the centre for modernising religious reform movements.

1.7 SUDAN (*Republic of Sudan/Al-Jamhuryat es-Sudan Al-Democratia*)

Capital:	Khartoum
Population:	25.5m
Muslim pop:	73% (mostly in north). 18% Animist, 6% Christian
GNP per cap:	$400
Sects:	Sunni-Maliki (75%), Ismailite Shi'i (20%).
Islam Founded:	c1000 by Muslim traders.
Ind. since:	1st January 1956 (Anglo-Egyptian administration).
Constitution:	Secular republic with *shari'ah* law.
Legal system:	Hybrid Islamic-European (Anglo-Muhammadan model). *Hadd* penal code enforced.
Int. rel'tns:	Firmly pro-Western since 1985 coup. Member of the Arab League Fund.
Fund. Movnts:	Islamisation campaign by small but influential Muslim Brotherhood is aimed at the consolidation of the *shari'ah* legal regime in the non-Muslim south of the country even at the cost of civil war and national disintegration.
Summary:	Islam is of the Maliki school and highly traditionalist.

11.8 MOROCCO (*Kingdom of the Maghreb/ al-Mamlaka al-Maghrebia*)

Capital:	Rabat
Population:	23 m

Muslim pop:	98%
GNP per cap:	$500
Sects:	Overwhelmingly Sunni-Maliki. Small groups of nomadic Bedouin Ibadites in the desert.
Islam Founded:	808 Fez conquered by the 'Umayyads.
Ind. since:	7th April 1956 (French Empire).
Constitution:	Constitutional monarchy, but King Hassan II retains right to dismiss parliament and is C-in-C of the armed forces and the supreme religious authority.
Legal system:	Hybrid Islamic-European (French model). *Ibadah* has enforceable legal status, though women may sue for divorce with the permission of the authorities.
Int. rel'tns:	Nominally non-aligned, member of the non-aligned movement, but in practice strongly pro-Western and pro-Saudi. At war with the Algerian-backed Polisario Liberation front in Western Sahara. Member of the Arab League.
Fund. Movnts:	'Islamic' opposition is suppressed but appears to be growing after destruction of secular opposition.
Summary:	Morocco is the ancient centre of Maliki traditionalism and hostility towards the heterodox Islam of Egypt and the Arab world.

11.9 ALGERIA (*Algerian Democratic People's Republic/al-Jumhuriyah al-Jazairiya ad-Dimuqratiya ash-Shabiya*)

Capital:	Algiers
Population:	22.6m
Muslim pop:	98%
GNP per cap:	$2,430
Sects:	85% Sunni-Maliki, 15% Ibadites and Sufi desert nomads.
Islam Founded:	699 'Umayyad conquest of Vandal Kingdom of Africa.

Ind. since:	25th September 1956 (French Empire).
Constitution:	Secular one-party republic under military dictatorship. Islam is the official state religion and socialism the official state ideology.
Legal system:	Hybrid Islamic-European (French model). Reformed *ibadah* is enforced (polygamy abolished). Islamic commercial courts enforce 'moral' contracts.
Int. rel'tns:	Non-aligned. Member of the Arab League.
Fund. Movnts:	Fundamentalist riots in 1982, inspired by groups allied to the Muslim Brotherhood.
Summary:	Algeria is the main centre for modern 'Islamic Socialism'.

11.10 UZBEKISTAN (*Uzbekistan Soviet Socialist Republic/Cumhuriyeti Ozebkiston Soviet Sotsialistik*)

Capital:	Tashkent
Population:	18 m
Muslim pop:	80% (est)
GNP per cap:	figures unavailable
Sects:	Sunni-Hanafi with very small Shi'i minorities and some Sufi and Isma'ilite missionary activity.
Islam Founded:	751 by conquering Abbasid armies from Persia.
Ind. since:	October 1917 (Russian Empire). Joined USSR 1925.
Constitution:	Secular one-party republic.
Legal system:	Soviet federal legal system. *Shari'ah* and *ibadah* have no legal validity.
Int. rel'tns:	Foreign policy directed at the federal Soviet level.
Fund. Movnts:	Fundamentalism is confined to the small and semi-clandestine Sufi orders, especially the Naqshbandi. The Sunni Uzbeks have little sympathy for Iranian Shi'ah fundamentalism.
Summary:	Uzbek Islam is moderate and highly secular and religious observance has declined throughout this century.

11.11 IRAQ (*The Republic of Iraq/al-Jumhouriya al-'Iraqia*)

Capital:	Baghdad
Population:	17.09m
Muslim pop:	95%
GNP per cap:	$2,140
Sects:	50% Sunni-Hanafi, 45% Twelver Shi'i, 5% other sects (Sufi orders, Shi'i Zaydis, Isma'ilites, etc).
Islam Founded:	C7th by the first Arabian Islamic Army.
Ind. since:	3rd October 1932 (British UN mandate administration).
Constitution:	Secular one-party republic under military dictatorship.
Legal system:	Hybrid Islamic-European (Anglo-Muhammadan model). All courts have *shari'ah* judges attached for trial of ibadah matters.
Int. rel'tns:	Non-aligned, but largely dependent on military aid from the USSR. Member of Arab League.
Fund. Movnts:	Unrest amongst the Shi'ah minority during the Iran-Iraq war.
Summary:	Sunni Islam is the focus for Arab nationalism against Iranian (Persian) Shi'ism.

11.12 MALAYSIA (*Federation of Malaysia*)

Capital:	Kuala Lumpur
Population:	16.2m
Muslim pop:	55%
GNP per cap:	$1,870
Sects:	Overwhelmingly Sunni-Shafi.
Islam Founded:	C16th by traders from Mogul India.
Ind. since:	16th September 1963 (Great Britain).
Constitution:	Federal monarchy. Islam recognised as state religion.
Legal system:	European secular (British model).
Int. rel'tns:	Pro-Western (ASEAN member).
Fund. Movnts:	No significant 'Islamising' movements.

Summary: Malaysian Islam is moderate and relatively
                    secular in outlook.

11.13 KAZAKSTAN (*Kazak Soviet Socialist Republic/Kazak Soviettik Sotsialistik Respublikasy*)

Capital:	Alma-Ata
Population:	16 m
Muslim pop:	60% (est)
GNP per cap:	figures unavailable
Sects:	Sunni-Hanafi with very small Shi'i minorities and some Sufi missionary activity.
Islam Founded:	751 by conquering Abbasid armies from Persia.
Ind. since:	October 1917 (Russian Empire). Joined USSR 1936.
Constitution:	Secular one-party republic.
Legal system:	Soviet federal legal system. *Shari'ah* and *ibadah* have no legal validity.
Int. rel'tns:	Foreign policy directed at the federal Soviet level.
Fund. Movnts:	Fundamentalism is confined to the small and semi-clandestine Sufi orders.
Summary:	Kazak Muslims are highly secularised and the republic contains the highest proportion of ethnic Russo-Ukrainians in central Asia.

11.14 AFGHANISTAN (*Democratic Republic of Afghanistan/Jamhuriat Democratek-e Afghani*)

Capital:	Kabul
Population:	15m (of which approx 5m are refugees)
Muslim pop:	98%
GNP per cap:	$250
Sects:	Sunni-Hanafi (90%), Twelver Shi'i (10%).
Islam Founded:	711 Conquest of the Hindu Kush by the 'Umayyads.
Ind. since:	1737 (Persia).
Constitution:	Secular republic under military dictatorship.

Legal system:	Secular (Soviet model). Lower courts use Sunni-Hanafi law where no new legislation has been enacted since the secularising revolution of 1978. *Hadd* penal code and aspects of the *ibadah* (eg denial of divorce) have been abolished.
Int. rel'tns:	Non-aligned. Dependent on USSR for economic and military aid.
Fund. Movnts:	Armed insurrection by alliance of fundamentalist groups supported by Pakistan, Iran, China and the USA.
Summary:	Islam in Afghanistan is highly traditionalist and linked to local tribalism and nationalism.

11.15 XINJIANG (*Autonomous Region of Xinjiang – People's Republic of China*)

Capital:	Ürümqi
Population:	13.44m
Muslim pop:	70% (est)
GNP per cap:	$250 (China average)
Sects:	Overwhelmingly Sunni-Hanafi.
Islam Founded:	c1250 by Mongol Khans.
Ind. since:	1911 (Manchu Empire) Autonomous status within PRC since 1955.
Constitution:	Autonomy with secular one-party republic.
Legal system:	Federal Chinese system. *Shari'ah* has limited legal validity but higher secular courts can overrule judgements.
Int. rel'tns:	Directed by central Chinese government.
Fund. Movnts:	Islamic opposition is suppressed. Recent demonstrations in Beijing for implementation of *shari'ah* in Muslim areas.
Summary:	The Muslims of Xinjiang form an ethnic as well as religious minority and have been repeatedly suppressed.

11.16 SAUDI ARABIA (*Kingdom of Saudi Arabia/ Al-Mamlaka al-'Arabiya as-Sa'udiyya*)

Capital:	Riyadh
Population:	11.52m
Muslim pop:	99%
GNP per cap:	$8,000
Sects:	Sunni-Hanbali (80%), Twelver Shi'i (15%), Zaydis and Bedouin Ibadites (5%)
Islam Founded:	Islam originated in Mecca and Medina 662.
Ind. since:	23rd September 1932 (British UN Mandate administration).
Constitution:	Absolute Islamic monarchy. No written constitution other than the Qur'an.
Legal system:	Entirely Islamic following the conservative Sunni-Hanbali school. *Hadd* penal code enforced.
Int. rel'tns:	Founder of the Arab League and World Muslim League. Militarily dependent on the USA. Declared official state of *jihad* (Holy War) against Israel in 1980.
Fund. Movnts:	The Saudi Arabian government is composed of descendants of the Wahhabis, the originators of modern Sunni fundamentalism.
Summary:	The Arabian peninsula was the cradle of Islam and a highly traditionalist version of the religion survives in the C20th hardly influenced by outside events.

11.17 SYRIA (*The Arab Republic of Syria/al-Jumhuriya al-Arabya as-Suriya*)

Capital:	Damascus
Population:	10.96m
Muslim pop:	80%
GNP per cap:	$2,000
Sects:	Sunni-Hanafi (75%), Twelver Shi'i (10%), Isma'ilites, Alawites (10%), Druze and Isma'ilite sub-sects (5%).
Islam Founded:	650 by 'Umar the Great.

Ind. since:	12th April 1946 (Anglo-French UN Mandate administration).
Constitution:	Secular one-party republic dominated by the Alawites.
Legal system:	Hybrid Islamic-European (French model). *Shari'ah* courts enforce the *ibadah*.
Int. rel'tns:	Non-aligned. Principal ally of the USSR in the Middle East. Member of the Arab League.
Fund. Movnts:	Internal dissent is illegal. Syria supports many fundamentalist terrorist groups in neighbouring Lebanon.
Summary:	Islam is manipulated as the focus of Syria nationalism in the war against Lebanon and continuing hostility against all other neighbouring states.

11.18 MALI (*Republic of Mali/République du Mali*)

Capital:	Bamako
Population:	8.73m
Muslim pop:	90%
GNP per cap:	$150
Sects:	Overwhelmingly Sunni-Maliki. Small numbers of nomadic Ibadites.
Islam Founded:	c1000 as the religion of the ruling Chieftain class. c1700 mass conversion of the population.
Ind since:	22nd September 1960 (Union of Senegal-Mali).
Constitution:	Secular one-party republic under joint military-civilian leadership.
Legal system:	Secular hybrid Islamic-European (French model).
Int. rel'tns:	Non-aligned.
Fund. Movnts:	All opposition is repressed and inactive.
Summary:	Islam is divided between the rigidly orthodox Maliki'ism of the northern Berbers and the magical 'African Islam' of the southern Negroes.

11.19 TUNISIA (*Republic of Tunisia/al-Jumhuriya at-Tunisiya*)

Capital:	Tunis
Population:	7.32m
Muslim pop:	90%
GNP per cap:	$1,250
Sects:	Overwhelmingly Sunni-Maliki. Small numbers of nomadic Ibadites.
Islam Founded:	698. 'Umayyad conquest of the Vandal kingdom of Africa-Carthage.
Ind. since:	20th March 1956 (French Empire).
Constitution:	Islam recognised as the state religion. Limited democracy with four official parties (all 'socialist').
Legal system:	Secular hybrid Islamic-European (French model). *Ibadah* enforced by *shari'ah* courts.
Int. rel'tns:	Non-aligned. Currently HQ for the PLO.
Fund. Movnts:	Considerable pressure for further Islamisation from urban-based fundamentalists. Growth of the Islamic Tendency Movement (linked to Muslim Brotherhood).
Summary:	Tunisian. Islam is more heterodox and Egyptian-influenced than that found in the neighbouring countries of North Africa.

11.20 AZERBAIJAN (*Azerbaijan Soviet Socialist Republic/Azarbaijchan Soviet Sotsialistik Respublikasy*)

Capital:	Baku
Population:	6.80m
Muslim pop:	78%
GNP per cap:	Figures unavailable
Sects:	Overwhelmingly Shi'i ithna ('Twelvers').
Islam Founded:	922 Conversion of the peoples of the Turkic Bulgar Kingdom.
Ind. since:	17th October (Russian Empire) joined USSR 1922 as part of the Transcaucasian Soviet Republic. Seceded from Transcaucasia to

form the Azerbaijani Soviet Republic. 1935-6. Joined the USSR as an autonomous republic in 1936.

Constitution:	Secular one-party republic.
Legal system:	Federal Soviet legal system. *Shari'ah* and *ibadah* have no legal validity.
Int. rel'tns:	Foreign policy directed at federal Soviet level.
Fund. Movnts:	All opposition parties, including Islamic opposition, are illegal. An Islamic-nationalist guerilla movement was sponsored by the Germans in the 1940s but was crushed in the 1950s.
Summary:	Although there is ethnic rivalry between Azerbaijan and neighbouring Christian Armenia, Islamic fundamentalism appears to play little role in the disturbances.

11.21 SENEGAL (*and The Gambia*) (*Republic of Senegal/République du Senegal*)

Capital:	Dakar
Population:	6.70m
Muslim pop:	91%
GNP per cap:	$360
Sects:	Overwhelmingly Sunni-Maliki.
Islam Founded:	c1000 by Muslim merchants from the Maghreb.
Ind. since:	22nd Aug 1960 (Federation of Mali).
Constitution:	Secular republic. Limited democracy.
Legal system:	Secular on the European (French) model.
Int. rel'tns:	Pro-Western, associate membership of the EEC.
Fund. Movnts:	No significant agitation.
Summary:	Senegalese Islam is highly influenced by both Sufi'ism and African mysticism.

11.22 NIGER (*Republic of Niger/République du Niger*)

Capital:	Niamey
Population:	6.60m
Muslim pop:	97%
GNP per cap:	$240
Sects:	Overwhelmingly Sunni-Maliki.
Islam Founded:	c1000 by Muslim merchants from the Maghreb.
Ind. since:	3rd August 1960.
Constitution:	Secular republic under military dictatorship.
Legal system:	Secular on European (French) model.
Int. rel'tns:	Pro-Western, associate member of the EEC.
Fund. Movnts:	Sufi networks, especially the Mooreves *tariqah* are highly influential.
Summary:	Islam is divided between official highly orthodox Maliki variety and local African mysticism.

11.23 NORTH and SOUTH YEMEN

Capital/Population:	North (Yemen Arab Republic) Sana'a, 6.53m South (People's Democratic Republic) Aden, 2.33m
Muslim pop:	99%
GNP per cap:	North – $ 510
	South – $ 500
Sects:	(Both): Shi'i Zaydis (59%), Sunni-Shafi (39%), desert Ibadites (2%).
Islam Founded:	625 by first Islamic Arab confederation.
Ind. since:	1937 (independent of rule by Saudi Arabia).
Constitution:	(Both): Formally secular republics under one-party rule. South Yemen is in addition a socialist country. In practice neither regime's rule extends to the tribal peoples of the interior who autonomously govern their affairs in line with ancient Arab custom based on enforcement of the *shari'ah*.
Legal system:	(Both): Shi'i version of the *ibadah* is enforced for personal and family matters.

Int. rel'tns:	North: Pro-Western. Member of the Arab League.
	South: Pro-Soviet with large Soviet Navy base at Aden. Sponsors Marxist Popular Front for the Liberation of Oman and the Gulf (PFLOAG) guerilla movement in several Gulf states.
Fund. Movnts:	(Both): Smouldering rebellion from the Zaydi tribes who favour full implementation of the *shari'ah* along Saudi Arabian lines.
Summary:	Yemeni Islam is ancient and highly traditionalist.

11.24 GUINEA (*Republic of Guinea/République de Guineé*)

Capital:	Conakry
Population:	6.33m
Muslim pop:	69%
GNP per cap:	$300
Sects:	Overwhelmingly Sunni-Maliki.
Islam Founded:	c1000 by Muslim merchants from the Maghreb.
Ind. since:	2nd October 1958 (French West Africa).
Constitution:	Secular republic under military dictatorship.
Legal system:	Secular on European (French) model. *Shari'ah* and *ibadah* have no legal validity.
Int. rel'tns:	Pro-Western. Associate member of the EEC.
Fund. Movnts:	No significant agitation.
Summary:	The only Muslim nation with an almost entirely Negro population many of whom have reverted to tribal religions which are only nominally Islamic.

11.25 SOMALIA (*Somalian People's Democratic Republic/Jamhuriyadda Dimugradiga Somaliya*)

Capital:	Mogadishu
Population:	6.11m
Muslim pop:	99%

GNP per cap:	$250
Sects:	Almost entirely Sunni-Shafi with strong Sufi influence. Zaydi Shi'i minority (about 10%).
Islam Founded:	C7th by Muslim settlers from the Arabian peninsula.
Ind. since:	1st July 1960 (Merger of British and Italian Protectorates).
Constitution:	One-party secular republic under military rule.
Legal system:	Hybrid Islamic-European (British model).
Int. rel'tns:	Somalia has moved away from its alliance with the USSR as a result of its war with Ethiopia.
Fund. Movnts:	All opposition is banned.
Summary:	Islam is divided into rival Sufi orders who compete for control of the country.

11.26 THE ARABIAN (GULF) STATES (*Kuwait, United Arab Emirates, Oman, Bahrain, Qatar*)

Capitals/ Populations:	Kuwait — Kuwait City, 1.77m
	UAE — Abu Dhabi, 1.77m
	Oman — Muscat, 1.20m
	Bahrain — Manama, 0.42m
	Qatar — Doba, 0.37m
Total pop:	5.53m (estimated 50% are guest workers).
Muslim pop:	91% (average).
GNP per cap:	Qatar — $22,940
	UAE — $19,270
	Bahrain — $11,708
	Kuwait — $11,510
	Oman — $7,080
Sects:	The Arabian Gulf states are overwhelmingly Sunni-Shafi or Sunni- Hanafi with small Shi'ah minorities. Bahrain and Kuwait have the largest Twelver Shi'i minorities and Oman has a tribal Shi'i Zaydi minority.
Islam Founded:	725 by the first Arab Islamic confederacy.
Ind. since:	Oman — 1744 (Portugese domination).
	Kuwait — 1961 (British Protectorate).

	UAE – 1971 (Abu Dahbi British Dependency).
	Bahrain – 1971 (British Protectorate).
	Qatar – 1971 (British Protectorate).
Constitution:	All the Arabian Gulf states are absolute monarchies. The UAE is a federation of Sultans each of whom has absolute power within his own territory.
Legal system:	In Oman and the Emirates the *shari'ah* and the monarch's word are the only source of law. Qatar has a hybrid system and *shari'ah* courts deal only with personal matters (*ibadah* and *mu'amalat*). Bahrain has a secular, European-type legal system (British model).
Int. rel'tns:	All the countries of the Gulf are pro-Western.
Fund. Movnts:	Islamic fundamentalism, in the form of conservative, Arabist versions of the *shari'ah* is the norm of government in the Gulf states. More radical fundamentalism, such as that practised in Libya and Iran, has little support except amongst the significant Shi'i minority. Radical opposition tends to come from secularists influenced by the PLO of the Iraqi Ba'th Party.
Summary:	The dominant type of Islam found in the Gulf is highly traditionalist and similar to that found in Saudi Arabia. Unlike in Saudi Arabia there are very large heterodox minorities, mainly Shi'ites.

11.27 CHAD (*Republic of Chad/République du Tchad*)

Capital:	N'Djamena
Population:	5.24m
Muslim pop:	55% (est. Many may in fact be followers of tribal cults).
GNP per cap:	$88
Sects:	Overwhelmingly Sunni-Maliki.
Islam Founded:	c1100 by Muslim merchants from the Maghreb.

Ind. since:	11th August 1960 (France).
Constitution:	Secular republic under military dictatorship.
Legal system:	Secular on the European (French) model.
Int. rel'tns:	Pro-Western (military and economic dependence on France).
Fund. Movnts:	No significant indigenous movements.
Summary:	Chad is in a state of constant civil war with power passing between secular, pro-French factions and 'Islamising' forces backed by Libya.

11.28 TADJIKSTAN (*Tadjik Soviet Socialist Republic/Respublikai Sovieth Sotsialistii Tojikiston*)

Capital:	Dushanbe
Population:	4.80m
Muslim pop:	80% (est)
GNP per cap:	figures unavailable.
Sects:	Sunni-Hanafi with Ithna Shi'ah minority.
Islam Founded:	751 by conquering Abbasid armies from Persia.
Ind. since:	October 1917 (Russian Empire). Joined USSR 1929.
Constitution:	Secular one-party republic.
Legal system:	Soviet federal legal system. *Shari'ah* and *ibadah* have no legal validity.
Int. rel'tns:	Foreign policy directed at the federal Soviet level.
Fund. Movnts:	All opposition, including Islamic parties, illegal.
Summary:	The Tadjiks are ethnically similar to the Iranians but are not Shi'ites.

11.29 KIRGHIZIA (*Kirghiz Soviet Socialist Republic/Kyrgyz Sovietik Sotsialistik Respublikasy*)

Capital:	Frunze
Population:	4.10 m
Muslim pop:	70%
GNP per cap:	figures unavailable

Sects:	Overwhelmingly Sunni-Hanafi.
Islam Founded:	751 by conquering Abbasid armies from Persia.
Ind. since:	October 1917 (Russian Empire). Joined USSR 1921.
Constitution:	Secular one-party republic.
Legal system:	Soviet federal legal system. *Shari'ah* and *ibadah* have no legal validity.
Int. rel'tns:	Foreign policy directed at the federal Soviet level.
Fund. Movnts:	No significant movements.
Summary:	Kirghizia is the most remote of the central Asian Republics and is home to a large number of Muslim Tartar exiles from the Volga region.

11.30 LIBYA (*The State of the Masses of the Democratic, Socialist, Arab Muslim Community of Libya/Al-Jamahiriya Al-Arabiya Al-Libiya Al-Shabiya Al-Ishtirakiya Al-Uzma*)

Capital:	Tripoli
Population:	3.96m
Muslim pop:	95%
GNP per cap:	$7,180
Sects:	Sunni-Maliki. About one third of the population are members of the extreme Maliki Sanusi sect.
Islam Founded:	647 by Uthman 'Umayyad.
Ind. since:	24th December 1951 (British-French mandate).
Constitution:	Jamahiriya 'state of the masses' — officially the Libyan state has been abolished and the affairs of the people are governed by local armed revolutionary committees.
Legal system:	*Shari'ah* personal law (*mu'amalat*) and *ibadah* are enforced by autonomous local religious courts (no right of appeal to higher courts).
Int. rel'tns:	Non-aligned, but effectively allied with the USSR on which Libya is dependent for the upkeep of its large armed forces.

| Fund. Movnts: | The Jamahiriya system attempts to keep the Muslim population in a permanent state of mobilisation in the interests of defending the official 'Green' ideology which is a mixture of Islam and extreme socialism (Maoist influence). |
| Summary: | Libyan Islam is based on the traditionalist Maliki school overlaid with the extremism of the secretive Sanusi Mahdist sect. |

11.31 TURKMENIA (*Turkmenistan Soviet Socialist Republic/Tiutkmenostan Soviet Sotsialistik Respublikasy*)

Capital:	Ashkabad
Population:	3.40m
Muslim pop:	70% (est)
GNP per cap:	figures unavailable
Sects:	Overwhelmingly Sunni-Hanafi.
Islam Founded:	751 by conquering Abbasid armies from Persia.
Ind. since:	October 1917 (Russian Empire). Joined USSR 1925.
Constitution:	Secular one-party republic.
Legal system:	Soviet federal legal system. *Shari'ah* and *ibadah* have no legal validity.
Int. rel'tns:	Foreign policy directed at the federal Soviet level.
Fund. Movnts:	Fundamentalism is confined to the small and semi-clandestine Sufi orders.
Summary:	Faith in Islam has been shaken by the momentous transition from nomadism to a settled agricultural way of life. Relatively few traces of older Turkomen traditions survive.

11.32 ALBANIA (*The People's Socialist Republic of Albania/ Republika Popullore Socialiste e Shqipërisë*)

| Capital: | Tirana |
| Population: | 3.08m |

Muslim pop:	70% (est – official statistics deny existence of Islam)
GNP per cap:	$930
Sects:	Overwhelmingly Sunni-Hanafi.
Islam Founded:	1389
Ind. since:	1913 (Ottoman Empire).
Constitution:	Secular one-party republic under strongly atheist Communist rule.
Legal system:	System of secular People's Courts.
Int. rel'tns:	Highly isolationist (previously pro-Chinese).
Fund. Movnts:	All opposition groups, including Islamic parties, are illegal. Regime closed all mosques in 1967.
Summary:	Islam has declined as a religion under extreme pressure from the regime.

11.33 JORDAN (*and Palestine*) (*The Hashemite Kingdom of Jordan /Al-Mamlaka al Urduniya al-Hashemiyah*)

Capital:	Amman
Population:	2.85m (plus est 800,000 Palestinians on the West Bank of the River Jordan which is occupied by the Israelis and is claimed as the territory of Jordan).
Muslim pop:	95%
GNP per cap:	$1,900 (excluding Palestinians)
Sects:	Overwhelmingly Sunni-Hanafi.
Islam Founded:	638 'Umayyad conquest of Jerusalem.
Ind. since:	1946 (British mandate administration).
Constitution:	Constitutional monarchy, limited democracy.
Legal system:	*Shari'ah* and *ibadah* are enforced. The King is the judge of last resort.
Int. rel'tns:	Strongly pro-Western. Member of the Arab League.
Fund. Movnts:	*Shari'ah* law is applied to the satisfaction of traditionalist Muslims. The main internal threat to Jordan is the Palestinian minority and the growing economic crisis.

Summary: The Kingdom of Jordan was established as
                            the first step in creating a conservative
                            Hashemite Kingdom encompassing the
                            entire Arab world.

11.34 MAURITANIA (*Islamic Republic of Mauritania/ République Islamique de Mauritanie*)

Capital: Nouakchott
Population: 2.01m
Muslim pop: 99%
GNP per cap: $450
Sects: Almost entirely Sunni-Hanafi with strong
                   Marabout ('African Muslim') and Qadiriyah
                   Sufi influence.
Islam Founded: c1000 by Muslim traders from the Maghreb.
Ind. since: 28th November 1960 (France).
Constitution: Islamic one-party republic under military
                   rule.
Legal system: *Shari'ah* law introduced in 1980.
Int. rel'tns: Mauritania is pro-Western, a member of the
                   Arab League and an associate member of the
                   EEC.
Fund. Movnts: The governing military junta seized power
                   in the name of Islam in 1979 and declared
                   the country an Islamic republic on similar
                   lines to Pakistan.
Summary: Islam is used as a national focus for a
                   country torn by ethnic and tribal differences.

11.35 THE INDIAN OCEAN ISLANDS (*Comoros, Zanzibar, Maldives, Laccadives*)

Capitals/   Comoros   – Moroni, 0.48m
Populations: Zanzibar   – Zanzibar Town, 0.37m
                   Maldives   – Malé, 0.21m
                   Laccadives – Androth, 0.06m
Total pop: 1.13m
Muslim pop: 99%
GNP per cap: Comoros   – $290

	Zanzibar – $210 (Tanzanian average)
	Maldives – $470
	Laccadives – $260 (Indian average)
Sects:	Almost entirely Sunni-Shafi.
Islam Founded:	c800–950 by Muslim traders from the Persian Gulf.
Ind. since:	Comoros – 1974 (French Empire/Madagascar).
	Zanzibar – 1963 (British mandate admin. Federated with Tanzania, 1964).
	Maldives – 1965 (Sri Lanka).
	Laccadives – 1947 (British Indian Empire, joined India as Union Territory, 1948).
Constitution:	Comoros – Federal Islamic republic.
	Zanzibar – Secular federal republic.
	Maldives – Parliamentary republic based on Islam.
	Laccadives – Secular Indian federal constitution.
Legal system:	Comoros – Hybrid French-Islamic legal.
	Zanzibar – Secular.
	Maldives – Entirely based on *shari'ah*.
	Laccadives – Federal Indian system.
Int. rel'tns:	The Comoros Islands, which occupy a vital strategic position in the Mozambique channel commanding the cape shipping routes, are pro-Western. The Maldives are a Commonwealth country, generally pro-Western and a tourist destination of growing significance. Zanzibar, as part of the Republic of Tanzania is firmly non-aligned and committed to 'African socialism'. The foreign policy of the Laccadives is directed by the Indian federal government.
Fund. Movnts:	No significant agitation.
Summary:	Shafi-Sunni'ism, an ancient and traditionalist version of Arabian Islam, has been preserved in isolation from the outside world.

11.36 DJIBOUTI (*Republic of Djibouti/Jumhouriyya Djibouti*)

Capital:	Djibouti
Population:	0.42m
Muslim pop:	99%
GNP per cap:	$760
Sects:	Overwhelmingly Sunni-Shafi. Small Shi'i Zaydi minority.
Islam Founded:	C7th by settlers from the Arabian Peninsula.
Ind. since:	27th June 1977.
Constitution:	Secular republic. Limited democracy.
Legal system:	Entirely based on the *shari'ah*.
Int. rel'tns:	Pro-Western.
Fund. Movnts:	None active.
Summary:	Islam in Djibouti is dominated by two rival tribes subscribing to different Sufi orders.

11.37 BRUNEI (*The Sultanate of Brunei/Negara Brunei Darussalam*)

Capital:	Bandar Seri Begawan
Population:	0.22m
Muslim pop:	63%
GNP per cap:	$16,000
Sects:	Entirely Sunni-Shafi.
Islam Founded:	C16th by Mogul merchants from India.
Ind. since:	31st December 1983 (Great Britain).
Constitution:	Unchallenged personal rule by the Sultan.
Legal system:	Criminal law based on the English model with final appeal function exercised by the British Privy Council in London. Separate *shari'ah* courts enforce Islamic law.
Int. rel'tns:	Pro-Western (member of ASEAN).
Fund. Movnts:	Opposition is mainly secular and firmly repressed.
Summary:	Islam in Brunei is used as the basis of the Sultan's rule. Otherwise it is a tolerant version of the Sunni-Shafi'ism found in neighbouring Malaysia.

SELECTED BIBLIOGRAPHY

The Qur'an. Tahrike Tarsile translation. TT Qur'an Inc, New York, 1989.

The Concise Encyclopaedia of Islam. Cyril Glasse. Stacey International, London 1989.

The Muslim World. Muslim Welfare House, London, 1989.

The Statesman's Yearbook 1988-89. John Paxton (editor). Macmillan, London, 1989.

The Politics of Satanic Verses – Unmasking Western Attitudes. Shoaib Qureshi and Javed Khan. Muslim Community Surveys No.3, London 1989.

An Introduction to Islam. Gerhard Endress. Edinburgh University Press, Edinburgh, 1988.

Discovering Islam. Akbar S. Ahmed. Routledge, London, 1988.

Islam – Beliefs and Teachings. Ghulam Sarwar. The Muslim Educational Trust, London, 1987.

The Encyclopaedia of Religion. Mircea Eliade (editor in chief). Macmillan, New York, 1987.

Muhammad. Michael Cook. Oxford University Press, Oxford, 1986.

Sufi'ism and Shari'ah. Muhammad Abdul Haq. The Islamic Foundation, Leicester, 1986.

Islam – Faith and Practice. Manazir Ahsan. The Islamic Foundation, London, 1985.

Atlas of the Islamic World since 1500. Frederick Robinson. Phaidon Press, Oxford, 1982.

The Lawful and the Prohibited in Islam. Yusef Al-Qaradawi. Shorouk International, London, 1985.

Islam and Revolution. Imam Khomeini. Mizan Press, Berkeley, 1981.

Selections from the Qur'an. Sidar Iqbal Ali Shah. The Octagon Press, London, 1980.

Towards Understanding Islam. Sayid Abdul Ala Mawdudi. The UK Islamic Mission, London, 1980.

Biography of the Holy Prophet Muhammad. Syed Ali Raza. Peermahomed Ebrahim Trust, Karachi, 1980.

Islam and Communism. Dr Abdullah Omar Naseef. Crescent Publishing Company, Delhi, 1980.

Family Life in Islam. Khurshid Ahmad. The Islamic Foundation, Leicester, 1974.

The Sufi Orders in Islam. Spencer Trimingham. Oxford University Press, Oxford, 1971.

History of the Islamic Peoples. Carl Brocklemann. Routledge and Kegan Paul, London 1948.